SELINUX

NSA's Open Source
Security Enhanced Linux

Other Linux resources from O'Reilly

Related titles

Building Secure Servers with Linux

Linux in a Nutshell

Linux iptables Pocket Reference

Linux Network Administrator's Guide

Linux Server Hacks

Managing Security with Snort and IDS Tools

Network Security Assessment

Network Security Hacks

Practical Unix and Internet Security

Secure Coding: Principles and Practices

Secure Programming Cookbook for C and C++

Security Warrior

Web Security, Privacy, and Commerce

Linux Books Resource Center

linux.oreilly.com is a complete catalog of O'Reilly's books on Linux and Unix and related technologies, including sample chapters and code examples.

ONLamp.com is the premier site for the open source web platform: Linux, Apache, MySQL, and either Perl, Python, or PHP.

Conferences

O'Reilly Media brings diverse innovators together to nurture the ideas that spark revolutionary industries. We specialize in documenting the latest tools and systems, translating the innovator's knowledge into useful skills for those in the trenches. Visit *conferences.oreilly.com* for our upcoming events.

Safari Bookshelf (*safari.oreilly.com*) is the premier online reference library for programmers and IT professionals. Conduct searches across more than 1,000 books. Subscribers can zero in on answers to time-critical questions in a matter of seconds. Read the books on your Bookshelf from cover to cover or simply flip to the page you need. Try it today with a free trial.

SELINUX
NSA's Open Source
Security Enhanced Linux

Bill McCarty

O'REILLY®

Beijing · Cambridge · Farnham · Köln · Paris · Sebastopol · Taipei · Tokyo

SELinux: NSA's Open Source Security Enhanced Linux
by Bill McCarty

Published by O'Reilly Media, Inc., 1005 Gravenstein Highway North, Sebastopol, CA 95472.

O'Reilly books may be purchased for educational, business, or sales promotional use. Online editions are also available for most titles (*safari.oreilly.com*). For more information, contact our corporate/institutional sales department: (800) 998-9938 or *corporate@oreilly.com*.

Editor:	Andy Oram
Production Editor:	Sanders Kleinfeld
Cover Designer:	Emma Colby
Interior Designer:	Melanie Wang

Printing History:

October 2004:	First Edition.

ISBN: 0-596-00716-7
[M]

Table of Contents

Preface

As a security researcher and author of computer books, I work hard to stay abreast of the latest technological developments. So, I'd been tracking Security Enhanced Linux (SELinux) on my technology radar for several years. But, frankly, it didn't seem to me easy enough, or robust enough, for dependable use by Linux system administrators.

About one year ago, SELinux seemed to grow up suddenly. I now believe that SELinux is the most important computing technology for Linux users that I've seen in the last several years. Obviously, others agree that SELinux is important and useful: SELinux has been incorporated into Fedora Core, Gentoo, and SUSE Linux. And by the time this book is in print, it's expected to be part of Red Hat Enterprise Linux.

Why the sudden popularity? In a nutshell, SELinux promises to change the way Linux users practice computer security from a reactive posture, based on applying patches intended to close published vulnerabilities, to a proactive posture that seeks to prevent even unpublished vulnerabilities from compromising systems. Properly configured and administered Linux systems already hold a well-deserved reputation for resistance to attack. SELinux significantly ups the ante on attackers and intruders by providing Linux system administrators with access to sophisticated security technology of a sort previously available only to administrators of high-security systems running expensive, military-grade operating systems.

Of course, as a good friend of mine—who happens to be an economist—is fond of saying, "There's no such thing as a free lunch." Like other security technologies, SELinux must be properly installed, configured, and maintained if it is to be effective. This book will help you understand and intelligently use SELinux. Whether you prefer to use the sample SELinux security policies delivered as part of a Linux distribution or to implement your own customized policies, this book will show you the way.

One thing *SELinux: NSA's Open Source Security Enhanced Linux* doesn't do is explain how to write programs that use the SELinux API. I anticipate that this book will be useful to those who want to write such programs. But *SELinux* is designed for system administrators, not programmers, and therefore doesn't assume programming skills or expertise. Consequently, those interested in using the SELinux API will have to supplement the material presented in this book with information obtained from SELinux documentation and other sources.

Organization of This Book

This book is divided into nine chapters and five appendixes. Here is a brief summary of each chapter's focus:

Chapter 1, *Introducing SELinux*, explains why SELinux is valuable and which common security flaws it addresses, including the concept of the 0-day vulnerability.

Chapter 2, *Overview of the SELinux Security Model*, explains such basic concepts as roles, domains, and transitions. It prepares the reader for SELinux installation.

Chapter 3, *Installing and Initially Configuring SELinux*, lays out the current state of SELinux support in several GNU/Linux distributions and provides guidance for installation.

Chapter 4, *Using and Administering SELinux*, is a basic SELinux system guide for system administrators, covering such techniques as user administration.

Chapter 5, *SELinux Policy and Policy Language Overview*, prepares the reader to write or revise policies, which is necessary when new software is installed on an SELinux system or when policies need to be adjusted to current system use. This chapter discusses the build process, the layout of policy-related files, and general issues such as macros.

Chapter 6, *Role-Based Access Control*, introduces the syntax of policy files and describes the directives that relate to user roles.

Chapter 7, *Type Enforcement*, discusses the next major aspect of SELinux policies, type-enforcement files.

Chapter 8, *Ancillary Policy Statements*, finishes the explanation of policy statements with a description of constraints and other miscellaneous directives.

Chapter 9, *Customizing SELinux Policies*, pulls together all the material from the book, provides concrete examples of how to adjust SELinux systems to users' needs, and introduces tools that help monitor the system and view policies.

Five appendixes list the classes, operations, macros, types, and attributes defined by SELinux policy files.

Conventions Used in This Book

This book uses the following typographical conventions:

Italic

> Used for commands, programs, and options. Italic also indicates new terms, URLs, filenames and file extensions, and directories.

Constant Width

> Used to show the contents of files or the output from commands. Constant width is also used to indicate domains, types, roles, macros, processes, policy elements, aliases, rules, and operations.

Constant Width Bold

> Used in examples and tables to show commands or other text that should be typed literally by the user.

Constant Width Italic

> Used in examples and tables to show text that should be replaced with user-supplied values.

 This icon signifies a tip, suggestion, or general note.

 This icon signifies a warning or caution.

A final word about syntax: in many cases, the space between an option and its argument can be omitted. In other cases, the spacing (or lack of spacing) must be followed strictly. For example, *-wn* (no intervening space) might be interpreted differently from *-w n*. It's important to notice the spacing used in option syntax.

Keyboard Accelerators

In a keyboard accelerator (such as Ctrl-Alt-Del), a dash indicates that the keys should be held down simultaneously, whereas a space means that the keys should be pressed sequentially. For example, Ctrl-Esc indicates that the Control and Escape keys should be held down simultaneously, whereas Ctrl Esc means that the Control and Escape keys should be pressed sequentially.

IF a keyboard accelerator contains an uppercase letter, you should not type the Shift key unless it's given explicitly. For example, Ctrl-C indicates that you should press the Control and C keys; Ctrl-Shift-C indicates that you should press the Control, Shift, and C keys.

Using Code Examples

This book is here to help you get your job done. In general, you may use the code in this book in your programs and documentation. You do not need to contact us for permission unless you're reproducing a significant portion of the code. For example, writing a program that uses several chunks of code from this book does not require permission. Selling or distributing a CD-ROM of examples from O'Reilly books does require permission. Answering a question by citing this book and quoting example code does not require permission. Incorporating a significant amount of example code from this book into your product's documentation does require permission.

We appreciate, but do not require, attribution. An attribution usually includes the title, author, publisher, and ISBN. For example: "*SELinux: NSA's Open Source Security Enhanced Linux*, by Bill McCarty. Copyright 2004 O'Reilly Media, Inc., 0-596-00716-7."

If you feel your use of code examples falls outside fair use or the permission given above, feel free to contact us at *permissions@oreilly.com*.

How to Contact Us

Please address any comments or questions concerning this book to the publisher:

O'Reilly Media, Inc.
1005 Gravenstein Highway North
Sebastopol, CA 95472
(800) 998-9938 (in the U.S. or Canada)
(707) 829-0515 (international/local)
(707) 829-0104 (fax)

We have a web page for this book, where we list errata, examples, and any additional information. The site also includes a link to a forum where you can discuss the book with the author and other readers. You can access this page at:

http://www.oreilly.com/catalog/selinux

To comment or ask technical questions about this book, send email to:

bookquestions@oreilly.com

For more information about books, conferences, software, Resource Centers, and the O'Reilly Network, see our web site at:

http://www.oreilly.com

Acknowledgments

Thanks to my editor, Andy Oram, who struggled alongside me through some difficult challenges of structure and design. This book wouldn't have been nearly as clear and readable without Andy's insights and patient influence.

Thanks also to Margot Maley of Waterside Productions, Inc., who brought this authorship opportunity to my attention.

Several reviewers, some working for O'Reilly Media and some working elsewhere, commented on the manuscript and suggested helpful corrections and improvements. In particular, I'd like to thank the following people for taking time to review this book: Dr. Steve Beatty, Joshua Brindle, David Castro, and George Chamales. I greatly appreciate their assistance and readily confess that any errors in the manuscript were added by me after their reviews, and so are entirely my responsibility.

My family—Jennifer, Patrick, and Sara—provided their customary compassion and assistance during this latest authorship experience. Thanks, guys!

I also acknowledge the faithfulness of my savior, Jesus Christ. His perfect love is entirely undeserved.

## CHAPTER 1

Introducing SELinux

This chapter explains the *what* and *why* of SELinux. It begins by describing the threat environment and why the prevalent model of security—patching against known vulnerabilities—is inadequate. The chapter goes on to describe several security mechanisms designed to protect against both known and unknown vulnerabilities. The chapter then presents an overview of SELinux, describing its main features, capabilities, and history. The chapter concludes with a survey of resources helpful to SELinux users.

Software Threats and the Internet

Because you're reading this book, it's likely that you're responsible for the management of one or more sensitive hosts. If that's the case, you're aware that the threat level for Internet-based attacks has increased rapidly over the last several years and continues to do so. One authoritative barometer of this trend is the number of incident reports logged by the Computer Emergency Response Team Coordination Center (CERT/CC) of Carnegie Mellon University's Software Engineering Institute. Table 1-1 shows the number of incident reports for 2000 through 2003. During this four-year period, incident reports increased at an average annual rate of almost 85 percent. That is, the number of incidents has roughly doubled each year. If this rapid rate of increase continues, the year 2010 will see over 10 million incident reports.

Table 1-1. CERT/CC incident reports[a]

Year	Reports
2000	21,756
2001	52,658
2002	82,094
2003	137,529

[a] Source: *http://www.cert.org/stats/cert_stats.html.*

Of course, the number of incident reports is an indirect rather than direct measure of the threat level. So some might argue that the threat level is unchanged, and the increase in incident reports is due to system administrators reporting a greater proportion of incidents.

Insider Threats

Not all threats arise from software or the Internet. So-called *insider threats*, which come from local-area networks or proprietary wide-area networks, can present even more serious risks. Insiders often attack systems by means other than software vulnerabilities. For instance, employees in two work groups may collude to falsify database records to steal from their employer. Such threats generally cannot be prevented by purely technical means. Gartner research has estimated that 70 percent of security incident costs are related to breaches committed by insiders.[a]

a. *Securing the Enterprise: The Latest Strategies and Technologies for Building a Safe Architecture* (Gartner, 2003), available at *http://www4.gartner.com/5_about/news/sec_sample.pdf*.

While available evidence does suggest that system administrators have historically been reluctant to report incidents and have become less reluctant lately, evidence also indicates that the threat level is substantial and is rising rapidly. As an information assurance researcher, I monitor several class-C networks for familiar and novel attacks. My data shows that a typical host on these networks is subject to attack every few seconds. An unprotected host can succumb to attack in less time than it takes to install a typical operating system or software patch. Therefore, those for whom the confidentiality, integrity, and availability of information are important must invest significant effort to protect their hosts, especially those that connect to the Internet.

To effectively protect hosts against threats, it's important to understand the nature of the threats and why they are increasing. Three of the most significant factors that have led to the increased level of software threats are software complexity, network connectivity, and active content and mobile code.

Software complexity. Because the human intellect is finite, software developers commit errors and leave omissions during the implementation of software systems. The defects resulting from their errors and omissions cause software systems to behave in unwanted or unanticipated ways when executed in untested or unanticipated ways. Attackers can often exploit such misbehaviors to compromise systems. As a general principle, the more complex a system, the greater the intellectual demands its implementation imposes upon its developers. Hence, complex systems tend to have relatively large numbers of defects and be relatively more vulnerable to attacks than smaller, simpler systems. Modern software systems, such as operating systems and standard applications, are large and complex. The Linux operating system, for instance, contains over 30 million source lines of code. And Red Hat Linux 7.1 was 60 percent larger than Red Hat Linux 6.2, which was released about one year earlier.* Therefore, contemporary systems are generally vulnerable to a variety of attacks and attack types, as explained in the following sections of this chapter.

Network connectivity. A second factor contributing to increased software threats is increased network connectivity and, in particular, the Internet itself. Connectivity provides a vector whereby attacks successfully launched against one networked host can be launched against others. The Internet, which interconnects the majority of networks in existence, is the ultimate attack vector. The recent popularity of consumer access to the Internet compounds the threat, since the computers of most consumers are not hardened to resist attack. Unsecured hosts easily fall prey to viruses and worms, many of which install backdoors or Trojan horses that enable compromised systems to be remotely accessed and controlled. Attackers can launch attacks by using these compromised hosts, thereby hiding their identity from the victims of their attacks and law enforcement. Many attackers attack from across international borders, which complicates the work of law enforcement. Because law enforcement generally has been ineffective in identifying and apprehending all but a handful of notorious computer criminals, attackers have believed themselves to be beyond the reach of prosecution and have acted out their whims and criminal urges with impunity. The recent advent of wireless connectivity exacerbates the risks, as several of the security facilities commonly used on wireless networks implementing the IEEE 802.11 standard (such as Wireless Encryption Equivalent Privacy (WEP)) have turned out to be flawed, and therefore vulnerable to attack.

Active content and mobile code. A third factor contributing to increased software threats is the use of active content and mobile code. *Active content* refers to documents that have the capability of triggering actions automatically without the intervention, or possibly even the awareness, of their user. Ordinary, ASCII-encoded documents are not active in this sense. However, a variety of modern document types can include active content such as Abobe PDF documents, MS Office documents, Java applets, and web pages containing JavaScript code or using browser plug-ins. Even Post-Script documents, which are widely thought to be safe, can contain active content. The danger of active content is that users generally perceive documents as benign, passive entities. However, malicious active content can compromise a user's computer as easily as any other form of malicious code. Opening, or even merely selecting and previewing, a document containing malicious active content may enable the malicious code to compromise a user's computer.

* Source: *http://www.dwheeler.com/sloc/*.

Mobile code is code designed to be transported across a network for execution on remote hosts. Mobile code is often designed to extend the capabilities of software programs and, because of users' desires for flexible and convenient software, has become ubiquitous. Email clients and web browsers, for example, accept and process a wide variety of mobile code types, including Java and JavaScript programs, Microsoft ActiveX controls, and others.

Unfortunately, active content and mobile code provide more than flexibility and convenience to users: they provide attackers with a flexible and convenient attack vector. Many Internet attacks take the form of active content or mobile code delivered via email. When a user views an email message containing malicious code, the malicious code may seize control of the user's computer. Especially sophisticated malicious code may not even require user action. Such code may be capable of compromising a vulnerable computer in a fraction of a second, without presenting the computer's user with an opportunity to refuse the code permission to execute or even receive notification of the event.

For more information on malicious mobile code in the context of Microsoft Windows, see *Malicious Mobile Code* (O'Reilly).

Privilege Escalation

Most common operating systems, including Microsoft Windows and Unix/Linux, provide multiple levels of authorization, thereby restricting the operations that some programs or users are permitted to perform. Multiple levels of authorization act as bulwarks against the damage done when a program is compromised. Many common operating systems have two primary levels of authorization—one for ordinary users and one for the system administrator. A handful of operating systems, such as those used on PDAs and small computing devices, do not impose any such restrictions.

Restricting programs to the few functions they need to perform is called the *principle of least privilege*. Operating systems that lack multiple levels of authorization cannot implement the principle of least privilege and are therefore inherently quite insecure. When an attacker compromises a program running under a single-level operating system, the attacker gains the ability to perform any operation of which the system is capable. However, an attacker who compromises a program on a system that has multiple levels of authorization obtains only the privilege to perform those operations for which the program is authorized. If the program performs tasks related to system administration, the attacker may gain wide-ranging privileges. However, if the program performs relatively mundane tasks, the attacker may achieve relatively little beyond gaining the ability to disrupt operation of the compromised program. Nevertheless, an attacker who compromises even a program that confers few privileges may achieve a significant victory, because the attacker can use the privileges conferred by the program as a beachhead from which to attack programs conferring additional or greater privileges. Alternatively, the attacker may intentionally disrupt operation of the compromised program in what is called a *denial of service*.

The Apache OpenSSL Attack

A popular Internet attack during 2002 and 2003 was the Apache OpenSSL attack, directed against the Apache web server. Most users configure Apache to run as an ordinary user, rather than as the system administrator. So, attackers who successfully exploited a web server using the Apache OpenSSL attack generally obtained only limited privileges. However, at the time of the attack's popularity, Linux systems were vulnerable to a second attack, one targeting the ptrace facility used to trace and debug processes. Unlike the Apache web service, which is available to remote users, the ptrace facility is available only to local users. Successful compromise of an Apache web server enabled attackers to access the ptrace facility and exploit a ptrace defect that conferred full system administration privileges.

The Patch Cycle and the 0-Day Problem

When a software vendor learns that one of its products is vulnerable to attack, the vendor will generally issue a *patch*. Users can install the patch, which modifies the vulnerable product in a way intended to eliminate—or at least mitigate—the vulnerability. Occasionally, a patch alleged to eliminate a vulnerability will fail to actually do so. Worse yet, occasionally a patch will introduce one or more new vulnerabilities. So patches are sometimes less than ideal solutions. But, as a means of defending against software attacks, patches suffer from a more fundamental flaw.

The essential problem with patches is that they are a reactive, rather than proactive, response. Patching is thus a continual process consisting of the following steps, known as the *patch cycle*:

1. A vulnerability in a software product is discovered.
2. The product's vendor prepares and publishes a patch for the vulnerability.
3. Users acquire, authenticate, test, and install the patch.

It may seem odd that security researchers publish vulnerabilities rather than privately inform vendors of them, because publication of a vulnerability may help attackers discover a way to exploit it. Indeed, most security researchers do prefer to inform vendors of vulnerabilities privately rather than publicly. But many vendors consistently fail to release patches in a timely manner. And some vendors fail even to acknowledge in a timely manner vulnerability reports submitted privately by researchers. So, many security researchers believe that it's necessary to force vendors to fix their products and therefore elect to publish vulnerabilities. In an effort to avoid giving attackers opportunity to exploit vulnerabilities, some researchers publish them only after first privately notifying the vendor and providing an opportunity to publish a patch before publication of the vulnerability.

Vendors can supply patches only for known vulnerabilities, so a fully patched computer remains vulnerable to attacks that are unknown to the vendor. Moreover, vendors require time to produce patches even for known vulnerabilities. So fully patched computers also remain vulnerable to known attacks for which vendors have not yet released patches. The interval between publication of a vulnerability and availability of a related patch is a time of especially high vulnerability. During the interval, vendors race to produce effective patches, while attackers race to produce effective exploits. This race generally favors the attackers, who do not have to test and analyze their exploits the same way that vendors must test and analyze their patches. So publication of a vulnerability amounts to initiation of a countdown to the widespread availability and use of exploits targeting the vulnerability.

Moreover, vulnerabilities are sometimes privately known and exploited well in advance of their publication. Vulnerabilities for which no patch is yet available are known as *0-day vulnerabilities* or simply *0-days* ("oh days"). The same term is often used to refer to attacks that target 0-day vulnerabilities. Attacks that target 0-days are a particularly potent form of attack, because even systems whose administrators have assiduously kept current with all vendor patches are vulnerable to them. Fortunately, most attacks do not target 0-days. The National Institute of Standards cites

CERT data indicating that 95 percent of attempted network intrusions target vulnerabilities for which patches are available.* However, patching is ineffective against the remaining 5 percent of network attacks, which target 0-day vulnerabilities.

Protecting Against 0-Days

Ordinary computer users may be content merely to patch their computers regularly, a practice that can protect them against 95 percent of attempted network intrusions. However, administrators of sensitive systems generally cannot afford to allow their systems to remain vulnerable to the 5 percent of attempted intrusions that target 0-day vulnerabilities. Although patching is, by definition, an ineffective defense against attacks targeting 0-day vulnerabilities, several types of defenses are more or less effective in protecting against them.

Defense by Layers

No software is known to be free of defects, and no means of producing defect-free software is known. Thus, no means of network or host defense that depends on the correct operation of software can be fully reliable. Hence, practical defense consists of implementing multiple defensive measures in hopes that if one defensive measure fails, one or more other measures will prove effective. This principle is known as *defense by layers*.

A corollary principle holds that imperfections in a defense mechanism do not preclude its use, since all defense mechanisms are considered to be imperfect. Instead, rational decisions concerning which defense mechanisms an organization should deploy are based on risk assessment and cost-benefit analysis.

Network and Host Defenses

Because hosts are generally subject to a variety of vulnerabilities for which no patch exists or has been installed, hosts must be protected against attack. Two basic sorts of defenses are employed:

Network defenses
    A defensive facility that protects an entire network

Host defenses
    A defensive facility that protects a single host

---

* *Procedures for Handling Security Patches*, NIST Special Publication 800-40, p. 2, available at *http://csrc.nist. gov/publications/nistpubs/800-40/sp800-40.pdf*.

Network defenses

Network defenses are often more convenient to deploy than host defenses, because a single network defense facility defends all hosts on a network. Host defenses, in contrast, must be implemented on each host to be protected. The two most widely used network defenses are firewalls and network intrusion detection systems. Neither is generally effective in protecting against 0-day attacks.

Network firewalls. Firewalls restrict the traffic flowing into and out of a network. The most basic sort of firewall restricts traffic by IP address. More sophisticated firewalls allow only designated application-layer protocols or requests having a specified form. For instance, some firewalls can block web client access to malformed URLs of the sort often associated with attacks. However, most currently deployed firewalls do not examine the application layer of traffic. Such firewalls are generally ineffective in protecting against 0-day attacks launched against ports to which the firewall is configured to allow access.

Network intrusion detection and prevention systems. Intrusion detection systems don't prevent attacks from succeeding; they merely detect them. To do so, they monitor network traffic and generate an alert if they recognize an attack. They typically use a database of signatures or rules to recognize the attacks. Thus, an intrusion detection system may not generate an alert for a particular 0-day attack, since the attack may not match any rule or signature within the system's database. Some intrusion detection systems do not rely on a database of signatures or rules. Instead they alert the user to unusual traffic. However, anomaly-based intrusion detection systems are not yet in widespread use.

An *intrusion prevention system* attempts to detect *and* prevent attacks. However, like anomaly-based intrusion detection systems, intrusion prevention systems are not yet in widespread use.

Host defenses

Host defenses may be more effective than network defenses in detecting or preventing 0-day attacks. Host defenses are more varied than network defenses. Some popular host defenses are:

- Host firewalls
- Host intrusion detection systems
- Logging and auditing
- Memory protection
- Sandboxes
- Access control lists

Host firewalls and intrusion detection systems. Firewalls and intrusion detection systems can be deployed on individual hosts as well as at the network level. Because host-based firewalls operate similarly to network-based firewalls, they are seldom more effective than network-based firewalls in protecting against 0-day attacks. Host-based intrusion detection systems are sometimes more effective in recognizing novel attacks than their network-based cousins. However, like their cousins, they detect rather than prevent attacks, so they are not an adequate solution to the 0-day problem.

Logging and auditing. Logs and other audit trails can provide indications or clues that an attack has succeeded. However, properly monitoring logs requires considerable effort, and many system administrators fail to take the time to regularly review logs. But even when logs are regularly monitored, they merely detect rather than prevent attacks.

Memory protection. One technique that is often effective in protecting against 0-day attacks is memory protection. Here are some of the most popular memory protection schemes:

Stack canaries
> Based on a concept originated by Crispin Cowan, a stack canary is a memory word containing a designated value, pushed onto the stack when a routine is called. When control returns to the calling routine, it verifies that the value of the stack canary has not been modified. Buffer overflow attacks that target the stack are likely to modify the value of the stack canary and therefore may be detected.

Nonexecutable stack
> Buffer overflow attacks that target the stack generally inject code into the stack and compromise the target host by executing the injected code. Since most programs don't require that stack contents be executable, buffer overflow attacks can be complicated or even thwarted by preventing execution of code residing on the stack. Many common microprocessors—including those having the Intel x86 architecture—can be configured to prohibit execution of stack contents.

Random assignment of memory
> Many exploits depend on knowledge of the specific memory locations occupied by the components of vulnerable programs. Specially modified compilers or loaders can randomize the addresses of memory into which program components are loaded, thereby breaking exploits that depend on fixed memory assignments.

Well-designed and well-implemented memory protection schemes tend to be effective even against attacks on 0-day vulnerabilities. However, some specific implementations of memory protection schemes can be circumvented relatively easily. In other cases, such as that of Microsoft's "security error handler" function added to its C++ compiler, the scheme itself is the source of vulnerabilities.*

SELinux does not incorporate memory protection facilities. However, SELinux consistently interoperates well with such facilities. Therefore, SELinux users can generally employ memory protection features when their operating system provides them.

Sandboxes. Yet another approach to defending hosts against 0-day attacks is running programs, especially services, within contexts called *sandboxes* that limit their capabilities. Sandboxing is common for programs running under Unix and Unix-like operating systems such as Linux, which includes the *chroot* command that creates such a sandbox. Sandboxing is also used for Java programs running within popular web browsers.

Sandboxing generally doesn't prevent the exploitation of an 0-day vulnerability. But, the attacker who successfully exploits an 0-day vulnerability in a sandboxed program gains access to only the capabilities afforded by the sandbox. Therefore, the sandbox limits the damage resulting from a successful attack.

However, sandboxes are software entities and thus are equally as imperfect: an attacker who gains access to a sandbox may be able to attack and escape it. In general, under Unix and Unix-like operating systems, it's possible for attackers to escape *chroot* sandboxes that contain programs running as the root user. However, sandboxes that contain programs running as a non-root user are less vulnerable. SELinux provides a special sort of sandbox, known as a *domain*, that is very difficult for attackers to escape—even if the domain contains programs running as the root user.

Access-control lists. An especially flexible form of sandbox is provided by mechanisms known as *access-control mechanisms*. In their simplest form, access-control mechanisms are found in every multiuser operating system that protects the files and resources owned by one user from unauthorized access by other users.

Access-control mechanisms are implemented by associating *access-control lists* (ACLs) with objects (e.g., files and directories), thereby limiting access to the protected objects. Essentially, the most familiar form of an ACL consists of three elements:

- A list of operations
- A list of subjects (users)
- A mapping that specifies which subjects (users) are authorized to perform which operations on the protected object

By associating an ACL with a file, for example, you can specify the users permitted to access the file. The familiar Unix *chmod* command accomplishes exactly this result. Representing many sorts of system objects, such as devices and FIFOs, this simple

---

* See "Microsoft Compiler Flaw Technical Note," by Chris Ren, Michael Weber, and Gary McGraw, and "Cigital Warns of Security Flaw in Microsoft .NET Compiler," both available at *http://www.cigital.com/news/index.php?pg=art&artid=70*.

mechanism enables system administrators and users to limit access to most system objects. ACLs can also specify access by subjects other than users, such as programs. Although several commercial operating systems based on Unix include ACLs, Linux does not. SELinux, on the other hand, goes beyond ACLs in providing a special type of access control known as mandatory access control (MAC). The following section explains MAC and contrasts it with the type of access control commonly used by Linux.

Discretionary and Mandatory Access Control

Most operating systems have a built-in security mechanism known as *access control*. Two main types of access control are commonly used:

Discretionary Access Control (DAC)
    Discretionary access controls are specified by the owner of an object, who can apply, modify, or remove them at will.

Mandatory Access Control (MAC)
    Mandatory access controls are specified by the system. They cannot be applied, modified, or removed—except perhaps by means of a privileged operation.

Discretionary access control

Linux employs discretionary access control. Under discretionary access control, a program runs with the permissions of the user executing it. For instance, if I log in as the user mccartyb and execute the program *mutt* to read my email, the program executes under my user ID and is capable of performing any operation that I'm permitted to perform. In particular, it can read and write files in my home directory and its subdirectories, such as the sensitive files holding SSH information. Of course, *mutt* doesn't need to access such files and generally wouldn't do so. But, by exploiting a vulnerability in *mutt*, an attacker may coerce *mutt* to access or modify sensitive files, thereby compromising the security of my user account.

Obviously, *mutt* doesn't need to be able to perform *every* operation that I'm permitted to perform. It has a well-defined purpose that requires only a handful of permissions, mostly related to network access. Granting *mutt* a broad array of permissions is inconsistent with the principle of least privilege. From the standpoint of the principle of least privilege, giving a program all the privileges of the user running the program is wretchedly excessive and highly risky.

Under discretionary access control, a compromised program jeopardizes every object to which the executing user has access. The risk is particularly great for programs that run as the root user, because the root user has unrestricted access to system files and objects. If an attacker can compromise a program running as the root user, the attacker can often manage to subvert the entire system.

Therefore, discretionary access control provides a rather brittle sort of security. When subjected to a sufficiently potent attack, discretionary access control shatters, giving the attacker a virtually free hand.

Mandatory access control

SELinux supplements the discretionary access control mechanism of Linux with mandatory access control. Under mandatory access control, each program runs within a sandbox that limits its permissions. A compromised program jeopardizes only the permissions available to the program. These are generally a small subset of all the permissions afforded the user executing the program.

Generally speaking, mandatory access controls are much more effective than Unix-style discretionary access controls, for the following principal reasons:

- Mandatory access controls are often applied to agents other than users, such as programs, whereas Unix-style discretionary access controls are generally applied only to users.
- Mandatory access controls cannot be overridden by the owner of the object to which they apply.
- Mandatory access controls may be applied to objects not protected by ordinary Unix-style discretionary access controls, such as network sockets and processes.

Thus, the mandatory access control facilities of SELinux provide stronger security than the discretionary access control facilities of Linux. Under SELinux, programs are generally assigned privileges according to the principle of least privilege; that is, they're generally granted permission to perform only a limited set of necessary operations. Therefore, an attacker who compromises a program running as the root user on an SELinux system does not generally gain an effective beachhead from which to successfully attack the entire system. Instead, the attacker gains control of only the compromised program and a handful of related operations.

SELinux Features

SELinux is a software product that includes several mechanisms that protect against attacks exploiting software vulnerabilities, including attacks on 0-day vulnerabilities. In particular, SELinux implements role-based access control and sandboxing.

SELinux also provides a logging and audit facility that records attempts to exceed specified permissions. By monitoring the system log, the administrator of an SELinux system can often discover attempts to escalate privileges and take action to prevent an intruder or insider from interfering with operation of the system.

SELinux is designed to protect against misuse and unauthorized use such as:

- Unauthorized reading of data and programs
- Unauthorized modification of data and programs
- Bypassing application security mechanisms
- Interfering with other processes
- Privilege escalation
- Information security breaches

How SELinux Works

Figure 1-1 depicts the operation of SELinux in a highly simplified fashion. SELinux works by associating each program or process with a sandbox known as a domain. Each domain is assigned a set of permissions sufficient to enable it to function properly but do nothing else. For instance, a domain is limited in the files it can access and the types of operations it can perform on those files. To enable specification of such permissions, each file is labeled with information called a *security context*. The definition of a domain spells out what operations it can perform on files having specific security contexts. A domain cannot access files having security contexts other than those for which it is explicitly granted access.

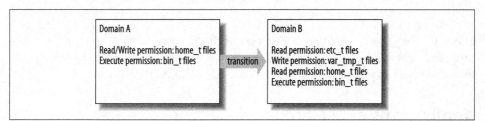

Figure 1-1. The operation of SELinux

Under specified conditions, a process that executes a program leaves its current domain and *transitions* to a new domain. Typically, transitions occur upon executing a program designated as an entry point to the new domain. The new domain may have more or fewer privileges than the original domain. Thus, programs can initiate other programs having more or fewer privileges than themselves.

An SELinux facility known as *type enforcement* (TE) ensures that the rules governing domains are always observed. SELinux also has a secondary facility known as *role-based access control* (RBAC). RBAC limits user access to domains. For instance, some domains are defined to be accessible only to the system administrator, whereas other domains are defined to be publicly available to any user.

An exciting aspect of SELinux is that the definitions of domains, security contexts, and transitions appear in files called *policy files* that can be modified by the SELinux system administrator. Thus, SELinux security policies are extremely flexible and can support a wide range of security needs. For instance, suppose that you want to install a program that neither you nor anyone you know has previously run under SELinux. Therefore, no policy specifying the operations that the program should and should not be allowed to perform exists. Nevertheless, you can create such a policy and enjoy the benefits of running the program in a manner consistent with the principle of least privilege.

SELinux Components and Linux Security Modules (LSM)

SELinux was originally implemented as a set of Linux kernel modules that worked with the Linux 2.2 kernel. SELinux has since been updated to work with Linux 2.4. SELinux can also work with the Linux Security Modules (LSM) feature of the Linux 2.6 kernel.

LSM consists of a set of hooks inserted into the Linux kernel. These hooks provide the means to notify a software unit, such as SELinux, whenever a process attempts to perform an operation on an object, such as opening a file for read access or deleting a file. LSM also provides a means whereby the software unit can prohibit the attempted access, making it straightforward for software developers to implement a security engine that oversees access to files and other objects, such as that used in SELinux.

In addition to kernel modules, SELinux includes a set of system administration programs that have been modified to be aware of the SELinux environment, and a set of programs used to administer SELinux itself. SELinux also includes a policy, implemented as a set of files, that defines users and roles and their permissions.

Applications of SELinux

To understand the value of SELinux, let's revisit the Apache and ptrace vulnerability mentioned earlier in the sidebar "The Apache OpenSSL Attack." Unknown to the administrator of the server, the version of Apache being run contains a vulnerability for which no patch is yet available. An attacker exploits this vulnerability to remotely compromise Apache, thereby gaining the privileges extended to the apache user account. Because the system's security is based on discretionary access control, these privileges are relatively extensive. In particular, they're sufficient to allow the attacker to execute the ptrace program, which also contains a vulnerability. Moreover, the ptrace program is a setsuid program that always runs as the root user regardless of the identity of the user who launches it. Thus, when the attacker compromises ptrace, he gains access to the root account and has unrestricted access to all system files and resources. The attacker establishes a backdoor by which to conveniently reenter the system at will, cleans the system logs to cover all traces of his intrusion, and adds the system to his list of owned hosts.

SELinux and User-Mode Linux (UML)

User-Mode Linux is an open source product that enables a single host to run multiple, sandboxed instances of the Linux kernel, referred to as *virtual machines*. UML's function is roughly comparable to that of commercial virtualization products, such as VMware and Microsoft's Virtual PC. However, UML supports only Linux, whereas VMware and Virtual PC support a variety of operating systems. Each virtual machine running under UML can run programs and applications, maintain a distinct filesystem separate from that of other virtual machines, and access the network. So if a program or an entire instance of a running kernel is compromised, the other programs and kernel instances may not be affected.

SELinux includes a set of policies that are intended to strengthen the UML sandbox and thereby improve system security and integrity. Using SELinux, you can make it less likely that a wayward application or a successful attack compromising one virtual machine will lead to the subversion or failure of other virtual machines. You can learn more about User-Mode Linux at *http://user-mode-linux.sourceforge.net*.

Alternatives to SELinux

An alternative product providing functions generally similar to those of SELinux is GRSecurity, described at *http://grsecurity.org*. Like SELinux, GR Security is supported only for Linux 2.*x*.

Developers of open source operating systems other than Linux are implementing products similar to SELinux. For example, the BSD community is creating TrustedBSD. To learn more about TrustedBSD, see its web site, *http://www.trustedbsd.org*.

If the web server had been running on an SELinux host with properly configured policies, the scenario would have proceeded differently. As before, the attacker would have been able to compromise Apache by using his 0-day attack. But, having done so, the attacker would gain only those permissions afforded the domain under which Apache was run. These would not permit the attacker to run the ptrace program, and so he would be prevented from using the ptrace vulnerability to seize control of the system. The domain associated with Apache would not provide the attacker with write access to the HTML files making up the web site. Thus the attacker would be prevented from defacing it. Unless the attack terminated the Apache process, the attack might not even interrupt the availability of web services. Under SELinux, the effects of the attack might be largely mitigated.

SELinux History

SELinux, though only recently released to the public as a software product, has a substantial heritage. SELinux descends from work that began several decades ago. In 1973, computer scientists David Bell and Leonard LaPadula defined the concept of a secure system state and published a formal model describing a multilevel security system.

Later, in the 1980s, the work of Bell and LaPadula strongly influenced the U.S. government's development of the Trusted Computer System Evaluation Criteria (TCSEC, popularly known as the Orange Book). The TCSEC defined six evaluation classes with progressively more stringent security requirements: C1, C2, B1, B2, B3, and A1. Class C1 and C2 systems, like Linux, depended upon discretionary access controls. Class B1 systems and systems of higher classes had to, like SELinux, implement mandatory access controls.

During the 1990s, researchers at the U.S. National Security Agency (NSA) worked with Secure Computing Corporation (SCC) to develop a strong and flexible mandatory access control architecture. Initially, their work focused on theoretical proofs of the properties and characteristics of the architecture. Eventually, working with a research team at the University of Utah, they developed a working prototype of the architecture called Flask within Fluke, a research operating system.

Later, NSA researchers worked with Network Associates and the R&D firm MITRE to implement the architecture within the open source Linux operating system. Their work was released to the public in December 2000, as an open source product.

Subsequently, Linux 2.5 was modified to incorporate LSMs, a kernel feature intended to simplify integration among SELinux, similar products, and the Linux operating system. This modification was carried forward to Linux 2.6 when development of Linux 2.5 was deemed complete.

More recently, several Linux distributors have announced plans to support SELinux within their Linux distributions. Among these are Red Hat, distributor of the commercial Linux distribution with the largest market share in the U.S. and worldwide, and SUSE, distributor of Europe's leading Linux distribution. SELinux is already a standard component of Fedora Core, the noncommercial Linux distribution whose development is sponsored by Red Hat, and several other noncommercial Linux distributions, including Debian GNU/Linux and Gentoo Linux.

Several Linux distributions augment SELinux with other security mechanisms. For instance, Gentoo Linux can be configured to compile the Linux kernel and applications to work with either of two mechanisms:

PaX
> Provides a variety of protections against attacks, including Address Space Layout Randomization (ASLR). See *http://pax.grsecurity.net/docs/pax.txt*.

Propolice
> Provides protection against stack-smashing attacks. See *http://www.research.ibm.com/trl/projects/security/ssp*.

Clearly, SELinux—originally a product of the highly secretive NSA—is becoming a mainstream technology.

Demo Systems

One of the best ways to observe the high level of security possible by using SELinux is to visit one of the SELinux demonstration systems provided for public use. Using an SSH client, you can remotely log into a demonstration system as the root user and try to hack your way to escalated privileges. Most likely, you'll completely fail.

One such system is the demonstration system hosted by Gentoo's Hardened Project, described at *http://selinux.dev.gentoo.org*. Another demonstration system, a Fedora Core system administered by Russell Coker, is described at *http://www.coker.com.au/selinux/play.html*. Finally, a demonstration system running Debian is described at *http://selinux.simplyaquatics.com*.

Web and FTP Sites

The main web site for SELinux is provided by the NSA:

The NSA's SELinux
> *http://www.nsa.gov/selinux*

The web site includes a FAQ, available at *http://www.nsa.gov/selinux/info/faq.cfm*.

In addition, various Linux distributors and interested parties provide SELinux-related web pages and FTP sites. Among the most popular and useful are:

Kerry Thompson's SELinux
> *http://www.crypt.gen.nz/selinux*

Network Associates SELinux
> *http://opensource.nailabs.com/selinux*

Russell Coker's SELinux
> *http://www.coker.com.au/selinux*

SELinux for Debian
     http://www.microcomaustralia.com.au/debian

SELinux for Distributions
     http://selinux.sourceforge.net

SELinux for Fedora Core
     http://fedora.redhat.com/projects/selinux

SELinux for Gentoo Linux
     http://www.gentoo.org/proj/en/hardened

SELinux for Red Hat Enterprise Linux
     http://www.redhat.com/solutions/security/SELinux.html

     ftp://people.redhat.com/dwalsh/SELinux

SELinux for SUSE
     http://leapster.org/linux/selinux/suse

SELinux Wiki (German and English)
     http://www.securityenhancedlinux.de

Sourceforge SELinux
     http://sourceforge.net/projects/selinux

Tresys Technology SELinux
     http://www.tresys.com/selinux

Mailing Lists

Several mailing lists address issues related to SELinux. Among these are:

The NSA's SELinux mailing list
     http://www.nsa.gov/selinux/info/list.cfm?MenuID=41.1.1.9

The Red Hat Fedora SELinux mailing list
     http://www.redhat.com/mailman/listinfo/fedora-selinux-list

The Gentoo Hardened mailing list
     http://www.gentoo.org/proj/en/hardened

You can use these lists to learn more about SELinux, get help in installing and using SELinux, and participate in the development of SELinux and related products.

## CHAPTER 2

Overview of the SELinux Security Model

The main purpose of this chapter is to introduce you to SELinux terms and concepts helpful in the installation and initial configuration of SELinux, which is covered in Chapter 3. This chapter presents an overview of the security model implemented by SELinux, which is based on the Flask architecture designed by the NSA. (SELinux is ultimately grounded on principles that have guided the design and administration of highly secure military systems for decades, such as those described in the so-called "Orange Book."*) Because of this chapter's practical aim, its emphasis is on basic Flask and SELinux concepts and terms. Chapter 5 explains the SELinux security model in greater detail. In addition to providing an overview of SELinux functions, Chapter 5 provides an overview of SELinux architecture, describing each major SELinux component.

Subjects and Objects

Like other onetime elementary and secondary students, you've probably endured many school lectures on the subject of English grammar. If you're old enough, you may even have endured that most feared exercise of secondary education (which is now largely extinct): the sentence diagram, like that shown in Figure 2-1.

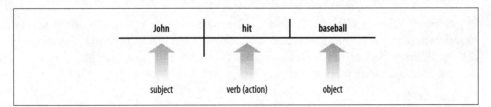

Figure 2-1. A simple sentence diagram

---

* *DoD Trusted Computer System Evaluation Criteria* (DoD 5200.28-STD), available from the U.S. National Institute of Standards, *http://csrc.nist.gov/secpubs/rainbow/nsaorder.txt*.

At the time of your elementary and secondary studies, the various parts of speech—nouns, verbs, adjectives, adverbs, and so on—and components of sentence structure—subjects, actions, direct and indirect objects, and so on—may not have seemed to you and your fellow students to be the most fascinating of topics. And, unless in adult life you've worked as a writer or editor, your aversion may seem to have been well-founded: many adults seem to get through life quite well with only a very fragmentary understanding of English grammar.

If I claimed that knowledge of English grammar would help you better secure your computer systems, would that influence your estimate of the value of its study? Perhaps not. But my claim would nevertheless be true. The security model that underlies SELinux is based on simple grammatical concepts common to English and most other human languages, as well as artificial languages such as computer programming languages. Some scientists believe that an understanding of these concepts is more or less intrinsic to humankind—encoded in the structure of the human mind itself—and quietly shapes the way we view and understand reality. Of course, if grammar is truly innate, one may well wonder why it's necessary to teach it to students. But rather than get sidetracked by a debate over psycholinguistics (as the study of the grammatical mind is called), let's explore the relationship between grammar, SELinux, and computer security.

At its root, the SELinux security model encompasses three elements:

- Subjects
- Objects
- Actions

Subjects are the actors within a computer system. You might initially think that users would be the subjects of the SELinux security model, especially if your experience with computer systems has been primarily with desktop—rather than server—systems. However, users don't crawl inside their computers and act directly on the bits and bytes that compose computer systems. Instead, processes are the true actors. However, processes often act as surrogates for human users. So subjects and users are closely associated, even though processes—not users—are the true actors.

In grammar, subjects operate on objects. The same is true in the SELinux security model, where subjects (processes) also operate on objects. As summarized in Appendix A, SELinux defines several dozen *security classes* (or, more simply, *classes*) of objects, including such workhorses as:

- Directories
- File descriptors
- Files
- Filesystems
- Links

Processes and Programs

If you're not a programmer, the distinction between processes and programs may not be obvious. Or even if you are a programmer, you may be confident that you understand the distinction, but be unable to readily articulate it.

Simply put, a program is an executable file, whereas a process is a program that has been read into memory and has commenced execution. For instance, if you start two identical terminal windows on your graphical desktop, you have started two processes that run the same program. Unlike a program, a process has state information. The state information associated with a process records the identity of the user account running the process, the instruction pointer (which indicates the next instruction to be executed), the value of every active program variable, and a variety of other information. Because processes and programs are closely related, some folks like to think of processes as programs in motion.

- Processes
- Special files of various types (block device, character device, socket, FIFO, and so on)

Notice that processes can serve as both subjects and objects of actions.

In Linux, many kinds of entities are represented as files. In particular, directories, devices, and memory can all be accessed as files. So the most common class of SELinux object that subjects act upon is a file. Table 2-1 describes the object security classes defined by SELinux.

Table 2-1. SELinux object security classes

Class	Description
File classes	
blk_file	Block device file
chr_file	Character device file
dir	Directory
fd	File descriptor
fifo_file	FIFO file
file	File
filesystem	Formatted filesystem residing on disk partition
lnk_file	Hard or symbolic link
Interprocess communication classes	
ipc	(Obsolete)
msg	Interprocess communication message within queue
msgq	Interprocess communication queue

Table 2-1. SELinux object security classes (continued)

Class	Description
sem	Interprocess communication semaphore
shm	Interprocess communication shared memory
Network classes	
key_socket	IPSec socket
netif	Network interface
netlink_socket	Socket used to communicate with kernel via the netlink syscall
node	TCP/IP network host, as represented by IP address
packet_socket	Obsolete object type used by Linux 2.0 programs invoking the socket syscall
rawip_socket	Raw IP socket
sock_file	Network socket file
socket	Generic socket
tcp_socket	TCP socket
udp_socket	UDP socket
unix_dgram_socket	Unix-domain datagram socket
unix_stream_socket	Unix-domain stream socket
Object class	
passwd	Linux password file
System classes	
capability	SELinux capability
process	Process
Security	Security-related objects, such as the SELinux policy
System	Kernel and system objects

The actions that SELinux subjects perform upon objects vary with the type of object. For instance, a subject can perform such operations as these on file objects:

- Append
- Create
- Execute
- Get attribute
- I/O control
- Link
- Lock
- Read
- Rename
- Unlink
- Write

The preceding list of actions is not comprehensive. As explained in Chapter 5, SELinux recognizes over one dozen actions that can be performed on files. And, as mentioned in the preceding text, other object classes exist. These classes have many related actions.

Using this simple framework—subjects, actions, and objects—we can identify the fundamental operation performed by the SELinux security server: determining whether a given subject is permitted to perform a given action on a given object. For instance, SELinux decides questions such as: *Is process 24691 permitted to read the file known as /etc/shadow?* To make such decisions, the SELinux security server consults its *policy database*. By basing security decisions on policies stored in a database, SELinux achieves a high degree of flexibility. Figure 2-2 illustrates this sample decision.

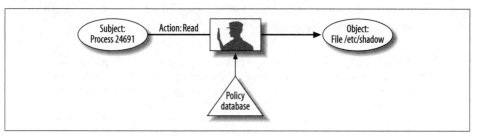

Figure 2-2. A typical SELinux decision

Linux and SELinux: Dueling Security Mechanisms?

As explained in the preceding chapter, Linux has its own system of discretionary access control (DAC). How does Linux DAC interoperate with the mandatory access control (MAC) provided by SELinux? Do we end up with dueling security mechanisms?

Fortunately, Linux DAC and SELinux MAC play well together. When making security decisions, SELinux first hands off the decision to Linux DAC. If DAC forbids an action, the action is not permitted. If, on the other hand, DAC permits an action, then SELinux performs its own authorization check, based on MAC. A requested action is allowed to occur only if both the Linux DAC and SELinux MAC authorizations are approved.

Security Contexts

The discussion in the preceding section might lead you to believe that SELinux makes security decisions based on the identity of individual subjects and objects. In principle, such a system could be made to work. But the system would be unnecessarily unwieldy. Because processes related to a single program can generally be treated the same, it's more convenient to make security decisions based on sets or classes of subjects and objects rather than on individual objects. For example, every instance of the SSH server should generally be given the same permissions, including read access to */etc/ssh/sshd_config*. Similarly, all the files within a given directory often can be manipulated by the same subject. For example, the DHCP service should be permitted to manipulate any of the files in */var/state/dhcp*. To simplify decision making, similar subjects can be grouped and similar objects can be grouped.

SELinux associates information called *security attributes* with subjects and objects and bases its security decisions on the values of these attributes. Three security attributes are used:

User identity

The user identity indicates the SELinux user account associated with a subject or object. In the case of a subject, the user identity gives the SELinux user account under which the process is running. In the case of an object, the user identity gives the user account that owns the object.

In tracking user identities, SELinux does not use the list of user accounts maintained by Linux in */etc/passwd*. Instead, it uses its own database and a mapping that associates SELinux users with Linux users. This approach is consistent with the philosophy that Linux access controls and SELinux access controls should be completely separate, so that changes to one don't affect the other. One important benefit of keeping separate user account databases is that changes to */etc/passwd* don't invalidate the SELinux security attributes of subjects and objects. Keeping separate user databases is not as cumbersome as it may seem, because most systems can be configured to use only a handful of SELinux user accounts. That is, many Linux user accounts can often be mapped to a single SELinux user account.

Role

Under SELinux, users are authorized to enter one or more roles, each of which defines a set of permissions a user can be granted. At a given time, a user can reside in only a single role. A user can transition from one authorized role to another by using the special command *newrole*. This command changes the user's SELinux role similar to the way the Linux *su* command changes a user's Linux identity. SELinux establishes a special role, sysadm_r, used for administering SELinux facilities.

Type

Types, which are also known as domains, divide subjects and objects into related groups. Types are the primary security attribute SELinux uses in making authorization decisions. They establish the sandboxes that constrain processes and prevent privilege escalation. Therefore, you can think of a type as naming a related sandbox.

In SELinux whitepapers, such as those available at the NSA web site and elsewhere, you may read that *type* and *domain* are distinct concepts that must never be confused. The original Flask model—and other computer security models—do carefully distinguish these terms. However, in SELinux the terms are synonymous, notwithstanding claims to the contrary.

Types are the workhorse security attribute: an SELinux policy typically defines only a handful of users and roles, but dozens or even hundreds of types.

Conventions help in distinguishing names that represent users, roles, and types. Table 2-2 summarizes the conventions.

Table 2-2. Naming conventions for security attributes

Security attribute	Standard name suffix	Example name
User	(None)	root
Role	_r	sysadm_r
Type	_t	sysadm_t

The three SELinux security attributes—user identity, role, and type—together make up what's called a *security context*. For convenience and efficiency, SELinux stores security contexts in a table. A *security identifier* (SID) identifies each table entry. Earlier, I implied that SELinux bases security decisions on security contexts. This is approximately correct. But, more precisely, SELinux makes security decisions based on SIDs rather than security contexts, thereby gaining some efficiency since SIDs are represented as integers and are therefore efficiently manipulated by the CPU.

Sometimes, a security context is loosely referred to as an SID. Because there is a one-to-one correspondence between security contexts and SIDs, such references are not too harmful or confusing.

During system initialization, the security context table is preloaded with a small number of SID values. These values are called *initial SIDs*.

Because subjects are active, they often can take on a variety of roles. Objects, on the other hand, are passive and seldom have need of roles. However, every subject or object must possess all three security attributes (user, role, and type). Objects that have no other need of a role are assigned the dummy role object_r.

Transient and Persistent Objects

Two kinds of objects exist within a Linux system: transient objects and persistent objects. A *transient object* has a quite limited lifetime, often existing merely as a data structure within kernel space. A process is the most common kind of transient object. SELinux can directly associate an SID with a transient object by keeping a memory-resident table that maps transient object identities to SIDs and thence to security contexts.

In contrast to transient objects, a *persistent object* has an indefinite lifetime. The most common persistent objects are files and directories. Because persistent objects, once created, generally exist until they're destroyed, a persistent object may exist across several system startups. Thus, a memory-resident table can't be used to associate persistent objects with their SIDs, because the contents of memory-resident tables are lost at system startup. Therefore, associating a persistent object with its security context is somewhat complicated.

In general, persistent objects are associated with Linux filesystems, which can be used to store their security contexts. Several Linux filesystem types, including the standard ext2 and ext3 filesystem types, provide an extended attribute feature that can be enabled during compilation of a Linux kernel. SELinux uses the extended attribute to store *persistent security identifiers* (PSIDs) on the filesystem. SELinux uses memory-resident tables to map PSIDs to SIDs, and thence to security contexts.

 An important operation performed when initially installing SELinux involves creating the PSIDs for persistent objects, a process known as *file labeling*, or merely *labeling*. A special utility named *setfiles* is used to perform the labeling, which is guided by a database called the *file context*. The file context identifies the initial security context that should be associated with specific files, and a default context that should be associated with files not explicitly identified in the file context. Once file labeling is complete, the file context is not needed except under extraordinary circumstances, such as recovery from filesystem damage.

Access Decisions

The SELinux security server makes two basic kinds of decisions:

Access decisions
> Access decisions determine whether a given subject is allowed to perform a given operation on a given object.

Transition decisions
> Transition decisions, also called *labeling decisions*, determine the types assigned to newly created objects, particularly processes and files.

This section explains access decisions—the more frequently made and important of the two kinds of decisions—and the following section explains transition decisions.

Conceptually, each object class has an associated bitmap called an *access vector,* containing one bit for each action defined for the class. Figure 2-3 shows a simplified bitmap for the file class. An actual bitmap for the file class would include each of the more than one dozen actions defined for the file class, rather than merely the common actions shown in the figure.

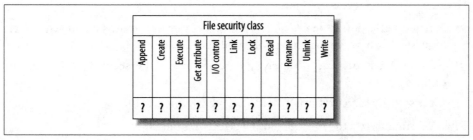

Figure 2-3. A simplified access vector for the file class

As explained earlier in this chapter, the SELinux security server makes access decisions by considering the security context of the subject and object of the action, the security class of the object, and the action requested. When the security server has made the access decision, it returns an access vector that indicates the allowed actions. More precisely, if the security server finds one or more policy rules matching the request, it returns three related access vectors, as shown in Figure 2-4. In the figure, the server has granted the subject permission to append to the object or create the object.

	File security class										
	Append	Create	Execute	Get attribute	I/O control	Link	Lock	Read	Rename	Unlink	Write
Allow	X	X	–	–	–	–	–	–	–	–	–
Auditallow	–	–	–	–	–	–	–	–	–	–	–
Dontaudit	–	–	–	–	–	–	–	–	–	–	–

Figure 2-4. A simplified access vector resulting from an access decision

The three access vectors have the following functions:

Allow

> The allow access vector identifies operations that the subject is permitted to perform on the object. No log entry is made of the operation.

Auditallow

> The auditallow access vector causes a log entry to be made when the indicated operation is performed. Despite its name, it doesn't allow any operation; only the Allow vector does so.

Dontaudit
  The dontaudit access vector identifies operations that the subject is not permitted to perform on the object, but that don't cause the denial to be logged.

Three rules govern access to objects:

- A requested action is denied unless the security server returns allow. Therefore, requests that have no matching policy rule are denied.
- If an action is denied, a log entry is made unless the security server returns dontaudit.
- If the security server returns auditallow, a log entry is made.

Table 2-3 summarizes the rules governing access to objects.

Table 2-3. Access to objects

Result	Access permitted	Result logged
No matching policy rule	No	Yes
allow	Yes	No, unless auditallow also specified
auditallow	No, unless allow also specified	Yes
dontaudit	No	No

 To improve the efficiency of its operation, the security server caches access vectors in a data structure called the *access vector cache* (AVC).

Transition Decisions

Access decisions are one of the two basic kinds of decisions made by the SELinux security server. Transition decisions—which are sometimes called labeling decisions—are the second.

Since every object has a security context, newly created objects must be labeled with some security context. A transition decision decides what security context is chosen. Transition decisions come up in two common contexts:

Process (subject) creation
  The new process may run in the same domain as its parent or in another authorized domain. If the process runs in another domain, a *domain transition* is said to have occurred.

File (object) creation

The new file (or file-like object, such as a directory) may be labeled with the security context of the directory containing it or with another authorized domain. If the file's security context pertains to a domain other than that of the directory that contains it, a *file-type transition*—or, more simply, a *type transition*—is said to have occurred.

 In SELinux, the terms *domain* and *type* are synonymous. The term *domain* is more often used in reference to processes, while *type* is more often used in reference to passive objects such as files.

Let's first consider process creation. Given permission, a running process—called a *parent process*—may invoke the exec syscall, creating a new process—called a *child process*—by executing a specified program file. Generally, the child process runs in the same SELinux domain as the parent process and receives the same SID and security context. However, some programs are defined in the SELinux policy as *entry points* to domains. When such a program is executed, the child process is given a new security context having another domain. The process is said to have *transitioned* to a new domain.

 Domain transitions occur only subject to policy restrictions. A process cannot transition to a domain other than one for which it has been authorized.

Processes can also transition to new domains by using the SELinux application programming interface (API). Programs that need to make special transitions (for example, the login and SSH daemons) have been modified to use the special SELinux APIs that accomplish them. In order that they not compromise system security, such programs permit their programmed transitions only under carefully regulated conditions.

Figure 2-5 illustrates process creation with and without a domain transition. In the left half of the figure, a user runs the *vi* editor in a domain named vi_t. When the user executes the *ls* command from within *vi*, both *vi* and the *ls* command run in the vi_t domain; no transition occurs. In the right half of the figure, the Init process is running in the initrc_t domain. When Init starts the SSH service daemon, a domain transition occurs, so that the SSH service daemon runs in its own domain, the sshd_t domain.

Recall that access decisions are generally based on the domain of the subject and object, along with the class of the object and the requested action. When a process transitions to a new domain, its permissions become those associated with the new domain. Thus, the permissions of processes can be specified with high granularity and flexibility.

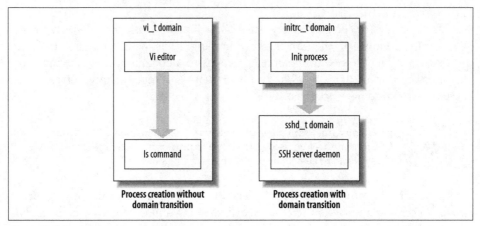

Figure 2-5. Process creation and domain transition

Transition decisions related to file creation work similarly. By default, a newly created file or file-like object receives the security context of the directory that contains it. However, an SELinux policy rule can specify that files created by a process running in a particular domain are specially labeled. Figure 2-6 illustrates the default situation and a situation influenced by a policy rule.

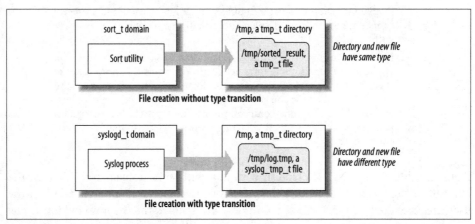

Figure 2-6. File creation and transition decisions

In the upper half of Figure 2-6, the *sort* utility runs in the sort_t domain. The utility creates a temporary file, */tmp/sorted_result*, which receives the same file type as that of its parent directory, */tmp*; namely, tmp_t. This demonstrates automatic inheritance of file type. In the lower half of the figure, an SELinux policy rule causes explicit assignment of a special file type. There, the */tmp/log.tmp* file created by the Syslog process receives the file type syslog_tmp_t rather than the file type of its parent directory.

Just as the SELinux API can override process transition decisions, it can override file creation transition decisions. But only specially designed and modified programs actually do so.

SELinux Architecture

The preceding sections of this chapter have provided an overview of the functions that underlie SELinux. This section provides an overview of the architecture of SELinux. SELinux consists of the following major components:

- Kernel-level code
- The SELinux shared library
- A security policy
- Tools
- Labeled SELinux filesystems (optional)

Kernel-Level Code

When active, the SELinux kernel code monitors system activity and ensures that requested operations are authorized under the currently configured SELinux policy, disallowing any operations not expressly authorized. It also generates system log entries for certain allowed and denied operations, consistent with policy specifications.

Originally, the SELinux kernel-level code was implemented as a patch to the Linux 2.2 kernel, and later the Linux 2.4 kernel. More recently, much of the SELinux kernel-level code has been integrated within the Linux 2.6 kernel. The Linux Security Modules (LSM) feature of Linux 2.6 was expressly designed to support SELinux and other potential security servers.

The principal SELinux facility omitted from Linux 2.6 concerns the labeling of network objects and the security decisions pertaining to them. Some Linux distributors have plans to make the missing SELinux capabilities available as one or more kernel patches, or otherwise.

Despite the integration of SELinux with the Linux 2.6 kernel, a given operational Linux 2.6 kernel may or may not support SELinux. Like many kernel features, the level of SELinux support can be configured when the kernel is built. SELinux can be:

- Incorporated directly within the kernel
- Entirely omitted from the kernel

Therefore, before attempting to configure SELinux on a system, you should determine whether any of the available kernels supports SELinux and, if not, obtain an appropriate kernel. Chapter 3 explains how to build a Linux 2.4 or Linux 2.6 kernel that supports SELinux.

The SELinux Shared Library

Most non-kernel SELinux components are linked against an SELinux shared library, currently named *libselinux1.so*. This library makes available the functions associated with the SELinux application programming interface (API). This library must be installed and available or programs linked against it will fail.

> It might seem that the absence of the SELinux shared library would be a relatively minor matter inhibiting the full and correct functioning of SELinux. However, as explained subsequently in this chapter, implementation of SELinux entails installation of modified versions of several critical system executables, which are linked against the SELinux shared library. Generally, if the SELinux shared library is not available, the system will be crippled. Recovery procedures will be necessary to restore proper system operation.

The SELinux Security Policy

As explained, the SELinux security server bases its decisions on a policy file that can be configured by the administrator. The policy file provides flexibility, enabling SELinux administrators to implement customized security policies that suit local needs, rather than one-size-fits-all boilerplate policies provided by a Linux distribution.

When an SELinux system starts up, it loads the local security policy from a binary policy file, which typically resides in */etc/security/selinux*; however, a Linux distributor may choose to place the file in another location.

The SELinux binary policy file is generated by a *Makefile*, which resides in the SELinux source directory, typically */etc/security/selinux/src/policy* or */etc/selinux*. Some Linux distributions, such as Fedora, do not install the SELinux source directory by default, so the directory and the *Makefile* may be absent from your system. The *Makefile* concatenates a variety of source files, expands the M4 macros they contain, and places the result in a file named *policy.conf*, which resides in the SELinux source directory. It then compiles the resulting SELinux policy statements within *policy.conf* into binary form. Figure 2-7 illustrates this process.

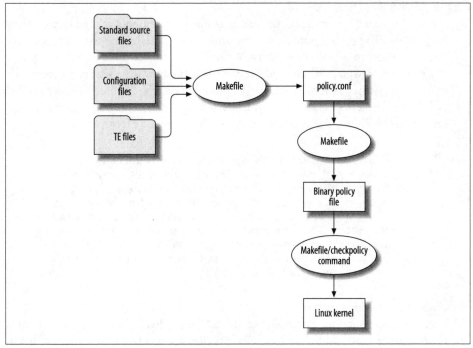

Figure 2-7. Creating and loading the SELinux binary policy file

 make is a Linux/Unix application that compiles source code—such as the Linux kernel—and performs other useful operations, under control of a configuration file called a *Makefile*. You don't need a detailed understanding of *make* to work with SELinux.

M4 is a macro processor commonly used in support of Linux applications, such as Sendmail. M4 is explained more fully in Chapter 5.

Roughly speaking, the SELinux source files are of four major types:

Standard source files that are seldom modified by the SELinux administrator
These files include such files as the SELinux *Makefile*, files defining standard M4 macros, and files that contain boilerplate policy language. Administrators may find it necessary to modify these files to support special, unusual policy requirements. These files typically reside in the SELinux source directory and a variety of subdirectories, including *domains*, *file_contexts*, *flask*, *macros*, and *types*.

Source files that are typically modified by the SELinux administrator during initial configuration of SELinux
These include such files as those defining the authorized SELinux users and their associated roles. They are few in number, relatively short, and easy to modify and maintain. The source files most likely to be modified reside in the SELinux source directory and its *types* subdirectory.

Type-Enforcement (TE) source files

Each TE file contains most of the policy language statements related to a particular domain. The package maintenance utilities of some Linux distributions have been modified to install automatically the TE file related to a package at package installation time. SELinux administrators may find it necessary to create TE files for programs lacking them, or to modify existing TE files to meet special policy requirements. These files typically reside in the *domains/programs* subdirectory of the SELinux source directory and have the file extension *.te*.

 SELinux administrators may also find it necessary to modify TE files to resolve problems arising from SELinux policy bugs. Unfortunately, SELinux policies are relatively large, typically consisting of over 10,000 source lines. Consequently, the typical SELinux policy contains a significant number of bugs, some of which an SELinux administrator may be compelled to fix in order to achieve satisfactory system operation. As SELinux matures, we can expect that the incidence of such problems will decrease significantly and that many SELinux users will be satisfied with default SELinux policies.

File Context (FC) source files

Each FC file contains specifications for labeling (that is, assigning types to) a related set of files and directories. The FC files are used to initially label filesystems and may be used to relabel all or part of a filesystem at special times, such as installation of a software package that creates new files or directories. The FC files typically reside in the *file_contexts/programs* subdirectory of the SELinux source directory and have the file extension *.fc*.

SELinux Tools

SELinux includes three main categories of tools:

- Special commands used to administer and use SELinux
- Modified versions of standard Linux commands and programs
- Supplementary SELinux tools, used for purposes such as policy analysis and development

The following sections describe these tool categories.

SELinux commands

SELinux includes a variety of tools for its administration and use. Chapter 4 describes these tools in detail. Among the principal tools are these:

chcon
> Labels a specified file, or set of files, with a specified security context.

checkpolicy
> Performs a variety of policy-related actions, including compiling policy sources to binary and loading a binary policy into a kernel. The command is typically invoked via the SELinux *Makefile* rather than directly.

getenforce
> Displays a message indicating whether SELinux is currently in permissive mode or enforcing mode. Useful only for kernels compiled with support for permissive mode.

newrole
> Enables a user to transition from one authorized role to another.

run_init
> Used to start, stop, or otherwise control a service. Ensures that the operation is executed in the same context used when services are automatically started, stopped, or controlled by Init.

setenforce
> If given the argument 0, places SELinux in permissive mode; if given the argument 1, places SELinux in enforcing mode.

setfiles
> Sets file labels for a specified directory and its subdirectories, based on the specifications provided in FC files. The command is typically invoked via the SELinux *Makefile* rather than directly, and is generally used only during initial SELinux configuration.

Older versions of SELinux included the following commands, which have been retained in the current version for the convenience of users familiar with them:

avc_enforcing
> Equivalent to *getenforce*.

avc_toggle
> Switches the system from enforcing to permissive mode, or vice versa.

Modified Linux commands and programs

In addition to special commands related to SELinux, an SELinux implementation typically includes modified versions of several Linux commands. Among these are the following commands:

cp, mv, install, and other basic commands
> Modified to label the new file with the security context of the source.

id
> Modified to include an option for displaying the user's current security context.

ls
Modified to include an option for displaying a file's current security context.

ps
Modified to include an option for displaying a process's current security context.

Several common programs are generally modified to support SELinux, including:

cron
Modified to set a standard security context for all *cron* jobs.

login
Modified to set the initial security context of a user when the user logs in.

logrotate
Modified to preserve the security context of log files being rotated.

pam
Modified to set the initial security context of a user and to use the SELinux API to obtain privileged access to password information.

ssh
Modified to set the initial security context of a user when the user logs in.

various programs that modify /etc/passwd or /etc/shadow
Modified to preserve the security context of the modified file.

Supplementary SELinux tools

A variety of supplementary SELinux tools is available, and others are under development. Among the most noteworthy are the tools provided by Tresys (*http://www. tresys.com*) and distributed under the GNU General Public License. These tools include:

Apol
A tool for analyzing the SELinux *policy.conf* file. Figure 2-8 shows a typical Apol screen.

SeAudit
A graphical user interface (GUI) tool for analyzing SELinux log entries.

SeCmds
A set of non-GUI tools for analyzing the SELinux *policy.conf* file.

SePCuT
A GUI tool for browsing and editing SELinux policy files.

SeUser
A pair of GUI and non-GUI tools for managing Linux and SELinux user accounts.

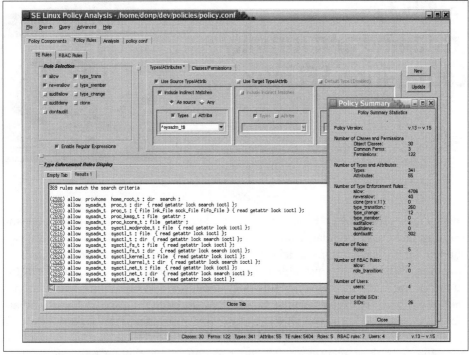

Figure 2-8. The Apol policy analysis tool by Tresys

References

To learn more about the SELinux security model, you can read Chapter 5 of this book. The description of the SELinux security model presented in this book is based primarily on the paper "Configuring the SELinux Policy," by Stephen Smalley. It is available on the NSA's SELinux web site, *http://www.nsa.gov/selinux/index.cfm*. The paper is somewhat out of date because SELinux has been developed further since its publication. However, for the most part, the information presented in the paper remains accurate, even if somewhat incomplete.

CHAPTER 3
Installing and Initially Configuring SELinux

This chapter presents step-by-step procedures for installing and initially configuring SELinux on several popular Linux distributions. At the time of writing, only two popular Linux distributions officially support SELinux: Fedora Core and Gentoo. However, SELinux is also available for Debian GNU/Linux and SUSE, thanks to the unofficial work of independent software developers. In addition, Red Hat has announced that Red Hat Enterprise Linux 4 will support SELinux. So those who are looking to install SELinux can choose from a variety of Linux distributions. You may also be able to download and apply the SELinux source release to a Linux distribution other than those mentioned. The final section of this chapter provides an overview of this process.

 This chapter contains step-by-step instructions for installing and initially configuring SELinux on several Linux distributions. I exercised care in writing and testing these instructions, which were also reviewed and tested by others. However, I can't promise that they'll work in every situation or in your particular situation. And directions such as these tend to become outdated quickly. So don't become alarmed if your system responds differently than expected. You'll likely find the instructions more useful as a rough guide than as a detailed road map.

SELinux Versions

Every implementation of SELinux is based on one of the official NSA versions. The NSA has published four major versions of SELinux:

Original (Pre-LSM) SELinux
    The original version of SELinux, which supported Linux 2.2 and Linux 2.4.

LSM-Based SELinux
    A version of SELinux that worked with the Linux Security Modules (LSM) patch to Linux 2.4 and 2.5.

SELinux for Linux 2.4

A version of SELinux that also worked with the LSM patch to Linux 2.4, but additionally required the extended attribute (EA) patch. Apart from differences in kernel support, this version is architecturally similar to SELinux for Linux 2.6 but is no longer under active development.

SELinux for Linux 2.6

The current version of SELinux, which works with standard Linux 2.6 kernels. The Linux 2.6 kernel natively supports SELinux and therefore does not have to be patched.

The application programming interface of the original and LSM-based versions of SELinux differs from that of current version. Therefore, although the older versions can still be downloaded from the NSA's web site, I don't recommend that the older versions—or third-party packages or source code based on the older versions—be used.

Similarly, although the Linux 2.4 version of SELinux is architecturally similar to the current Linux 2.6–based SELinux release, it is not under active development and therefore lacks useful functions present in the current release. At the time of writing, implementations of SELinux for Linux distributions not integrally supporting SELinux tend to be based on SELinux for Linux 2.4 and are therefore somewhat out of date. Consequently, my own preference and recommendation is that you install one of the following SELinux implementations:

- Red Hat Enterprise Linux 4 (when available)
- Fedora Core 2

Nevertheless, in the following sections I give procedures and suggestions for installing SELinux for Debian GNU/Linux—owing to its high popularity and ready availability—and Gentoo Linux. Although Gentoo Linux does not support SELinux integrally, Gentoo's Hardened Project does officially support Gentoo's implementation of SELinux.

Installing SELinux

SELinux can be installed in three fundamental ways:

- As an integral component of a Linux distribution, installed at the same time as the distribution
- By using binary or source packages, such as the *.deb* packages used by Debian GNU/Linux; the ebuilds used by Gentoo Linux; or the RPM packages used by Fedora Core, Red Hat Enterprise Linux, and SUSE Linux
- By downloading, compiling, and installing the sources provided by the NSA

At the time of writing, only Fedora Core and Gentoo contain SELinux as a fully supported, native facility. So unless you choose one of those distributions, you must install SELinux yourself. If you install SELinux yourself, it's generally much more convenient to do so using packages. However, prebuilt packages are not available for every Linux distribution. Those who are unable or unwilling to use a distribution for which packages are available must compile the sources provided by the NSA. In many cases, the sources must be modified in order to work properly with the distinctive characteristics of a specific Linux distribution.

The following sections explain how to install and initially configure SELinux for several popular Linux distributions. The final section of this chapter explains how to install SELinux using the source code provided by the NSA.

Using X with SELinux

Coaxing SELinux into working with X has proven to be somewhat difficult. Recent releases of SELinux perform much better in this regard than older releases. But they still fall short of perfection. It's common for SELinux users to find that the login screen doesn't appear or that they can't log in.

The KDE Desktop has so far proven more resistant to interoperation with SELinux than its rival desktop, GNOME. The central problem is that various KDE programs run as identically named processes. Thus, SELinux cannot assign these KDE processes to distinct domains. One result of this inability is that KDE's temporary files sometimes cannot be labeled with appropriate domains. Thus, with respect to KDE, SELinux policies tend either to be too restrictive or too lax. We can hope that a future release of KDE or SELinux will somehow address this problem. In the meantime, for those using SELinux, GNOME is generally a better desktop choice than KDE.

If you find yourself unable to log into X, try returning to a text-mode console by pressing Ctrl-Alt-F1. Then log in and reboot the system in non-SELinux mode, as explained in Chapter 4.

Linux Distributions Supporting SELinux

Currently only Fedora Core supports SELinux by providing it as an integral component that is installed without special effort on the part of the installing user. However, Red Hat has announced that Red Hat Enterprise Linux 4 (RHEL 4) will support SELinux. The RHEL 4 implementation of SELinux is expected to closely resemble the one in Fedora Core 2.

Fedora Core 2

Fedora Core is a Linux distribution sponsored—but not supported—by Red Hat that uses the distribution as a test bed for new technologies being considered for incorporation in Red Hat's supported distributions, such as Red Hat Enterprise Linux. Fedora Core is freely available at *http://fedora.redhat.com*. Unlike Red Hat Enterprise Linux, which contains proprietary components, Fedora Core is fully redistributable under the terms of the GNU GPL.

Fedora Core 2 presents the most convenient implementation of SELinux available to date. To install SELinux, you must respond `selinux` to the boot prompt that appears after booting from the installation media.* During the installation procedure, the Firewalls screen (see Figure 3-1) provides the user with the opportunity to choose from three levels of SELinux support:

Disabled
  Disables SELinux.

Warn
  Enables SELinux to log, but not prevent, attempted violations of the SELinux policy.

Active
  Enables SELinux to fully enforce its policy.

When the system boots after installation, SELinux immediately assumes the mode specified during installation—no further configuration is necessary. Of course, the system administrator can reconfigure the system to operate in a different SELinux mode by modifying the boot configuration (*/boot/grub/grub.conf*) or the SELinux configuration (*/etc/sysconfig/selinux*), either manually or by using the GUI Security Level tool.

Moreover, the RPM package manager included in Fedora Core is SELinux-aware. It automatically labels files and directories when new packages are installed. Thus, running SELinux under Fedora Core may involve relatively little ongoing administration.

The default SELinux policy implemented by Fedora Core is termed a "relaxed policy," meaning that it seeks to protect potentially vulnerable services and daemons without strictly imposing the principle of least privilege on every user action. Thus, the policy represents a compromise between ease of use and security that is appropriate for many users. The system administrator, of course, is free to tailor the SELinux policy to better suit local needs. In particular, the system administrator may find it necessary to do so if the system hosts binaries other than those distributed as part of Fedora Core, or if the system administrator wants to restrict the privileges available

---

* Fedora Core 2 test versions do not require you to use this special boot option.

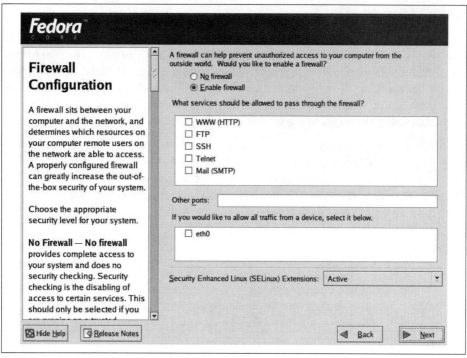

Figure 3-1. The Fedora Core firewalls screen

to scripts such as *cron* jobs. Chapters 5–8 of this book explain the procedures for doing so.

Installation Overview

The procedure for installing SELinux varies according to the target Linux distribution. However, it generally includes the following operations:

- Configuration, compilation, and installation of a kernel supporting SELinux
- Modification of the bootloader configuration to include the new, SELinux-capable kernel
- Installation and configuration of SELinux-related userland libraries, utilities, and commands
- Compilation and installation of an SELinux policy
- Labeling of the filesystems

The operations can be performed in any of a variety of sequences. A few of these operations can be entirely omitted if precompiled packages are used. And additional operations are generally required, as explained in the following sections.

Installing SELinux from Binary or Source Packages

Unless you choose a Linux distribution that includes built-in support for SELinux, you'll have to install and configure SELinux yourself. It's generally easier to do so using binary or source packages than using the source code tarballs released by the NSA. This section explains how to install and initially configure SELinux on:

- Debian GNU/Linux
- Gentoo Linux
- SUSE Linux 8.2

In addition, the section gives advice on installing and configuring SELinux to work with Red Hat Enterprise Linux 3. As explained earlier, the forthcoming Red Hat Enterprise Linux 4 is planned to integrally support SELinux.

Debian GNU/Linux

At the time of writing, two releases of Debian GNU/Linux are currently in use, and a third is under development. The two commonly used releases are:

- Debian GNU/Linux 3.0 stable, known as Woody
- Debian GNU/Linux 3.0 unstable, known as Sid

As the release names indicate, Woody is considered the more reliable release; its component packages have been subject to more extensive, and more thorough, testing and use than those of Sid. However, the C compiler and libraries and other components of Woody are too old to work well with SELinux. Consequently, this section presents an SELinux installation procedure appropriate for Sid.

If you're interested in using SELinux with Woody, you can use special packages created by Brian May, available at *http://www.microcomaustralia.com.au/debian*. You can find brief instructions for using them at *http://www.coker.com.au/selinux*. Because these packages are subject to change, I don't present step-by-step instructions for installing and configuring SELinux under Woody. If you plan to install SELinux under Woody, you can request assistance by posting to the SELinux mailing list, to which you can subscribe using the web page identified in Chapter 1.

To install SELinux under Sid, perform the following steps. Since I presume you know how to install Debian Sid, the steps include only general explanations of the associated operations. If you're unfamiliar with the installation procedure for Debian, please see the installation manual available at *http://www.debian.org/releases/stable/i386/install*.

1. Obtain bootable media for Debian Sid and boot the system using them. I recommend the media available at *http://people.debian.org/~dwhedon/boot-floppies*, especially *bf2.4-3.0.23-netinst.iso* because of its relatively small size (10 MB). If you like, you can choose from other media available at *http://www.debian.org/CD/netinst*.

2. Burn the ISO image to a CD-RW or CD-R and boot the system using it. Choose the language to be used during installation and your keyboard type.

3. Partition the target system's primary hard disk and create Linux filesystems as usual. The simplest installation consists of three partitions: a boot partition (*/boot*), a root partition (*/*), and a swap partition. The swap partition should have partition type 82, whereas the other two partitions should have type 83.

   The installer encourages you to choose the ext2 filesystem type for the boot and root partitions. I suggest that you ignore the default and choose ext3 as the filesystem type for the root filesystem, because the journaling provided by ext3 will improve the reliability of your filesystem. You can choose either ext2 or ext3 as the filesystem type of the boot partition. I myself prefer to choose ext3 for consistency.

4. Install a kernel and any drivers necessary for devices you plan to use during, and immediately after, installation. In general, you should ensure that a driver is available for your system's network interface. The installation program may automatically recognize your system's devices, in which case you don't need to explicitly load any drivers.

5. Set up networking by specifying a hostname, domain name, and network configuration. If a DHCP or BOOTP server is available, you can request automatic network configuration, which identifies the system IP address, network mask, gateway IP address, and DNS server IP address for you; otherwise, you must specify these yourself.

6. Install the bootloader. Generally, you should install LILO, the default Debian bootloader, to the MBR (master boot record) of the primary hard drive. If your system is configured to boot multiple operating systems, special considerations are necessary. Consult the Debian installation manual for details.

7. Reboot the system. When the system configuration screen appears, specify configuration options, including the time zone, MD5 passwords (which should generally be enabled), a shadow password file, a root password, and a non-root user.

8. When prompted to run *apt*, decline to do so by pressing Cancel. Likewise, decline to run *tasksel*. When *dselect* runs, allow it to continue and also allow it to delete any previously downloaded *.deb* files that are no longer needed.

If you allow *apt* to run, it may install updated packages that conflict with SELinux packages to be installed later in this procedure. Declining to run *apt* avoids this problem.

9. Respond to the installation program prompts that lead you through the configuration of installed packages such as mail.

10. When configuration is complete, log in as the root user. Use a text editor to create the file */etc/apt/apt_preferences*, specifying the following contents:

```
Package: *
Pin: release o=etbe
Pin-Priority: 1100
```

This configuration file will prevent critical SELinux packages from being overwritten by updated non-SELinux packages.

11. Use a text editor to modify the file */etc/apt/sources.list*, deleting any existing entries and specifying the following contents:

```
deb http://www.coker.com.au/newselinux/ ./
deb ftp://ftp.us.debian.org/debian/ sid main
```

The web site *www.coker.com* is a repository of Debian SELinux packages, maintained by Russell Coker.

12. Issue the command:

```
# apt-get update
```

to update the list of available packages.

13. Use *apt-get* to install the libselinux1 package. Then install the following packages:

```
checkpolicy
coreutils
cron
dpkg
fileutils
initscripts
libpam0g
libpam0g-dev
libpam-cracklib
libpam-doc
libpam-modules
libpam-runtime
libselinux1
logrotate
policycoreutils
procps
selinux-doc
selinux-policy-default
selinux-utils
shellutils
strace
sysvinit
```

```
sysv-rc
textutils
```

These packages contain versions of standard utilities that have been modified to work with SELinux, SELinux-specific utilities, the SELinux policy, and SELinux documentation.

You may be prompted to update Glibc, which you should approve. You will then be prompted to accept a series of files contained in the *selinux-policy-default* package; you may accept all such files.

14. Launch *dselect*, and use it to install any available updates to Sid. If *dselect* does not propose installation of a Linux 2.6 kernel, manually select an appropriate *kernel-image* package for installation. In any case, manually select a *kernel-source* package corresponding to the kernel that *dselect* automatically selected or that you manually selected. Finally, be sure that the *ncurses-dev* package is selected for installation. Allow *dselect* to install the selected packages.

15. Now, you're ready to build an SELinux kernel. Move to the directory */usr/src*, unpack the kernel sources, and set up a symbolic link named *linux*, pointing to the directory containing the unpacked sources. If you're unfamiliar with the procedure for manually configuring, compiling, and installing a Linux kernel, consult the Debian installation guide.

16. Enter the directory containing the kernel sources. Using a text editor, open the *Makefile* and change the EXTRAVERSION variable to a distinct value. This value is used to name and identify the directory containing loadable kernel modules that work with your kernel.

17. Choose an installed */boot/config* file and copy it to the current directory, naming it *.config*. Doing so will conveniently set default values for many configuration options.

18. Issue the command:

```
# make menuconfig
```

19. Choose kernel configuration options appropriate to your system, overriding default values as necessary. I personally like to omit support for devices and filesystems that I don't use and specify that support for needed devices and filesystems should be compiled integrally in the kernel, rather than as modules. But, other preferences are acceptable.

Also specify the following SELinux-related options. Under Code Maturity, specify:

```
Prompt for development and/or incomplete code/drivers
```

Under Device Drivers → Character Devices, specify:

```
Unix98 PTY
No Legacy (BSD) PTY support
```

Under File systems, specify:

```
Second extended fs support
Ext2 extended attributes
```

```
Ext2 security labels
Ext3 journalling file system support
Ext3 extended attributes
Ext3 security labels
```

Do not specify POSIX access control lists for either ext2 or ext3.

Under Pseudo filesystems, specify:

```
/dev/pts Extended Attributes
/dev/pts Security labels
```

Do not specify:

```
/dev file system support
```

Finally, under Security options, specify:

```
Enable different security models
Socket and networking security hooks
Default Linux capabilities
NSA SELinux
NSA SELinux boot parameter
NSA SELinux Development support
```

20. Compile and install the kernel, by issuing the commands:

```
# make clean
# make install modules modules_install
```

If you compiled all features integrally within the kernel, omitting support for modules, use the following command instead:

```
# make clean && make install
```

21. Modify the */etc/lilo.conf* bootloader configuration to boot the new kernel in SELinux mode, by adding the following LILO option to the stanza pertaining to the new kernel:

```
append="selinux=1 enforcing=0"
```

Issue the */sbin/lilo* command to update the boot record.

22. Create the special directory used by the SELinux kernel during system startup:

```
# mkdir /selinux
```

23. Add the following line at the end of the */etc/fstab* configuration file:

```
none /selinux selinuxfs defaults 0 0
```

24. Modify the PAM configuration by adding the following line at the end of the files */etc/pam.d/login* and */etc/pam.d/ssh*:

```
session required pam_selinux.so
```

25. Compile the SELinux policy and label the filesystem:

```
# cd /etc/selinux
# make policy
# make relabel
```

Labeling the filesystem associates a security context with each existing file. As explained in Chapter 5, a file's security context identifies the SELinux user, role, and type of the file. The SELinux policy specifies the label to apply to each file.

Unfortunately, it's not unusual for errors to appear during compilation of the SELinux policy. These are generally typographical errors or other gross errors in policy files specifying domains, such as *domain/ programs/*.te*. To work around such errors, create the directory */etc/ selinux/domain/programs/error*, move any defective files to this directory, and remake the policy file. You may need to read material in the following several chapters of this book to successfully complete this process. You can also post a request for help on the SELinux mailing list, identified near the end of Chapter 1.

26. Reboot your system. When the system starts up, relabel the filesystem a second time so that any files creating during the reboot are properly labeled:

```
# cd /etc/selinux
# make relabel
```

27. Your Debian SELinux system should now be ready for use. The information in the following chapters will help you better understand how to use, maintain, and improve it.

The Debian developers do not officially support SELinux. However, they tend to be both technologically keen and helpful in responding to questions that interest them. Understandably, the developers are sometimes nonresponsive to questions posed by users who seem to them to be lazy or unskilled. In a few cases, they may even seem to respond contemptuously or with hostility. To make good use of their time and avoid taxing their patience, be sure to put forth a good-faith effort to troubleshoot and resolve problems before posting questions to the Debian mailing lists, such as *debian-security*.

Gentoo Linux

Unlike Debian GNU/Linux, Gentoo Linux specifically supports SELinux. However, SELinux has not been integrated into the standard Gentoo release. This section explains how to install SELinux under Gentoo to a fresh or bare-metal system. The following section explains how to install SELinux to a preexisting Gentoo Linux system.

At the time of writing, Gentoo supports SELinux only on servers, not workstations, due primarily to interoperability problems between SELinux and X. However, the Gentoo developers suggest that SELinux workstation may be available in a future Gentoo release.

Installing SELinux to a fresh Gentoo system

The "Gentoo x86 SELinux Installation Guide," available at *http://www.gentoo.org/ selinux*, gives the official Gentoo instructions for installing Gentoo SELinux. The online instructions are likely to be more up to date than the following procedure;

however, you may find the following procedure helpful in explaining how the Gentoo procedure works. Ideally, when installing SELinux under Gentoo, you should consult both the online instructions and this book.

To install SELinux under Gentoo, perform the following steps:

1. Obtain a current Gentoo LiveCD image, available from a Gentoo mirror site listed at *http://www.gentoo.org/main/en/mirrors.xml*. Burn the image to CD-R or CD-RW and boot your system from it. Choose a kernel from those listed as available. For installation, you don't need to choose an SELinux kernel; a standard Gentoo kernel such as *gentoo* or *nousb* is satisfactory.

2. After booting, the system automatically logs you in as the root user. The system probably loaded appropriate kernel drivers for your system's devices automatically. But, if not, you can manually load a driver by issuing the *modprobe* command. Use the *lsmod* command to verify that the driver appropriate for your network interface was loaded. If it was not loaded, manually load a driver from */lib/modules*/kernel/drivers/net*. If a required SCSI driver was not loaded, manually load one in the same manner.

3. Issue the */sbin/ifconfig* command to verify that networking has been configured. If networking has been configured, verify that it's working by pinging your DNS server or accessing a web site. The *lynx, ping, scp, ssh, wget,* and other network commands are available and should work. If networking is not properly operational, consult the Gentoo installation guide for troubleshooting and problem resolution hints.

4. Use the *date* command to set your system's date and time. For instance, you can set the date and time to 2:27 a.m. on July 1, 2004, by issuing the command:

   ```
   022707012004
   ```

5. Use *fdisk* to establish appropriate partitions on your system's primary hard drive.

6. Use *mkswap* to prepare a swap partition for use and use *mke2fs* to prepare ext3 (preferred) or ext2 filesystems on the non-swap partitions. Activate the swap partition and mount the filesystems. For instance:

   ```
   mkswap /dev/hda2  # prepare swap partition
   mke2fs -j /dev/hda1 # make /boot filesystem
   mke2fs -j /dev/hda3 # make / filesystem
   swapon /dev/hda2  # activate swap partition
   mount /dev/hda3 /mnt/gentoo  # mount / partition
   mkdir /mnt/gentoo/boot  # create mount point
   mount /dev/hda1 /mnt/gentoo/boot # mount /boot
   ```

7. Download the installation tarball, *stage1-x86-1.4_rc4.tar.bz2*, using the *lynx* or *wget* command, from a Gentoo mirror such as *http://gentoo.oregonstate.edu/experimental/x86/stages*, and place the tarball in the */mnt/gentoo directory*. Extract the tarball contents, enter the *chroot*ed filesystem just created, and update your shell context:

```
# tar jxvpf stage1-*.tar.bz2
# mount -t proc proc /mnt/gentoo/proc
# mount -t selinuxfs none /mnt/gentoo/selinux
# cp /etc/resolv.conf /mnt/gentoo/etc/resolv.conf
# chroot /mnt/gentoo /bin/bash
# env-update
# source /etc/profile
```

8. Update the portage tree:

```
# emerge sync
```

9. Use a text editor, such as Nano, to customize the build settings, if desired. The settings reside in the file */etc/make.conf*, which is heavily commented and therefore largely self-explanatory. Generally, the default values are acceptable. But, you should check the values of CHOST, CFLAG, and CXXFLAGS to ensure they're consistent with the processor type of your system.

 Detailed information on the configuration options provided by the *make.conf* file is available at *http://www.gentoo.org/doc/en/use-howto.xml* and *http://www.gentoo.org/dyn/use-index.xml*.

10. Initiate the bootstrap process, which builds the GNU C library, the C compiler, and other fundamental programs:

```
# export PORTAGE_TMPDIR=/var/tmp
# cd /usr/portage
# scripts/bootstrap.sh
```

The bootstrap process is relatively time-consuming, as you might suspect. You can specify a directory other than */var/tmp*, if you prefer. The directory should provide several hundred megabytes of free space.

11. Build the non-bootstrapped programs:

```
# emerge system
```

This process generally takes even longer than the bootstrap process.

12. Set the time zone:

```
# ln -sf /usr/share/zoneinfo/path /etc/localtime
```

where *path* denotes the subpath corresponding to your time zone. For instance, */usr/share/zoneinfo/America/Los_Angeles* denotes the U.S. Pacific time zone.

13. Install a kernel by issuing any *one* of the following commands:

```
# emerge sys-kernel/selinux-sources
# emerge sys-kernel/hardened-sources
# emerge sys-kernel/gentoo-dev-sources
# emerge sys-kernel/devlopment-sources
# emerge sys-kernel/mm-sources
```

 Issue only one of the preceding commands; don't issue all of them.

---

14. Now, you're ready to build an SELinux kernel. To begin doing so, issue the following commands:

```
# cd /usr/src/linux
# zcat /proc/config.gz > .config
# make menuconfig
```

Specify the following SELinux-related options. Under Code Maturity, specify:

```
Prompt for development and/or incomplete code/drivers
```

Under Device Drivers → Character Devices, specify:

```
Unix98 PTY
No Legacy (BSD) PTY support
```

Under File systems, specify:

```
Second extended fs support
Ext2 extended attributes
Ext2 security labels
Ext3 journalling file system support
Ext3 extended attributes
Ext3 security labels
```

Do not specify POSIX access control lists for either ext2 or ext3.

Under Pseudo filesystems, specify:

```
/dev/pts Extended Attributes
/dev/pts Security labels
```

Do not specify:

```
/dev file system support
```

Finally, under Security options, specify:

```
Enable different security models
Default Linux capabilities
NSA SELinux
NSA SELinux boot parameter
NSA SELinux Development support
```

Do not specify:

```
Socket and networking security hooks
NSA SELinux MLS policy
```

15. If needed, configure kernel support for PPPoE and IDE CD burning. Be sure the kernel includes support for your system's Ethernet card. See the Installation Guide for details.

16. Compile and install the kernel:

```
# make dep
# make clean bzImage modules modules_install
# cp /usr/src/linux/arch/i386/boot/bzImage /boot
```

17. Install any kernel-related software needed by your system. For instance, you might issue one or more of the following commands:

```
# emerge e100   # Intel e100 NIC
# emerge e1000  # Intel e1000 NIC
# emerge emu10k1 # Creative SBLive!
```

18. Install a system logging service. Under Gentoo, you can choose any one of four logging services. I prefer the Unix de facto standard, Syslog. To install Syslog, issue the following commands:

```
# emerge -k app-admin/sysklogd
# rc-update add sysklogd default
```

 If you prefer to configure a logging service other than Syslog, see the Installation Guide.

19. Install the *cron* service:

```
# emerge -k sys-apps/vixie-cron
# rc-update add vixie-cron default
```

20. First, use *nano* (or another editor of your choice) to create an */etc/fstab* file that mounts your Linux *ext2* and *ext3*, *swap*, *proc*, *tmpfs*, and *cdrom* filesystems. A typical file looks like this:

```
/dev/hda1 /boot     ext3   ro,noatime           1 1
/dev/hda2 /         ext3   noatime              0 0
/dev/hda4 /space    ext3   noatime              0 0
/dev/hda3 none      swap   sw                   0 0
none      /proc     proc   defaults             0 0
none      /dev/shm  tmpfs  defaults             0 0
/dev/cdroms/cdrom0 /mnt/cdrom iso9660 noauto,ro 0 0
```

Then, add the following two SELinux-related lines to the file:

```
none      /selinux selinuxfs defaults           0 0
none      /dev/pts devpts    defaults           0 0
```

The first line causes the system to automatically mount the SELinux pseudofile-system during system startup. The second line causes the system to automatically mount the *devpts* pseudofilesystem. This is needed because the current release of Gentoo SELinux uses *devpts* rather than the Gentoo-default *devfs* pseudofilesystem.

21. Set the password for the root user, by issuing the *passwd* command. You should also create one or more non-root users, by issuing the *adduser* command. You should also set a password for each non-root user you create.

```
# passwd
New UNIX password: (password not echoed)
Retype new UNIX password: (password not echoed)
# adduser staff
# passwd staff
New UNIX password: (password not echoed)
Retype new UNIX password: (password not echoed)
```

22. Specify the host and domain names. To set the host name, issue the command:

```
# echo hname > /etc/hostname
```

where **hname** is the host name. To set the domain name, issue the command:

```
# echo dname > /etc/dnsdomainname
```

where *dname* is the domain name. If your system is to be part of an NIS domain, also set the name of the NIS domain:

```
# echo nisname > /etc/nisdomainname
```

where *nisname* is the NIS domain name.

Also, modify the */etc/hosts* file to include a line such as the following:

```
xxx.xxx.xxx.xxx hname.dname hname
```

where *xxx.xxx.xxx.xxx* is the primary IP address of your system, *hname* is its host name, and *dname* is its domain name.

 If your system receives its network configuration dynamically, via DHCP or BOOTP, you may omit this step.

23. Specify the kernel modules that should be loaded at system startup. To do so, add their names (and any desired options) to */etc/modules.autoload*.

 If the driver for your system's network adapter was compiled as a module, it's especially important that the corresponding module is specified in */etc/modules.autoload*. You can determine the name of the module by inspecting the names of the driver files located in */lib/ modules/`uname –r`/kernel/drivers/net*.

24. Configure your system's IP address, network mask, and other TCP/IP parameters in */etc/conf.d/net*. Then set networking to start at the default run level:

```
# rc-update add net.eth0 default
```

 If your system has multiple network adapters or a PCMCIA network adapter, consult the Installation Guide for the proper configuration procedure.

25. Set system preferences in */etc/rc.conf*. Comments in the file explain the functions of the configuration options. In particular, be sure the CLOCK setting has the correct value (UTC or local).

26. Compile, install, and configure the GRUB bootloader.

 If your system uses hardware RAID, your system is configured for multiple boot, your kernel is configured to use framebuffer video, or if you prefer to configure the LILO bootloader rather than GRUB, see the Installation Guide for further instructions.

To compile GRUB, issue the command:

```
# emerge grub
```

To install GRUB, enter its command-line environment and issue the GRUB *root* and *setup* commands:

```
# grub
grub> root (hd0,0)
grub> setup (hd0)
grub> quit
```

The GRUB root command shown is appropriate only if your */boot* partition is the first partition on the primary hard drive, the most common case. If the */boot* partition is the second partition, use the command:

```
grub> root(hd0,1)
```

To configure GRUB, use an editor to create the */boot/boot/grub.conf* file. A typical file might resemble the following:

```
default 0
timeout 30
splashimage=(hd0,0)/boot/grub/splash.xpm.gz
title=Gentoo SELinux
root (hd0,0)
kernel (hd0,0)/boot/bzImage root=/dev/hda3 gentoo=nodevfs
```

This configuration file assumes that the boot partition is */dev/hda1* and the Linux root partition is */dev/hda3*. It won't work if your hard drive is differently configured. In that case, you must adjust the configuration parameters. If you're unfamiliar with the contents of GRUB's configuration file, or uncertain what values to specify, see the Installation Guide.

If your system fails to boot, it's handy to have available a GRUB boot disk. To create one, put a blank floppy in the drive and issue the following commands:

```
# cd /usr/share/grub/i386-pc/
# cat stage1 stage2 > /dev/fd0
```

27. Update any out-of-date configuration files, by issuing the command:

```
# etc-update
```

28. Compile the SELinux policy and label the filesystem, by issuing the following commands:

```
# cd /etc/security/selinux/src/policy/
# make install
# make chroot_relabel
```

Labeling the filesystem associates a security context with each existing file. As explained in Chapter 5, a file's security context identifies the SELinux user, role, and type of the file. The SELinux policy specifies the label to apply to each file.

Unfortunately, it's not unusual for errors to appear during compilation of the SELinux policy. These are generally typographical errors or other gross errors in policy files specifying domains, such as *domain/programs/*.te*. To work around such errors, create the directory */etc/selinux/domain/programs/error*, move any defective files to this directory, and remake the policy file. You may need to read material in the following several chapters of this book to successfully complete this process. You can also post a request for help on the SELinux mailing list mentioned near the end of Chapter 1.

29. Exit the *chroot*ed shell, and reboot the system:

```
# exit
# cd /
# umount /mnt/gentoo/boot
# umount /mnt/gentoo/proc
# umount /mnt/gentoo/selinux
# umount /mnt/gentoo
# reboot
```

30. When the system has booted, relabel the filesystem for the second time, so that files created during rebooting will be properly labeled:

```
# cd /etc/security/selinux/src/policy
# make relabel
```

Your Gentoo SELinux system should now be ready for use. The information in the following chapters will help you better understand how to use, maintain, and improve it.

Installing SELinux to an existing Gentoo Linux system

The preceding section explains how to install a Gentoo SELinux system onto a bare-metal system. It's also possible to install SELinux to a working Gentoo Linux system. This section explains how to do so. The "Gentoo Linux SELinux Quick Start Guide," available at *http://www.gentoo.org/proj/en/hardened/selinux/selinux-quickstart.xml*, gives the official Gentoo instructions for installing Gentoo SELinux to an existing Gentoo Linux system. The online instructions are likely to be more up to date than the following procedure; however, you may find the following procedure helpful in explaining how the Gentoo procedure works. Ideally, when installing SELinux under Gentoo, you should consult both the online instructions and this book.

1. First, check whether your system is compatible with Gentoo SELinux. Your system should be a server, not a workstation. And, it should use the Linux ext2 or ext3 filesystem rather than a more exotic filesystem such as ReiserFS.

 Gentoo SELinux also supports the XFS filesystem. However, this book does not explain how to configure SELinux to work with that filesystem. See the Quick Start Guide for instructions on doing so.

2. Issue the following instructions to switch to the SELinux profile:

```
# rm -f /etc/make.profile
# ln -sf /usr/portage/profiles/selinux-x86-1.4 \
/etc/make.profile
```

3. Check whether any USE flags need to be reenabled in *letc/make.conf*:

```
# emerge info
```

Edit *letc/make.conf* as appropriate, based on any messages you see.

> You may see the message "!!! SELinux module not found. Please ver-ify that it was installed," which you may safely ignore. The cause of this message will be fixed by a subsequent step of this procedure.

4. Check that the C headers are sufficiently up to date:

```
# emerge -s linux-headers
```

If the version of the headers is older than 2.4.20, merge new headers by issuing the command:

```
# emerge \>=sys-kernel/linux-headers-2.4.20
```

5. Next, recompile the C library, by issuing the command:

```
# emerge glibc
```

This step generally takes a significant amount of time to complete.

6. Merge an appropriate Linux 2.4 or Linux 2.6 kernel, by issuing any *one* of the following commands:

```
# emerge sys-kernel/selinux-sources
# emerge sys-kernel/hardened-sources
# emerge sys-kernel/gentoo-dev-sources
# emerge sys-kernel/devlopment-sources
# emerge sys-kernel/mm-sources
```

> Issue only one of the preceding commands; don't issue all of them.

7. Now, you're ready to build an SELinux kernel. To begin doing so, issue the following commands:

```
# cd /usr/src/linux
# make menuconfig
```

Specify any options needed to support devices or facilities installed on your system. Also, specify the following SELinux-related options. Under Code Maturity, specify:

```
Prompt for development and/or incomplete code/drivers
```

Under Device Drivers → Character Devices, specify:

```
Unix98 PTY
No Legacy (BSD) PTY support
```

Under File systems, specify:

```
Second extended fs support
Ext2 extended attributes
Ext2 security labels
Ext3 journalling file system support
Ext3 extended attributes
Ext3 security labels
```

Do not specify POSIX access control lists for either ext2 or ext3.

Under Pseudo filesystems, specify:

```
/dev/pts Extended Attributes
/dev/pts Security labels
```

Do not specify:

```
/dev file system support
```

Finally, under Security options, specify:

```
Enable different security models
Default Linux capabilities
NSA SELinux
NSA SELinux boot parameter
NSA SELinux Development support
```

Do not specify:

```
Socket and networking security hooks
NSA SELinux MLS policy
```

8. Compile and install the kernel:

```
# make dep
# make clean bzImage modules modules_install
# cp /usr/src/linux/arch/i386/boot/bzImage /boot
```

9. Add the following lines to /etc/fstab:

```
none /selinux selinuxfs gid=5,mode=620 0 0
none /dev/pts devpts    defaults      0 0
```

The first line causes the system to automatically mount the SELinux pseudofile-system during system startup. The second line causes the system to automatically mount the *devpts* pseudofilesystem. This is needed because the current release of Gentoo SELinux uses *devpts* rather than the Gentoo-default *devfs* pseudofilesystem.

10. Edit /boot/grub/grub.conf, adding gentoo=nodevfs to the kernel line; for instance:

```
kernel /bzImage root=/dev/hda3 gentoo=nodevfs
```

 If your system boots using LILO rather than GRUB, add append="Gentoo=nodevfs" to the proper stanza within /etc/lilo.conf.

11. Make two directories needed by SELinux:

```
# mkdir /selinux
# mkdir /sys
```

12. Reboot the system.

13. Merge packages required by SELinux:

```
# emerge libselinux checkpolicy policycoreutils
# emerge selinux-base-policy
```

14. Load the precompiled SELinux policy:

```
# cd /etc/security/selinux/src/policy
# make load
```

15. Merge packages modified to work with SELinux:

```
# emerge baselayout coreutils findutils openssh \
pam pam-login procps psmisc python-selinux shadow \
util-linux
```

16. Merge any of the following packages that are already installed:

```
# emerge app-admin/logrotate
# emerge sys-apps/vixie-cron
# emerge sys-libs/pwdb
```

vixie-cron is the only *cron* package compatible with SELinux. If you have another *cron* package installed, you should remove it and, optionally, replace it with *vixie-cron*.

17. Remove the following packages:

```
# emerge -C fileutils sh-utils textutils
```

18. Compile and install the SELinux policy, and label the files:

```
# cd /etc/security/selinux/src/policy
# make install
# make relabel
```

Labeling the filesystem associates a security context with each existing file. As explained in Chapter 5, a file's security context identifies the SELinux user, role, and type of the file. The SELinux policy specifies the label to apply to each file.

Unfortunately, it's not unusual for errors to appear during compilation of the SELinux policy. These are generally typographical errors or other gross errors in policy files specifying domains, such as *domain/programs/*.te*. To work around such errors, create the directory */etc/selinux/domain/programs/error*, move any defective files to this directory, and remake the policy file. You may need to read material in the following several chapters of this book to successfully complete this process. You can also post a request for help on the SELinux mailing list, identified near the end of Chapter 1.

19. If using GRUB, reinstall GRUB to the MBR:

```
# grub
grub> root (hd0,0)
grub> setup (hd0)
grub> quit
```

If GRUB is installed to a location other than the MBR, or your system's */boot* filesystem resides on a partition other than the first partition of the primary hard drive, see the Quick Start Guide for instructions.

20. Reboot the system.

21. Relabel the files again, to ensure that files created during rebooting are properly labeled:

```
# cd /etc/security/selinux/src/policy
# make relabel
```

Your Gentoo SELinux system should now be ready for use. The information in the following chapters will help you better understand how to use, maintain, and improve it.

RPM-Based Distributions

Installing SELinux using RPM packages is fast and convenient. And assuming that the packages are fully compatible with the target system, it's also effective. SELinux RPM packages are available for two Linux releases: Red Hat Enterprise Linux and SUSE Linux.

Red Hat Enterprise Linux

At one time, Red Hat engineer Dan Walsh, who's a member of the team responsible for implementation of SELinux under Fedora Core 2, made available SELinux binary and source RPM packages for RHEL3, on his FTP site, *ftp://people.redhat.com/dwalsh/SELinux/RHEL3/*. However, the packages available there at the time of writing are not fully compatible with RHEL3; they have have dependencies unsatisfied by packages available from the site or the RHEL3 release.

Those who are handy with source RPMs can likely hack the packages available at *ftp://people.redhat.com/dwalsh/SELinux/srpms/* to work with RHEL3, by tweaking them a bit and by installing updated versions of Autoconf, Automake, and other source code tools available under Fedora Core 2. Alternatively, it's possible to install Fedora Core 2 binary packages that satisfy the dependencies. I have installed SELinux on RHEL3 using both approaches. Nevertheless, I do not include instructions here for doing so, for two reasons:

- At the time of writing, the packages are being regularly updated due to ongoing work for Fedora Core 2. Therefore, it's not possible to provide step-by-step instructions that can be expected to be accurate at the time of this book's publication.

- Notwithstanding that the SELinux packages for RHEL3 were made by a Red Hat engineer, Red Hat does not support SELinux under RHEL3. Therefore, installation by a user of SELinux under RHEL3 would likely void the user's support agreement with Red Hat.

Those who want to use SELinux with RHEL are likely better served by installing a beta or production release of RHEL4, which should be available by the time of publication of this book.

SUSE Linux

The latest SUSE Professional Linux release available at the time of writing, SUSE Professional Linux 9.1, includes an SELinux-capable Linux kernel and SELinux-patched utilities. However, the distribution reportedly does not include the SELinux tools and includes a very old version of the SELinux sample policy. Consistent with that report, searching the SUSE web site for the word *SELinux* did not return any information about SELinux and SUSE 9.1. And a web search failed to turn up information about using SELinux with SUSE 9.1. However, a Novell representative has announced that a forthcoming SUSE Linux release will include a fully supported implementation of SELinux.

SELinux RPM packages for SUSE 8.2 have been independently released by Paul Dwerryhouse, a system and network engineer employed at the time of this writing by Versatel b.v., in Amsterdam, Netherlands. His work is available at *http://leapster.org/ linux/selinux/suse*.

To install SELinux under SUSE 8.2 using Paul's packages, you must download and install:

- His modified kernel (or download his kernel patches and apply them against Linux 2.4).
- His modified *initrd*.
- His userspace RPM packages, of which there are currently 27. These are available individually, or combined within a single 78 MB tarball.

Paul provides special instructions for installing his kernel. He also cautions not to use his kernel on production hosts, since—as Paul himself explains it—he "cheated in a couple of places when porting the SELinux patch to [the Linux 2.4] kernel," by removing the variable HZ feature and taking other shortcuts.

 SELinux for SUSE 8.2 is not officially supported by SUSE. Users who install SELinux under SUSE 8.2 may void any support agreement with SUSE.

 Those interested in using SELinux with SUSE may find helpful information on the SELinux Wiki and file repository maintained by Tom Vogt and others. The Wiki is available at *http://www. securityenhancedlinux.de/index_orig.html,* and the file repository is available at *http://selinux.lemuria.org*. Much of the information in the Wiki is in German, the native language of many SUSE users and developers.

Installing from Source

If you want to install SELinux on a system running a Linux distribution other than one for which SELinux support is available, you may be able to do so by using the NSA's SELinux release, available at *http://www.nsa.gov/selinux/code*. However, the release is not a generic, cross-platform release. Instead, the current release is designed to work with Fedora Core 2.

The NSA's SELinux release has the following components:

- Kernel patch
- SELinux shared library
- SELinux utilities for managing policies and users
- SELinux reference policy
- Modified Linux programs, including *SysVinit* (modified to load SELinux policy during boot), PAM, Linux utilities (*vipw*, *chsh*, *chfn*, *passwd*), OpenSSH, *vixie cron*, Shadow utilities (programs that modify */etc/passwd* and */etc/shadow*), GNU core utilities, *procps* (modified to display process context information), and *star* (backup and recovery utility)
- SELinux documentation

To adapt the NSA's release to a new platform generally requires modifications to build files and may require modifications—potentially significantly difficult modifications—to userland and kernel source code. Therefore, it's not recommended that those other than skilled programmers attempt to implement SELinux on an unsupported platform.

CHAPTER 4

Using and
Administering SELinux

At this point we'll assume your SELinux system has been installed and that you are ready to log in. This chapter lays out the first administrative tasks you need to do and some ongoing administrative tools you'll want to know about as you continue to add software and users to your system.

As with any multiuser system, you have to create accounts for users and assign them the proper privileges. In SELinux these tasks are not much more complicated than in other systems, although you'll have to learn some new commands to carry them out. And in the future, after SELinux has become widely adopted, the wrinkles have been ironed out, and thoroughly tested policy files are available, these typical sysadmin tasks may be all that's involved for most people running SELinux.

But unfortunately, we are not yet at that stage of maturity. As explained in earlier chapters, each release of SELinux on each distribution has its own rough spots. These will be manifested in various hard-to-diagnose ways, including:

- Users being unable to log in
- Users logging in but having their X desktops or particular applications freeze
- Applications failing (silently or with obnoxious complaints) because they cannot access files or other necessary resources

Thus, basic sysadmin tasks for SELinux include checking log files and tracing what has happened to users and applications. This chapter contains a substantial section to help you understand SELinux logging and make use of that information to change permissions on users and files.

Furthermore, SELinux has a built-in troubleshooting method known as permissive mode to help you figure out what changes to make. In permissive mode, SELinux does not actually stop anybody from doing anything. In other words, you do not actually have a secure SELinux system. (Traditional Unix security is still operational, though.) You should learn how to switch to and from permissive mode—on a nonproduction system in a safe environment, of course—in order to find out what changes you need to make in order to let users and applications run on your system.

When you make changes to your system, you may have to rebuild the policy files SELinux uses to control access or relabel files. Sometimes you can install software seamlessly, and SELinux automatically does the right thing. But in other cases, the policies or labels become out of sync with the system.

The topics in this chapter include:

- Permissive mode
- Rebuilding policies
- Labeling files
- Routine system administration (changing roles, adding users, and checking file contexts)
- Monitoring SELinux through log files
- Miscellaneous troubleshooting

Some administrative tasks go beyond the use of SELinux commands and require you to actually change SELinux policy files. These will be the subjects of several later chapters.

System Modes and SELinux Tuning

As mentioned, SELinux provides a special mode called *permissive mode* that's useful for policy troubleshooting and system maintenance. SELinux's other operating mode is called *enforcing mode* (sometimes called *enforcement mode*). Enforcing mode is the normal mode of SELinux operation. Under enforcing mode, operations that violate the SELinux security policy are prevented. Generally, when an operation is prevented, an entry is also written to the system log so that a system administrator can learn what operations have been prevented and why. Some operations may be prevented due to an incorrect or incomplete SELinux security policy, whereas others may be prevented due to an attempted system compromise. The system log provides administrators with data useful in determining the reason operations were prevented so that appropriate action can be taken. The section of this chapter titled "Monitoring SELinux" explains the format of the log entries made by SELinux.

Permissive mode is available only if your system's kernel was compiled with the option *NSA SELinux Development support*. Generally, Linux vendors compile their standard kernels with this option. However, if you compiled your own kernel, you may have omitted the option, in which case permissive mode won't be available.

If you're especially concerned about the security of your system, you may prefer to compile a kernel without the *NSA SELinux Development support* option. Doing so ensures that the system always operates in enforcing mode. However if you do so, you may find it cumbersome to administer the system. For instance, you may install a new software package and find that the associated policy file isn't quite accurate or complete, causing the application to operate imperfectly. Without the ability to enter permissive mode, it may be difficult to troubleshoot and correct the problems with the policy file.

Permissive mode is used when configuring, testing, and troubleshooting SELinux and the SELinux security policy. Under permissive mode, SELinux permits all operations, even those that violate the SELinux security policy. Nevertheless, SELinux writes log entries that would have been written had the system been in enforcing mode. Permissive mode enables a system administrator to observe the effects of experimental SELinux security policies without affecting the operation of the system. SELinux includes a special utility, Audit2allow, that can recommend SELinux policy changes based on log entries; the section of this chapter titled "Monitoring SELinux" explains this utility and how to use it to revise the SELinux security policy.

Because an SELinux system operating in permissive mode does not prevent operations that violate its security policy, you generally should not put an SELinux system that resides in a hostile environment into permissive mode. Before putting the system into permissive mode, you should relocate it to a protected network, shut down vulnerable services, restrict remote logins, or otherwise secure the system.

Controlling SELinux

Controlling SELinux entails three primary operations:

- Switching the SELinux mode
- Loading a security policy
- Labeling files

The following subsections explain how to perform these operations.

The available commands and the associated command options provided by a given implementation of SELinux may differ a bit from those described in the following subsections. When you encounter such differences, you should check your system man pages and other available documentation to understand the operation of your system.

Switching Modes

If your Linux kernel was compiled with the *NSA SELinux Development support* option, you can specify the SELinux operating mode that should be entered when your SELinux system is booted. And, unless the SELinux security policy specifies otherwise, you can dynamically change the operating mode of a running SELinux system. Additionally, if your Linux kernel was compiled with the *NSA SELinux boot parameter* option, you can entirely disable SELinux via a boot parameter. The following subsections explain how to do so.

Setting the initial operating mode

The initial operating mode of an SELinux system can be set via the boot parameter enforcing. To boot the system into enforcing mode, assign this boot parameter the value 1; to boot the system into permissive mode, assign this boot parameter the value 0.

If you use GRUB to boot your system and want the system to automatically boot into enforcing mode, you might specify a kernel directive such as the following in your GRUB configuration file (generally, */boot/grub/grub.conf*):

```
kernel /vmlinuz-2.6.4-1.305 ro root=LABEL=/ enforcing=1
```

If you use LILO to boot your system and want the system to automatically enter permissive mode after booting, you might specify an append directive such as the following in your LILO configuration file (generally, */etc/lilo.conf*):

```
append="enforcing=0"
```

Whether you use GRUB or LILO, you may find it convenient to configure two boot configurations: one booting into enforcing mode and another booting into permissive mode. Doing so makes it easy to interactively choose the SELinux mode each time the system is booted.

GRUB optionally supports interactive editing of boot configurations. If you use GRUB, you may find it convenient to specify only an enforcing-mode boot configuration. When you want to boot the system into permissive mode, you can interactively edit the kernel directive to specify the value 0 for the enforcing option.

> If you specify multiple boot configurations, and your system resides in a hostile environment, be sure to configure the boot manager to load the enforcing-mode configuration by default; otherwise, if someone untrained in SELinux or too much in a hurry reboots your system, it will enter permissive mode when booted and may be compromised.

To ameliorate the difficulty of troubleshooting an inaccurate or incomplete TE file in enforcing mode, you can install two kernels on your system: one compiled without the *NSA SELinux Development support* option and one compiled with the option. To help ensure that the system remains secure under normal circumstances, specify the configuration without the *NSA SELinux Development support* option as the default boot configuration. When you need to troubleshoot the system, you can reboot the system using the alternate kernel compiled with the *NSA SELinux Development support* option.

If you're especially concerned about security, you may feel that including a kernel capable of permissive mode in your system's boot configuration is too risky. In that case, you can prepare a boot disk or boot CD containing a permissive kernel and boot the system from your external media when troubleshooting is necessary.

You may find it impractical to reboot your system to perform troubleshooting. Indeed, a popular Linux mantra has it that "rebooting is only for installing new hardware." In this case, you may find it necessary to maintain a clone of your production system, so that you can verify that activities such as installation of a new software package will work correctly and not interfere with system operation.

Dynamically setting the operating mode

Unless your SELinux security policy or the absence of the *NSA SELinux Development support* option dictate otherwise, you can set the operating mode of a running SELinux system dynamically. To ensure system integrity, the SELinux security policy prohibits nonprivileged users from dynamically setting the SELinux operating mode. Even the root user cannot do so unless operating within the sysadm_r role. The section of this chapter titled "Changing Roles" explains user roles and how to enter the sysadm_r role. If you possess the necessary privileges, you can dynamically set the SELinux operating mode either by manipulating a file within the */selinux* filesystem or by issuing a special command.

The */selinux* filesystem is a virtual filesystem resembling the familiar */proc* or */sys* filesystem. That is, it looks just like a filesystem but doesn't reside on a hard drive or other physical media. Instead, it's automatically generated by the kernel. The file */selinux/enforce* indicates the current SELinux mode. Manipulating the file changes the current SELinux mode.

You can determine the current SELinux mode by issuing the command:

```
cat /selinux/enforce
```

The value that is displayed indicates the current mode: the value 0 indicates permissive mode and 1 indicates enforcing mode.

To enter enforcing mode, issue the command:

```
echo "1" > /selinux/enforce
```

Similarly, to enter permissive mode, issue the command:

```
echo "0" > /selinux/enforce
```

Many users find it inconvenient to directly access or modify the contents of the */selinux/enforce* file. SELinux implementations provide commands that enable a properly privileged user to determine, or set, the current SELinux mode. In earlier SELinux releases, the command used to determine the current SELinux mode was avc_enforcing. Issuing this command printed the value "permissive" or "enforcing" according to the current

SELinux mode. And, generally, the command avc_toggle was available to toggle the current SELinux mode, changing from permissive to enforcement or vice versa.

Under the current SELinux release, which breaks with tradition, the command *getenforce* reports the current SELinux mode as "permissive" or "enforcing." The *setenforce* command changes the current SELinux mode. However, unlike the avc_toggle command, the *setenforce* command does not toggle the current mode. Instead, the *setenforce* command takes an argument that specifies the desired SELinux mode: 0 for permissive mode and 1 for enforcing mode. For instance, to enter permissive mode under Fedora Core 2, you issue the command:

```
setenforce 0
```

Disabling SELinux at boot time

If a Linux kernel was compiled with the *NSA SELinux boot parameter* option, it's possible to completely disable SELinux at boot time. To do so, specify the boot parameter and value selinux=0 in the boot configuration, or interactively specify this parameter-value pair in response to a boot prompt or menu.

By disabling SELinux, you preclude it from prohibiting actions based on its security policy and from generating log entries. You also avoid the overhead entailed by SELinux itself, which some estimate consumes roughly seven percent of CPU resources. In essence, your system operates as though it were using a non-SELinux kernel.

You may find it convenient to disable SELinux when SELinux is operating improperly or entirely failing to operate. Booting in disabled mode may enable you to troubleshoot and repair the problem.

However, when SELinux is disabled, it's not available to write appropriate file labels for newly created files, including files replaced after editing. Consequently, your system almost certainly will not operate correctly if you subsequently boot with SELinux enabled. To avoid this problem, you must relabel the filesystems—or at least all new files—before booting the system with SELinux enabled. The section of this chapter titled "Labeling Files" explains how to do so.

Loading the SELinux Security Policy

If you configure your system to boot into enforcing mode, it will automatically load the SELinux security policy at boot time. However, you may find it necessary or convenient to load the SELinux security policy at another time. For instance, you may modify the security policy and desire to replace the current security policy with the modified policy. This section explains how to load the security policy and perform several related operations.

The SELinux Makefile

As explained in Chapter 5, the */etc/security/selinux/src/policy* directory contains a *Makefile* and related files that enable a system administrator to manipulate the security policy. SELinux prevents ordinary users from manipulating the security policy; only the root user in the sysadm_r role can manipulate the policy.

 If your system does not include the *src/policy* directory and the *Makefile* that resides there, it's likely that you've installed SELinux only partially. For instance, under Fedora Core 2, it's likely that you haven't installed the *checkpolicy* and *policy-sources* RPM packages.

 You may choose to delete the policy source files from your system. Doing so may complicate the work of an intruder seeking a way to circumvent the SELinux security policy.

The *Makefile* supports five operations related to the security policy. In addition, it supports one operation related to file labeling, which is explained in the following section. Table 4-1 summarizes the operations supported by the *Makefile*, which are known as *targets*.

Table 4-1. Policy Makefile targets

Make target	Compiles the policy from source?	Installs the policy?	Loads or reloads the policy?
policy	Yes	No	No
install	Yes	Yes	No
load	Yes	Yes	Yes
reload	Yes	Yes	Yes
relabel	No	No	No

 If you're not familiar with *Makefile*s and their use, I suggest that you consult *Managing Projects with Make* (O'Reilly).

The three steps that can be performed through the *Makefile* are:

Compiles the policy from source
  Checks the syntax of the policy source files and verifies that no policy constraints are violated.

Installs the policy
  Creates the binary SELinux policy.

Loads or reloads the policy

Currently, the load and reload targets work the same way. Each loads the binary SELinux policy into the running kernel and begins using it to make security decisions.

To use the *Makefile* to perform a supported operation, follow this procedure:

1. Be sure your current role is sysadm_r. The section "Routine SELinux System Use and Administration" of this chapter explains how to do so:

   ```
   # id -Z
   root:staff_r:staff_t# newrole -r sysadm_r
   Authenticating root.
   Password:
   # id -Z
   root:sysadm_r:sysadm_t
   ```

2. If you're not logged in as the root user, issue the *su* command to become the root user:

   ```
   su -
   ```

3. Fedora Core automatically transitions you to the sysadm_r role when you issue the *su* command. If you're not using Fedora Core, you must explicitly transition to the sysadm_r role:

   ```
   newrole -r sysadm_r
   ```

4. Change the current working directory to */etc/security/selinux/src/policy*:

   ```
   cd /etc/security/selinux/src/policy
   ```

5. Invoke the desired operation:

   ```
   make target
   ```

   where target is the desired operation. For instance, to reload the security policy, issue the command:

   ```
   make reload
   ```

6. Observe any error messages that appear on the console and take appropriate action.

Depending on the target you specify, the *Makefile* invokes one or both of the following SELinux utilities:

checkpolicy

The SELinux policy compiler

load_policy

A utility that loads the SELinux binary policy into the running kernel

It's generally best to use the *Makefile* to perform policy-related operations. But, you may find it useful or necessary to understand how the *Makefile* does its work. The following sections explain the main utilities invoked by the *Makefile*: *checkpolicy* and *load_policy*.

The SELinux policy compiler (checkpolicy)

The SELinux policy compiler *checkpolicy* reads an SELinux policy source file and creates a binary policy file. In preparation for policy compilation, the SELinux *Makefile* provides the compiler with a single policy source file that includes all the installed TE files and other policy source files. The *Makefile* also expands M4 macros contained in those files.

The SELinux policy compiler has the following syntax:

```
checkpolicy [-b] [-c policyvers] [-d] [-o output_file] \
    [input_file]
```

The *-b* option instructs the policy compiler to read a binary policy file (contained in a file named *policy*) rather than a source policy file. This flag is rarely used.

The *-c* flag specifies the policy version number. If the flag is omitted, the latest policy version is assumed.

The *-d* option instructs the policy compiler to enter debug mode after it loads the policy.

The *-o* option specifies the name of the binary policy file that the compiler will write.

The input_file argument specifies the name of the policy source file that the compiler will process. If the argument is omitted, the compiler reads the *policy.conf* file (unless the *–b* option appears, in which case the compiler reads the binary policy file named *policy*).

For more information on the policy compiler and the compilation process, see the paper "Configuring the SELinux Policy," by Stephen Smalley, available at *http://www.nsa.gov/selinux/info/docs.cfm*.

The load_policy utility

The *load_policy* utility reads a binary policy file, the name of which is specified as a command argument, and loads the policy into the running kernel. The utility provides no other arguments or options.

Labeling Filesystems and Files

As explained in Chapter 3, SELinux requires that files be labeled with extended attributes indicating their security context. Available filesystems are typically labeled when SELinux is installed.

It's not routinely necessary to relabel filesystems and files after installation. However, it sometimes is necessary to do so. For instance, installation of a new filesystem may require the filesystem to be labeled. Or booting a system from a non-SELinux kernel may result in the creation of unlabeled files or the removal of labels from labeled files. Under such circumstances, you can use the *Makefile* in */etc/security/selinux/src/policy* to label or relabel all available filesystems. Alternatively, you can use any of several commands to label or relabel just the filesystems or files that lack proper labels. This section explains how to perform these operations.

 Some filesystem types do not support the extended attributes used to store file context labels. The *src/policy/genfs_contexts* file provides default contexts for files residing in such filesystems.

Depending on the size of the system's hard drives and the number of files they store, the relabeling operation may require many minutes, perhaps more than an hour. When only a few files require relabeling, it's inefficient to relabel by using the *Makefile*. In such cases, it's better to perform the relabeling by using an SELinux utility. The next section explains how to do so.

Using the Makefile to label or relabel filesystems

To relabel all available filesystems by using the *src/policy Makefile*, follow this procedure:

1. Be sure your current role is sysadm_r. The section "Routine SELinux System Use and Administration" of this chapter explains how to do so:

    ```
    # id -Z
    root:staff_r:staff_t
    # newrole -r sysadm_r
    Authenticating root.
    Password:
    # id -Z
    root:sysadm_r:sysadm_t
    ```

2. If you're not logged in as the root user, issue the *su* command to become the root user:

    ```
    su -
    ```

3. Fedora Core automatically transitions you to the sysadm_r role when you issue the *su* command. If you're not using Fedora Core, you must explicitly transition to the sysadm_r role:

    ```
    newrole -r sysadm_r
    ```

4. Change the current working directory to */etc/security/selinux/src/policy*:

    ```
    cd /etc/security/selinux/src/policy
    ```

5. Invoke the relabel operation:

    ```
    make relabel
    ```

6. Observe any error messages that appear on the console and take appropriate action.

Using commands to label or relabel files or filesystems

SELinux provides several utilities that report or manipulate file labels. The utilities differ primarily in whether they operate on files or filesystems and whether they label by using a fixed, specified context or by using a specification file. One or another of the utilities is apt to be more convenient in any particular situation. The available utilities include:

/usr/bin/chcon
> Labels one or more files with a specified security context

/sbin/fixfiles
> Labels all available filesystems according to the contents of the standard specification file, *src/policy/file_contexts/file_contexts*

/sbin/restorecon
> Labels one or more files according to the contents of the standard specification file, *src/policy/file_contexts/file_contexts*

/usr/sbin/setfiles
> Labels one or more files or filesystems according to the contents of a specification file

The following subsections explain each utility in more detail.

The chcon utility. The *chcon* utility labels one or more filesystems with a security context. The command has two forms. The first form is used to label a file with a specified security context. The second form is used to label a file with the security context associated with a specified reference file.

The first form has this syntax:

```
chcon [options] context path...
```

For the moment, please ignore the command options. The remaining arguments represent a security context and one or more paths to be labeled or relabeled. For example, to set the security context of the files */etc/hosts* and */etc/hosts.allow* to *system_u:object_r:etc_t*, issue the command:

```
chcon system_u:object_r:etc_t /etc/hosts /etc/hosts.allow
```

The second form has this syntax:

```
chcon [options] --reference=rfile path...
```

The security context associated with the reference file, `rfile`, is used to label or relabel the specified paths. For example, to set the security context of the files */etc/hosts.allow* and */etc/hosts.deny* to the current security context of the file */etc/hosts*, issue the command:

```
chcon --reference=/etc/hosts /etc/hosts.allow /etc/hosts.deny
```

In addition, the *chcon* utility supports several options:

-c, --changes
> Print a message for each change made.

-h, --no-dereference
> Operate on symbolic links instead of files they reference.

-f, --silent, --quiet
   Suppress noncritical error messages.

-R, --recursive
   Change files and directories recursively.

-r, --role ROLE
   Set role *ROLE* in the target security context.

-t, --type TYPE
   Set type *TYPE* in the target security context.

-u, --user USER
   Set user *USER* in the target security context.

-v, --verbose
   Print a message for each file processed.

--help
   Print a help message and then exit.

--version
   Print version information and then exit.

The fixfiles utility. The *fixfiles* utility labels all available filesystems according to the contents of the standard specification file, *src/policy/file_contexts/file_contexts*. The form of the command is:

```
fixfiles [check | restore | relabel]
```

That is, exactly one of the following arguments must appear:

check
   Show any incorrect file labels, but do not change any file labels.

restore
   Change the labels of any incorrectly labeled files.

relabel
   Relabel all available filesystems.

For example, to check the file labels on all mounted filesystems, issue the command:

```
fixfiles check
```

The restorecon utility. The *restorecon* utility labels one or more files according to the contents of the standard specification file, *src/policy/file_contexts/file_contexts*. The command has the following form:

```
restorecon [-n] [-v] path...
```

One or more path names must be specified as arguments. For example, to label the file */etc/hosts* according to the standard specification file, issue the command:

```
restorecon /etc/hosts
```

The command options have the following meanings:

-n

Do not change any file labels; merely print the changes that would be made.

-v

Show changes to file labels.

The setfiles utility. Whereas the *fixfiles* utility labels all available filesystems, the *setfiles* utility labels one or more specified filesystems. The command has the following form:

```
setfiles [options] spec_file path...
```

The *spec_file* argument specifies the file containing the specifications used to determine file labels. It has the same form as the FC files, which will be described in Chapter 5. The *path* argument specifies the files to be labeled. For example, to label the */etc/hosts* file using the specifications contained in the file *src/policy/file_contexts/file_contexts*, issue the command:

```
setfiles src/policy/file_contexts/file_contexts /etc/hosts
```

The available command options include:

-d

Show the specification that matched each file.

-n

Don't change any file labels.

-q

Suppress noncritical messages.

-s

Take a list of files from standard input rather than use a pathname on the command line.

-v

Show changes in file labels if type or role is changed.

-vv

Show changes in file labels if type, role, or user is changed.

-W

Print warnings about specification entries that have no matching files.

Tuning Fedora Core 2 SELinux

Because of the SELinux policy language and Flask architecture, SELinux is highly flexible. A system administrator can tailor—or entirely replace—the standard SELinux security policy with a customized policy that better suits the local environment. However, some implementations of SELinux provide very simple means for

---

tailoring policy operation. In particular, the Fedora Core 2 implementation of SELinux provides two convenient ways of tailoring SELinux operation:

- Macros
- Policy Booleans

The following subsections describe these means. If you're using an SELinux implementation other than that associated with Fedora Core 2, you may find that your implementation provides similar features, though perhaps in a different way. And even if your SELinux implementation entirely lacks features like those described in the upcoming sections, the sections may suggest useful ways in which to modify your SELinux security policy. So you're likely to find it worthwhile to read the sections, even though they deal specifically with the Fedora Core 2 SELinux implementation.

Tuning via macros

The file *src/policy/tunable.te* defines two to three dozen M4 macros that you can use to tailor the operation of SELinux. Doing so is simple: you merely comment or uncomment a macro definition.

M4 does not use the hash mark (#) to denote comments, as many other Linux programs do. Instead, M4 prefixes comments with the characters dnl ("do not list"), followed by a space. If you've configured Sendmail, which uses M4, you're familiar with M4's rather odd convention.

Table 4-2 summarizes the macros defined in *tunable.te*.

Table 4-2. Policy macros

Policy macro	Active by default?	Description
allow_user_direct_mouse	Yes	Allow regular users direct access to the mouse device file (otherwise allow only the X server to do so).
allow_user_dmesg	Yes	Allow users to run the dmesg command
allow_user_tcp_server	Yes	Allow users to run TCP servers (bind to ports and accept connection from the same domain and outside users). Disabling this Boolean forces FTP passive mode and may affect other protocols (including IRC if single_userdomain is defined).
allow_xserver_home_fonts	Yes	Allow X server to check for fonts in ~/.gnome or ~/.kde.
allow_ypbind	Yes	Allow ypbind to run with NIS.
direct_sysadm_daemon	Yes	Allow sysadm_t to start daemons directly.
ftp_home_dir	No	Allow FTP to read/write files in user home directories.
ftpd_is_daemon	Yes	Allow FTP to run from inetd instead of as a stand-alone daemon.
hide_broken_symptoms	No	Adds dontaudit rules for broken polices that are not security risks.

Table 4-2. Policy macros (continued)

Policy macro	Active by default?	Description
nfs_export_all_ro	No	Allow reading on any filesystem.
nfs_export_all_rw	Yes	Allow read/write/create on any filesystem.
nfs_home_dirs	Yes	Allow NFS home directories.
nscd_all_connect	Yes	Allow all domains to access NSCD.
read_default_t	Yes	Allow ordinary users to read any file having type default_t.
readhome	Yes	Allow Mozilla to read files in the user home directory.
run_ssh_inetd	No	Allow SSH to run from inetd instead of as a daemon.
secure_levels	No	Allow only administrator to log in at the console and forbid direct access to disk devices.
single_userdomain	No	Make processes other than *newrole* and *su* run by a user domain stay in the same user domain.
ssh_sysadm_login	Yes	Allow SSH logins to the sysadm_r:sysadm_t security context; otherwise, remote SSH users cannot enter this context.
staff_read_sysadm_file	No	Allow staff_r users to search the system administrator's home directory (generally */root*) and read its files.
unlimitedServices	Yes	Allow processes under initrc and xinetd to run with all privileges.
unlimitedUsers	No	Allow users to have full access.
unrestricted_admin	Yes	Allow sysadm_t to do almost everything.
use_games	Yes	Allow users to run games.
user_can_mount	Yes	Allow users to execute *mount* command.
user_canbe_sysadm	Yes	Allow normal users to enter sysadm_r role.
user_net_control	Yes	Allow users to control network interfaces (also needs USERCTL=true).
user_rw_noexattrfile	Yes	Allow users to read/write noexattrfile (FAT, CDROM, FLOPPY).
writehome	Yes	Allow Mozilla to write files in the user home directory.
xdm_sysadm_login	Yes	Allow xdm logins as sysadm_r:sysadm_t.

 The description of *tunable.te* macros given in Table 4-2 is based on the Test 2 release of Fedora Core 2. It's possible—even likely—that the contents of the file will differ in subsequent releases.

To tailor the security policy using *tunable.te*, follow this procedure:

1. Make the current working directory */etc/security/selinux/src/policy*.

2. Using a text editor, comment or uncomment macros in *tunable.te*, by adding or deleting the *dnl* token.

3. Compile the policy sources and load a revised binary policy by issuing the command make reload.

Tuning via policy Booleans

Fedora Core 2 introduces *Policy Booleans* (generally referred to as simply *Booleans*), a new SELinux feature that enables modification of a running SELinux security policy. Booleans are true-false values that can be tested by security policy rules. The unique aspect of Booleans is that special commands can query and change their values at any time. The commands, of course, are available only to system administrators.

At the time of writing, the Fedora Core 2 security policy defines only one Boolean: user_ping. The value of the user_ping Boolean specifies whether ordinary users are permitted to use the *ping* command. Admittedly, this Boolean enables a rather trivial policy tweak. However, it's likely that subsequent releases of Fedora Core 2 and releases of other SELinux implementations will include additional Booleans.

Two commands are used in working with Booleans:

change_bool
　　Changes the value of a Boolean.

show_bools
　　Prints all available Booleans and their values.

The *change_bool* command has the following form:

```
change_bool boolean [0|1]
```

where *boolean* is the name of the Boolean whose value is being set. The value 0 stands for false and 1 stands for true. For example, to set the value of the user_ping Boolean to false, issue the command:

```
change_bool user_ping 0
```

The *show_bools* command, which reports the value of available Booleans, requires no options or arguments. Typical output of *show_bools* follows:

```
# show_bools
user_ping --> active: 0 pending: 0
```

Notice that the output of the *show_bools* command distinguishes two values for each listed Boolean: the *active value* and the *pending value*. When setting Boolean values via *change_bool*, this distinction is not important. Internally, SELinux allows revised Boolean values to be designated in a way that enables the system administrator to cause the changes to several different values to take effect simultaneously. However, the *change_bool* command immediately commits changes to Booleans. Therefore, when using the *change_bool* command to set Boolean values, the active and pending values should always be the same.

Setting Booleans via the /selinux filesystem. Rather than use the *change_bool* command to set the value of a Boolean, you can manipulate nodes within the */selinux/boolean* directory of the */selinux* filesystem. The names of those nodes are identical to the names of the corresponding Booleans. For example, to set the value of the user_ping Boolean to *false*, issue the command:

```
echo 0 > /selinux/booleans/user_ping
```

Unlike changes made via the change_bool command, changes made via the */selinux* filesystem do not immediately take effect. To commit the changes, issue the command:

```
echo 1 > /selinux/commit_pending_bools
```

All pending changes take effect immediately upon issuance of this command.

Routine SELinux System Use and Administration

SELinux is largely transparent to ordinary system users and presents system administrators with few complications. This section describes the handful of issues that users and administrators need to be aware of when using and administering an SELinux system. The issues fall into the following broad categories:

- Entering a role
- Viewing security contexts
- Adding users and groups
- Starting and controlling daemons
- Tuning SELinux

Entering a Role

Recall that, as explained in Chapter 2, SELinux users have one or more associated roles and, at any time, are bound to exactly one of these. Users are initially bound to a role at login time. Thereafter, a user can issue a special command to replace this binding with a binding to any role for which the user is authorized. System administrators may use this command to transition back and forth between the staff_r and sysadm_r roles. Otherwise, role transitions are relatively rare.

The sestatus Command

The Gentoo and Fedora Core 2 implementations of SELinux include a useful new command: *sestatus*. As the name of the *sestatus* command suggests, the command lets you view SELinux status information. Here's a typical example:

```
# sestatus
SELinux status:         enabled
SELinuxfs mount:        /selinux
Current mode:           enforcing
Policy version:         17

Policy booleans:
user_ping               inactive
```

As you can see, the command reports the SELinux status and mode, the mount point of the selinuxfs filesystem, and the policy version. The command also reports the value of any policy Booleans. Policy Booleans are an SELinux feature introduced in Fedora Core 2, and are described in the "Tuning SELinux" section of this chapter.

The *sestatus* command can be issued with a *-v* option, which instructs the command to issue more verbose output that includes information concerning process and file contexts. An example follows:

```
# sestatus -v
SELinux status:         enabled
SELinuxfs mount:        /selinux
Current mode:           enforcing
Policy version:         17

Policy booleans:
user_ping               inactive

Process contexts:
Current context:        root:sysadm_r:sysadm_t
Init context:           system_u:system_r:init_t
/sbin/mingetty          system_u:system_r:getty_t
/usr/sbin/sshd          root:system_r:sshd_t

File contexts:
Controlling term:       root:object_r:sysadm_devpts_t
/etc/passwd             system_u:object_r:etc_t
/etc/shadow             system_u:object_r:shadow_t
/bin/bash               system_u:object_r:shell_exec_t
/bin/login              system_u:object_r:login_exec_t
/bin/sh                 system_u:object_r:bin_t -> system_u:object_r:shell_exec_t
/sbin/agetty            system_u:object_r:getty_exec_t
/sbin/init              system_u:object_r:init_exec_t
/sbin/mingetty          system_u:object_r:getty_exec_t
/usr/sbin/sshd          system_u:object_r:sshd_exec_t
/lib/libc.so.6          system_u:object_r:lib_t -> system_u:object_r:shlib_t
/lib/ld-linux.so.2      system_u:object_r:lib_t -> system_u:object_r:ld_so_t
```

The standard SELinux security policy defines four roles:

staff_r
>   Used for users permitted to enter the sysadm_r role

sysadm_r
>   Used for the system administrator

system_r
>   Used for system processes and objects

user_r
>   Used for ordinary users

 The flexibility of SELinux makes it possible for SELinux administrators to define additional roles. However, few administrators find any need to do so. The four canonical roles are the only roles found on most SELinux systems.

When a user logs into an SELinux system, the system will either:

- Automatically assign a default role.
- Present a convenient menu that enables the user to choose from the roles the user is authorized to enter.

If the user is authorized to enter only one role, no menu is presented. Instead, the user is automatically placed in the role. Since the *su* - command initiates a login shell, the menu may also appear when that command is issued. Fedora Core works this way, but other SELinux implementations may not.

Here's a typical example of the menu:

```
$ su -
Password:
Your default context is root:sysadm_r:sysadm_t.

Do you want to choose a different one? [n]y
[1] root:staff_r:staff_t
Enter number of choice: 1
```

When the menu appears, it displays the default context and asks the user whether another context is preferred. If the user responds affirmatively, the menu lists the contexts for which the user is authorized, associating a number with each context. By typing the number associated with a listed context, the user can enter that context.

Changing roles

After login, a user may wish to enter a role other than the one assigned at login. For instance, a user who is authorized to enter the sysadm_r role may wish to do so in order to issue one or more commands that are restricted to system administrators.

To enter a new role, a user issues the *newrole* command. The simplest and most common form of the *newrole* command has this syntax:

```
newrole -r role
```

where *role* identifies the role to be entered. If the user is not authorized to enter the role, the command fails. Otherwise, the command creates a new shell in a context labeled with the user's identity, the new role, and a default type derived from the new role. However, before the shell is instantiated, the user is prompted to confirm her identity by entering her Linux password.

> Please bear in mind that only users who are associated with the staff_r role can transition to the sysadm_r role by issuing the *newrole* command. Your SELinux user configuration determines whether a user is associated with the staff_r or user_r role. Also, if you're using Fedora Core, recall that its *su* command has been modified to automatically transition to the sysadm_r role when you become the root user. Other implementations of SELinux do not currently share this characteristic.

Here's a typical usage of the *newrole* command. Suppose you are a system administrator currently logged in to the staff_r:staff_t security context rather than the sysadm_r:sysadm_r security context. You need to add a new user, a task that requires you to enter the sysadm_r:sysadm_t security context. Here's how you might do so:

```
# id -Z
root:staff_r:staff_t
# newrole -r sysadm_r
Authenticating root.
Password:
# id -Z
root:sysadm_r:sysadm_t
```

The *id -Z* command, explained in the following section, reports the user's security context. You don't need to issue the *id* command when you change roles, but doing so makes it possible to verify that you have indeed left your original role and entered the desired one. As you can see in the example, the *newrole* command changed the role from staff_r to sysadm_r.

The full form of the *newrole* command is:

```
newrole [[-r|--role] ROLE] [[-t|--type] TYPE] [-- [ARGS]...]
```

The *-t* option, which can also be specified as *--type*, enables a type to be explicitly specified rather than inferred from the role. The option also enables transitioning to a new type without changing role, though this is seldom done. The *ARGS* arguments let the user specify arguments to be passed to the new shell.

Viewing Security Contexts

SELinux provides modified versions of several familiar commands, extending them with the capability of reporting security contexts. The commands include:

id
> View the user context.

ls
> View a file context.

ps
> View a process context.

The following subsections explain how to use the modified commands.

Viewing the user security context

Under Linux, the *id* command reports real and effective user IDs and group IDs. Under SELinux, the *id* command has been modified to also report the security context of the current user:

```
# id
uid=0(root) gid=0(root)
groups=0(root),1(bin),2(daemon),3(sys),4(adm),6(disk),10(wheel) context=root:sysadm_
r:sysadm_t
```

The command has also been modified to include a special -Z option that causes the command's output to include the security context of the current user:

```
# id -Z
root:sysadm_r:sysadm_t
```

Although the *id* command continues to support an argument specifying the name of the user to be reported, the security context is printed only when this argument is omitted. The command is capable of reporting the security context of only the current user. For instance, suppose you issue the following command:

```
# id bill
uid=1001(bill) gid=100(users) groups=100(users),10(wheel)
```

The command doesn't report the security context associated with the user `bill`.

Viewing a file security context

Under Linux, the *ls* command lists directory contents. Under SELinux, the *ls* command has been modified to also report the security context of directory contents. This behavior is triggered by including one of the following options:

--context
> Prints a partial file context designed to generally fit on a single line.

--lcontext
> Prints the full file context.

--scontext

>Prints only the file context.

-Z

>Same result as *--context*.

Sample output of the *ls* command follows:

```
# ls -l /etc/hosts
-rw-r--r-- 2 root root 191 Apr 18 20:09 /etc/hosts
# ls --context /etc/hosts
-rw-r--r--+ root     root     system_u:object_r:etc_t          /etc/hosts
# ls --lcontext /etc/hosts
-rw-r--r-- 2 system_u:object_r:etc_t          root root 191 Apr 18 20:09 /etc/hosts
# ls --scontext /etc/hosts
system_u:object_r:etc_t          /etc/hosts
# ls -Z /etc/hosts
-rw-r--r--+ root     root     system_u:object_r:etc_t          /etc/hosts
```

Viewing a process security context

Under Linux, the *ps* command gives a snapshot of the current process or a specified process or processes. Under SELinux, the *ps* command has been modified to also report the security context of processes. This behavior is specified by use of the *-Z* option or *--context* option:

```
# ps
  PID TTY          TIME CMD
 8433 pts/1    00:00:00 su
 8436 pts/1    00:00:00 bash
 8800 pts/1    00:00:00 ps
# ps -Z
  PID CONTEXT                             COMMAND
 8433 bill:sysadm_r:sysadm_su_t           su -
 8436 root:sysadm_r:sysadm_t              -bash
 8801 root:sysadm_r:sysadm_t              ps -Z
# ps --context
  PID CONTEXT                             COMMAND
 8433 bill:sysadm_r:sysadm_su_t           su -
 8436 root:sysadm_r:sysadm_t              -bash
 8803 root:sysadm_r:sysadm_t              ps --context
```

As you can see, either option has the same result.

You can use the modified *ps* command to snapshot processes other than the current process, and can use any of the options or arguments supported by the standard Linux *ps* command. For instance:

```
# ps -Z 1
  PID CONTEXT                             COMMAND
    1 system_u:system_r:init_t            init [2]
```

Adding Users

Under SELinux, users' home directories are labeled with the special security context user_home_dir_t. When you create a new user account by using the *useradd* command, SELinux automatically labels the user's home directory with the proper security context. However, before creating a new user account, you should first enter the sysadm_r role so that you have the permissions necessary to set the security context.

Here's an example showing how a user account is added, and the security context assigned to the new user's home directory:

```
# id -Z
root:staff_r:staff_t
# newrole -r sysadm_r
Authenticating root.
Password:
# id -Z
root:sysadm_r:sysadm_t
# useradd -c "test user" -m -d /home/testuser -g users -s /bin/bash testuser
# finger testuser
Login: testuser                          Name: test user
Directory: /home/testuser                Shell: /bin/bash
Never logged in.
No mail.
No Plan.
# ls -ld -Z /home/testuser/
drwx------+ testuser users     root:object_r:user_home_dir_t
  /home/testuser/
```

Associating a user with a nondefault role

By default, users are associated with the SELinux role user_r, which is appropriate for users who are not authorized to enter the sysadm_r role. If you wish to authorize the user to enter the sysadm_r role, you must:

1. Edit the *src/policy/users* file.

2. Recompile the security policy.

3. Load the generated binary policy file into the kernel.

You can edit the *src/policy/users* file with your preferred text editor, such as *vi*. Add a line having the following form to the file:

```
user username roles { staff_r sysadm_r };
```

where *username* is the name of the user account that you want to authorize to enter the sysadm_r role.

To recompile and load the security policy, make */etc/security/selinux/src/policy* the current working directory and issue the following command:

```
make reload
```

How default roles are assigned

As explained in Chapter 5, the *src/policy/appconfig/default_contexts* file specifies default roles for user logins, SSH sessions, and *cron* jobs. The file is a simple text file consisting of two columns. The first column specifies a partial context (the role and domain) for the system process (login, sshd, or crond). For instance, the fourth line, which refers to the sshd_t domain, pertains to the sshd process. The second column specifies one or more security contexts, each of the form user:role:type. A typical *default_contexts* file follows:

```
system_r:sulogin_t        sysadm_r:sysadm_t
system_r:local_login_t    staff_r:staff_t user_r:user_t sysadm_r:sysadm_t
system_r:remote_login_t   user_r:user_t staff_r:staff_t
system_r:sshd_t           user_r:user_t staff_r:staff_t sysadm_r:sysadm_t
system_r:crond_t          user_r:user_crond_t staff_r:staff_crond_t
sysadm_r:sysadm_crond_t   system_r:system_crond_t mailman_r:user_crond_t
system_r:xdm_t            staff_r:staff_t user_r:user_t sysadm_r:sysadm_t
staff_r:staff_su_t        staff_r:staff_t user_r:user_t sysadm_r:sysadm_t
sysadm_r:sysadm_su_t      staff_r:staff_t user_r:user_t sysadm_r:sysadm_t
user_r:user_su_t          staff_r:staff_t user_r:user_t sysadm_r:sysadm_t
sysadm_r:sudo_t           sysadm_r:sysadm_t
staff_r:sudo_t            sysadm_r:sysadm_t staff_r:staff_t
user_r:sudo_t             sysadm_r:sysadm_t user_r:user_t
```

When SELinux must determine the default role for a login, session, or job, it consults the *default_contexts* file and selects the first line matching the partial context of the system process. SELinux then assigns the first security context that the user is permitted to enter; or, in the case of an interactive shell, SELinux may present a menu prompting the user to choose from among the available contexts. For instance, during a local login, SELinux consults the line:

```
system_r:local_login_t  staff_r:staff_t user_r:user_t sysadm_r:sysadm_t
```

This line tells SELinux to present a menu enabling the user to select from among the following security contexts:

- staff_r:staff_t
- user_r:user_t
- sysadm_r:sysadm_t

However, SELinux won't present a given menu item unless the user is authorized to enter the related security context. An ordinary user can enter only the user_r:user_t context and thus no menu is presented.

> If, as an ordinary user, you find that the default roles provided by the *default_contexts* file fail to meet your needs, you can create your own *default_contexts* file, *~/default_contexts*. However, the file merely specifies your preferences; it does not permit you to enter security contexts other than those authorized by the system administrator.

Setting user passwords

When setting user passwords, it's generally convenient to use the standard Linux *passwd* command. Under SELinux, this command has been modified to preserve the security contexts associated with the */etc/shadow* file.

If you use *vipw*, *vi*, or some other means to modify */etc/passwd*, */etc/group*, or */etc/shadow*, you'll likely remove the security context labeling the file, which will make the file inaccessible. If you discover that you've disrupted the file label, you can repair the damage by using the *restorecon* command, described earlier in this chapter. For instance, to repair the file label associated with the */etc/shadow* file, issue the command:

```
restorecon /etc/shadow
```

 If the *restorecon* command is not available in your SELinux implementation, you can use the *setfiles* command or one of the other file labeling commands explained earlier in this chapter.

Starting and Controlling Daemons

The init process generally starts several daemons when the system is booted or the current runlevel is changed. To do so, init uses init *scripts* that reside in the */etc/init.d* directory. The init process ensures that such scripts are started in a proper security context by referring to the *src/policy/appconfig/initrc_context* file.

When the system administrator manually starts an init script, the script must similarly be started in a proper security context. Establishing a proper security context is simplified by the *run_init* command, which runs an init script or program in the proper context.

The *run_init* command has this form:

```
run_init script [[arg]...]
```

where *script* is a path associated with the init script to be started and *arg* (which can be multiple arguments) optionally provides the init script with run arguments. For example, to start the NTP daemon via its init script, */etc/init.d/ntpd*, issue the command:

```
run_init /etc/init.d/ntpd start
```

Daemons started without using the *run_init* command are likely to be run in an incorrect security context and therefore fail.

 By default, Fedora Core 2 allows a role transition from sysadm_r to system_r, the role used by init. Therefore, unless you've specially configured Fedora Core 2 to disable this transition, it's not necessary to invoke the *run_init* command explicitly.

Starting non-init daemons and programs

Just as an init script may fail when started in an inappropriate security context, other programs may require that they be started in a specific context. To facilitate starting such programs, SELinux provides the *run_con* command, which lets you specify the security context in which a program runs.

The *run_con* command has the following form:

```
runcon [-t TYPE] [-u USER] [-r ROLE] COMMAND [ARGS...]
```

where *TYPE*, *USER*, and *ROLE* specify the security context under which the program should run, and *COMMAND* and *ARGS* specify the program to be run and its arguments.

For example, suppose the *cron* daemon has died and you want to restart it. The easiest way to do so is by using the *run_init* command or, on Fedora Core, the *service* command. But, suppose you tried to start the daemon like this:

```
# /usr/sbin/crond
```

The result will not be felicitous because the *cron* daemon will execute in the security context root:system_r:system_t, whereas it should execute in the security context system_u:system_r:crond_t. As a result, if you check your log files, you'll find that the *cron* daemon is unable to properly start *cron* jobs.

The *run_con* command enables you to start *cron* in the proper context. To do so, simply issue the command:

```
runcon -u system_u -r system_r -t crond_t /usr/sbin/crond
```

An alternative form of the command is convenient when all the components of the security context are specified, as in the example:

```
runcon CONTEXT COMMAND [args...]
```

The *CONTEXT* argument consists of a security context that includes a user identity, role, and type, specified in that order—for example, system_u:system_r:crond_t.

To use this form of the *run_con* command to run the command *run_con* in the security context system_u:system_r:crond_t, issue the command:

```
runcon system_u:system_r:crond_t /usr/sbin/crond
```

Monitoring SELinux

SELinux writes log entries that enable system administrators to monitor its operation. The following subsections explain the format of SELinux log messages, some logging subtleties, and how to use the Audit2allow utility to automatically generate rules to allow operations logged as denied.

SELinux Log Message Format

When a program attempts an operation that is checked by the SELinux security engine, SELinux may make a log entry. As more fully explained in Chapter 2, operations that are denied generally cause a log entry to be made, whereas permitted operations generally do not. However, SELinux policy rules can override this principle.

Apart from the timestamp and other information that accompanies every system log message, SELinux log messages have the following general format:

```
avc: result { operation } for pid=pid exe=exe path=opath dev=devno:ptno ino=node
scontext=source tcontext=target tclass=class
```

 A given SELinux log message may omit one or more of the attribute-value pairs given in the general format. Log messages include only the applicable attribute-value pairs.

The variable fields within the log message have the following meanings:

result
: The value granted or denied, indicating whether SELinux permitted or prohibited the operation.

operation
: The operation that was attempted, such as read or write. SELinux defines about 150 operations. Appendix B summarizes the SELinux operations that can appear in log messages.

pid
: The process ID of the process that attempted the operation.

exe
: The absolute path of the text file (executable) associated with the process that attempted the operation.

path
: The absolute path of the object on which the operation was attempted.

devno
: The block device number associated with the object on which the operation was attempted.

ptno
: The partition number associated with the object on which the operation was attempted.

node
: The inode number of the object on which the operation was attempted.

source
: The security context of the process that attempted the operation.

---

target
> The security context of the target object.

class
> The type of the target object, such as `file`. Table A-1 summarizes the SELinux object classes.

Let's parse a typical log message, which follows:

```
avc: denied { write } for pid=10400 exe=/usr/bin/nmap lport=255 scontext=root:
staff_r:nmap_t tcontext=root:staff_r:nmap_t tclass=rawip_socket
```

This message indicates that a `write` operation was denied. The process that attempted the operation, */usr/bin/nmap*, had process ID 10400. The security context of the process was `root:staff_r:nmap_t` and the security context of the object was `root:staff_r:nmap_t`. The target object class was `rawip_socket`. In addition, the message indicates the logical (source) port which was requested, 255. So, the messages tells us that the security engine has prevented Nmap from writing to a socket.

Let's now parse a log message that presents a common complication:

```
avc: denied { read } for pid=12999 exe=/usr/bin/slocate name=slocate.db dev=03:02
ino=391745 scontext=bill:staff_r:staff_t tcontext=system_u:object_r:var_lib_t
tclass=file
```

This message indicates that a read operation was denied. The process that attempted the operation, `/usr/bin/slocate`, had process ID 12999.

When the object path appears in the log message, we immediately know the identity of the object. However, SELinux often does not include the object path. In such cases, we must determine the object's identity from the information that is available. In this example, we have the device, partition, and inode numbers. We'll identify the object by using these.

The log entry shows that the process attempted to access partition 2 of block device 3. If Linux kernel sources are installed, we can determine the identity of this device by searching the file */usr/src/linux/Documentation/devices.txt*, which indicates that block device 3 is associated with */dev/hda*. We can verify this result by issuing the *ls* command:

```
# ls -l /dev/hda
brw-rw---- 1 root     disk     3, 0 Oct 4 2003 /dev/hda
```

If the *devices.txt* file is not available, we can search the */dev* directory for a device having the indicated device number.

To determine the partition related to the log message, we can use the *df* command:

```
# df
Filesystem           1K-blocks     Used Available Use% Mounted on
/dev/hda1              102454      13311     83853 14% /boot
/dev/hda2             3854576    2930172    728600 81% /
/dev/hda4            73854600   65026572   5076380 93% /space
none                    63272          0     63272  0% /dev/shm
```

From the command output, we learn that partition 2, */dev/hda2*, is associated with the root filesystem, /.

Skipping several intervening attribute-value pairs to which we'll return in a moment, we learn from the `tclass` attribute that the object in question has type `file`. To determine the path associated with the `file` object, we can use the *-inum* option of the *find* command, which searches for a node having the specified inode number. The following command searches the filesystem mounted at / for a node having inode number 391745:

```
# find / -inum 391745
/var/lib/slocate/slocate.db
```

The `file` object is identified as the file */var/lib/slocate/slocate.db*, which is not surprising in view of */usr/bin/slocate* being the process that attempted the read operation.

 Inodes can be deleted and reused. So, if enough system activity has occurred between generation of a log entry and an attempt to identify the referenced object by its inode number, the attempt is likely to fail or turn up an incorrect path.

Returning now to the attribute-value pairs we skipped, `scontext` and `tcontext`, we can infer the reason that led to denial of the operation. As indicated by the value of the `scontext` attribute, the `slocate` process was running in the security context `bill: staff_r:staff_t`. Apparently, this context is not permitted to perform the read operation on `file` objects having the type indicated by the value of the `tcontext` attribute, `system_u:object_r:var_lib_t`. The most likely cause is that the `slocate` process should have been run in some other context, such as `sysadm_t`.

SELinux Logging Subtleties

To avoid excessive overhead, SELinux attempts to curtail unnecessary logging. To do so, it uses separate strategies for permissive and enforcing mode.

In permissive mode, SELinux attempts to log each denial only once, avoiding a flood of identical and therefore redundant messages. To do so, SELinux maintains a cache of log entries. Before making a log entry, SELinux checks whether the entry resides in the cache. If so, SELinux suppresses the log entry.

Under some circumstances, this caching behavior may become confusing to a system administrator, who wonders why a denied operation is not accompanied by a log entry. This is particularly likely if a long interval passes between the original denial that resulted in a cache entry and subsequent denials. If you suspect that you're confronted with such a situation, you can prompt SELinux to clear its cache of log entries. You can do so either of two ways:

- Change to the policy source directory and reload the security policy:

```
cd /etc/security/selinux/src/policy
make reload
```

- Toggle between modes. For instance, in Fedora Core, you can issue the commands:

```
setenforce 1
setenforce 0
```

In enforcing mode (1), SELinux limits the rate at which log entries are made. This is necessary because some programs don't properly check error return codes. So, when SELinux prohibits an operation, these programs could cause large numbers of repeated log entries if SELinux didn't have limits on logging.

When rate limiting is occurring, log entries are lost. Obviously, this can complicate diagnosis and troubleshooting. Unfortunately, SELinux does not provide system administrators with a means of controlling its rate-limiting functionality. Nor does SELinux provide a log entry informing a system administrator that a rate limit has been initiated or terminated. Consequently, system administrators should bear in mind the possibility that SELinux log entries may be missing during intervals of high activity. Eventually, SELinux developers hope to stop depending on the system logging facility by implementing a separate logging facility designed expressly for SELinux.

 Occasionally, you may find that your console is being flooded by log messages from SELinux or another facility. When this occurs, you can regain control of the console by turning off the logging of kernel messages to the console. To do so, issue the command:

```
dmesg -n 1
```

The Audit2allow Utility

SELinux includes a special utility, Audit2allow, that scans the system log, looking for entries pertaining to denied operations and generating a file of allow rules that—if added to the security policy—would prevent those operations from being denied. Using the utility is a nontrivial matter, because the rules it generates are not always optimal. To ensure proper security, it's often necessary to define new domains or make other structural changes rather than blindly add the generated rules to the security policy. Chapter 9 gives tips and procedures for using the Audit2allow utility.

Troubleshooting SELinux

SELinux is generally stable and free of trouble. But sometimes, particularly during the initial period when a system administrator is unfamiliar with SELinux, problems crop up. The following five subsections provide troubleshooting tips that address the most common problems encountered. These problems are classified into the following five categories:

- Boot problems
- Local login problems
- Program execution problems
- Daemon problems
- X problems

Boot Problems

It's relatively common to misconfigure or otherwise break an SELinux system in a way that prevents it from booting. If you find that you've done so, try to boot into permissive mode (enforcing=0) or with SELinux disabled (selinux=0). If your kernel does not support these options, boot the system using a non-SELinux kernel, such as one residing on rescue media. Generally, you can then troubleshoot and repair the problem.

 If you boot with SELinux disabled or by using a non-SELinux kernel, the system will likely create unlabeled files or disturb existing file labels during your session. To repair the damage, you should reboot into permissive mode, relabel the filesystems, reboot, and relabel the filesystems once again.

Local Login Problems

Another relatively common problem is inability to log into the system. A likely cause is that the user's home directory is not labeled or is labeled with an incorrect security context. You can fix this problem by using the *fixfiles* utility:

```
fixfiles restore
```

Alternatively, if you're confident that only *one* user's home directory is badly labeled, you can fix the problem by using the *setfiles* utility:

```
cd /etc/security/selinux/src/policy
setfiles file_contexts/file_contexts /home/bill
```

Program Execution Problems

If an application program fails to work properly, the program is likely attempting to violate the security policy. To troubleshoot the problem, inspect the system log for SELinux denial messages related to the application. If the system is running in enforcing mode but temporarily running the system in permissive mode would not pose an unacceptable risk, you may find it convenient to switch modes. Doing so should enable the program to execute properly and should provide log messages that point out the problem.

To avoid the problem, you may simply need to start the program in an appropriate security context. Alternatively, you may need to modify the security policy. Chapters 5–9 provide you with the information and techniques for doing so.

Daemon Problems

Problems with daemons, particularly *crond* and *SSHd* are also relatively common. *cron* jobs often fail to start because the associated scripts are not properly labeled. You can relabel the troublesome scripts by issuing the *fixfiles* command:

```
fixfiles restore
```

or by issuing the setfiles command:

```
cd /etc/security/selinux/src/policy
setfiles file_contexts/file_contexts cron_files
```

where *cron_files* is the path of the script or scripts to be relabeled.

If you can't log in via SSH, consider the following possibilities:

The user account may not be properly configured.
    Verify that you can log into the user account from the console.

The user account is not associated with staff_r *or* user_r.
    If the user account is associated only with the sysadm_r role, the user won't be able to log in via SSH.

The SSH daemon is not running in the proper context.
    SSH should run in the security context root:system_r:sshd_t. Use ps -Z to determine the context actually used. If the context is not correct, restart the process using the correct context. For instance, issue the command:

```
    run_init /etc/init.d/sshd restart
```

More generally, programs started by init scripts may fail to operate correctly. This problem is generally due to improper labeling of one or more init scripts. You can relabel the scripts by issuing the *fixfiles* command:

```
fixfiles restore
```

or by issuing the *setfiles* command:

```
cd /etc/security/selinux/src/policy
setfiles file_contexts/file_contexts /etc/init.d/*
```

X Problems

Most SELinux users run servers, not desktops. So, the community has less collective experience running the X server under SELinux than other servers—too little, it seems, to ensure trouble-free operation. So, you may find it prudent to avoid using X and SELinux together. However, SELinux is achieving a new level of popularity with the release of Fedora Core 2, and many Fedora Core 2 users operate desktops. Moreover, an experimental branch of Xorg improves integration between X and SELinux by implementing policy restrictions on X objects such as windows, frames, and so on. We can reasonably expect that the quality of the X-SELinux experience will soon improve. In the meantime, I can offer some tips based on my experience and that of others.

If you're running X as the root user, you may find that the system hangs. However, you shouldn't run X as the root user whether your system runs SELinux or not. So, to avoid such system hangs, log in as a user other than the root user. Alternatively, if you insist on running X as the root user, transitioning to the sysadm_r:sysadm_t role before starting X may avoid the system hangs.

When using KDE, you may find that several graphical applications or features don't work properly. This occurs because KDE starts a variety of executables with the same process name, kdeinit. No simple fix exists for such problems, since a simple fix would entail loosening security to an unacceptable extent. You may find it more convenient to use a desktop other than KDE—such as GNOME—when running SELinux.

A workaround is to log out of KDE and remove all KDE-related temporary files from /var/tmp. Then log into KDE and see if the problems persist.

## CHAPTER 5

SELinux Policy and Policy Language Overview

Chapter 2 examined the SELinux security model from a bird's-eye perspective. The purpose of that chapter was to acquaint you with SELinux just enough to enable you to understand the procedure for installing and initially configuring SELinux. In the long run, you're likely to need to know significantly more about the SELinux security model. So this chapter picks up where Chapter 2 left off, explaining the SELinux security model and SELinux policies in greater detail and laying the groundwork for the following chapters, which explain the SELinux policy language in detail.

> For convenience, this chapter recapitulates some of the key concepts and terms introduced in Chapter 2. However, I assume that you're generally familiar with and able to recall the material from that chapter. If you find this chapter difficult to follow, I suggest that you revisit Chapter 2 and then return to this chapter. I anticipate that you'll find this chapter much clearer when the material from Chapter 2 is fresh in your mind.

The SELinux Policy

General systems theory arose in the middle of the last century, as systems analysts discovered that systems of a variety of types share common characteristics. One such characteristic is that systems can often be understood at any of several levels, sometimes referred to as *levels of abstraction*. For example, scientists tell us that interactions among atoms and molecules are governed by the quantum mechanical properties of elementary particles. But much of chemistry can be understood without reference to these fundamental structures. Indeed, chemistry arose and prospered as a discipline before the discovery of quantum mechanics and elementary particles.

To understand SELinux, it's important that its internal mechanisms—such as access vectors—be understood, because these govern the security decisions SELinux makes.

Yet because SELinux is highly configurable, the runtime behavior of an SELinux system can be viewed as effectively determined by the system's SELinux policy, which operates at a higher level of abstraction than low-level mechanisms such as access vectors.

The high flexibility of SELinux is due to the configurability of its policy. Hence the SELinux policy of any given system—though likely to be more or less based on the SELinux sample policy distributed with the NSA's SELinux release—is unlikely to exactly match the sample policy. Moreover, the SELinux sample policy is itself a living document. At the time of writing, work is underway to polish the SELinux implementation to be released as part of Fedora Core 2, and the policy is being updated regularly, even daily.

The configurability of policy and the high frequency of policy change complicate explication of the policy in two ways. First, they raise the question: what version of the policy is being explained? And second, they imply that any explanation is likely to be quickly outdated.

Fortunately, this analysis overstates the degree of difficulty. Over an extended period of time, the main features of the SELinux sample policy have remained relatively constant. And, as mentioned, most actual SELinux policies are based on the NSA's sample policy. So although policies vary and are subject to change, they remain more alike than different.

In this chapter, I explain a generic SELinux policy based on the SELinux policy associated with Fedora Core 2. The policy is hypothetical in the sense that it's not identical to any actual policy at any actual time. But that's not to say that it's irrelevant or even artificial. Instead, it's intended to be representative of a cross-section of actual SELinux policies and therefore serve as a baseline for understanding other, more highly customized or developed policies. You'll find the generic SELinux policy described in this chapter a useful point of reference in understanding the behavior of typical SELinux systems. However, please bear in mind that the policy of your own SELinux system is unlikely to match precisely the one described in this chapter.

More particularly, this chapter explains:

- The two forms (source and binary) of an SELinux policy
- The component files associated with a typical SELinux policy domain
- The structure of the directory tree that contains the SELinux source policy and the contents of each component directory

Two Forms of an SELinux Policy

If you're familiar with a programming language, such as C, you'll find that working with an SELinux policy resembles working with a program. Programs generally have two forms: a source form and an object form. Programmers work with the source form of a program, which resides in one or more ordinary text files. These files can be created and changed using a text editor or interactive development environment (IDE). However, you can't load and run the source form of a program. Instead, you must use a compiler to translate the source form into object form. The file that contains the object form of a program is a binary file that cannot be viewed or changed using a text editor. Figure 5-1 shows the process that transforms a program from source to object form.

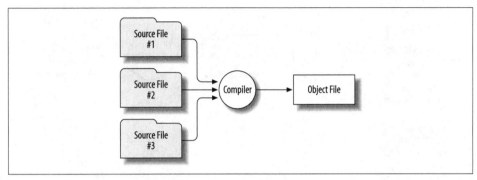

Figure 5-1. Transforming a program from source to object form

Figure 5-2 shows the process that transforms an SELinux policy from source to binary (object) form. The *checkpolicy* command is analogous to the compiler that converts a program from source to object form. Sometimes, therefore, the *checkpolicy* command is referred to as the *SELinux policy compiler*.

Unlike a typical compiler used to translate computer programs, the *checkpolicy* command can take input from only one source file. So, all SELinux policy source files are concatenated and written to the *policy.conf* file. The *checkpolicy* command reads the *policy.conf* file and writes a *policy.??* file containing a binary policy. The replaceable part of the binary policy filename indicates the version number of the SELinux policy language that was used to create the binary policy. For instance, a binary policy having filename *policy.17* would relate to Version 17 of the SELinux policy language.

The binary form of an SELinux policy can be loaded into a running Linux kernel by issuing a *load_policy* command specifying the binary policy filename as an argument. However, as explained in Chapter 4, the system administrator generally uses the SELinux *Makefile* to load a policy. The *make install*, *make load*, and *make reload* commands cause the SELinux *Makefile* to issue the *load_policy* command.

Because the SELinux policy compiler can read only one file, it may seem odd that an SELinux policy is organized as a set of files. Indeed, it would be possible for the policy to reside only in *policy.conf*. However, a typical SELinux policy contains almost 250,000 lines of code. Editing such a large file would be quite cumbersome. So the SELinux policy is distributed throughout a directory tree, typically rooted at */etc/security/selinux/src/policy*. The principal subdirectories of this directory tree include:

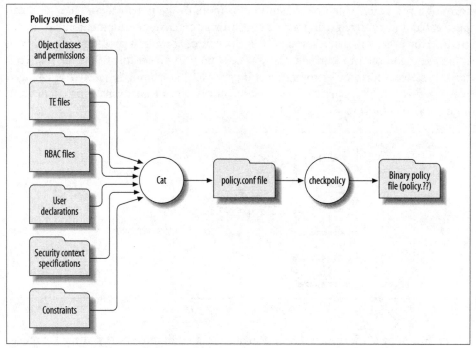

Figure 5-2. Transforming an SELinux policy from source to binary form

appconfig
> Defines default types and security contexts for several special circumstances.

domains
> Defines the type-enforcement domains.

file_contexts
> Defines the security contexts of persistent files.

flask
> Defines symbols used by the SELinux-capable kernel.

macros
> Defines M4 macros used in policy source files.

tmp
> Concatenates policy source files during policy compilation.

 The *tmp* directory is merely a working directory used during SELinux *Makefile* operations and therefore has no permanent contents. It is not further explained in this chapter.

types
> Defines several *general types*—that is, types not associated with particular domains.

Because the contents of the SELinux policy files are concatenated and written to *policy.conf* before being compiled, the SELinux policy compiler isn't aware which SELinux policy file contains the policy statements it compiles. But humans find it convenient to place related policy statements in a single file. Doing so makes it easier to understand the policy, which can be studied a file or two at a time, rather than all at once. And distributing statements among a set of files makes it easier to locate a statement of interest, because you can often deduce which files are most likely to contain it. So when creating or revising an SELinux policy, it's important to observe the conventions used by the original developers of the policy. These conventions are described more fully in the section of this chapter titled "SELinux Policy Structure."

Anatomy of a Simple SELinux Policy Domain

Let's switch our view of the SELinux policy from wide-angle to close-up and examine a simple component of an SELinux policy, to better understand how an SELinux policy operates. Recall that the SELinux type enforcement mechanism is based on domains. At any given time, a running process is associated with a domain that determines its permissions. The SELinux policy statements that establish a domain are generally grouped as two files:

FC file
> The file context (FC) file, which has the filename extension *.fc*, resides in the *file_contexts/program* subdirectory of the policy source directory. The file specifies the security contexts of directories and files associated with the domain.

TE file
> The type enforcement (TE) file, which has the filename extension *.te*, resides in the *domains/program* subdirectory of the policy source directory. The file specifies the access vector rules and transitions associated with the domain.

An SELinux policy contains many files other than FC and TE files. However, most of the work you do with an SELinux policy will involve the FC and TE files. Because FC and TE files are central to SELinux, understanding the function of these files takes you a long way toward understanding SELinux policies. So in this section, we'll overview the FC and TE files. The following chapters will explain more fully the FC and TE files as well as the other files that comprise an SELinux policy.

The FC and TE files that establish a domain generally carry the name of the principal program associated with the domain. For instance, the files associated with the domain that regulates the behavior of the Snort intrusion detection application are named *snort.fc* and *snort.te*. Let's begin by examining the *snort.fc* file.

The snort.fc File

The *snort.fc* file specifies security contexts for directories and files related to Snort:

```
# SNORT
/usr/sbin/snort       --   system_u:object_r:snort_exec_t
/usr/local/bin/snort  --   system_u:object_r:snort_exec_t
/etc/snort(/.*)?           system_u:object_r:snort_etc_t
/var/log/snort(/.*)?       system_u:object_r:snort_log_t
```

The first line in the file is a comment, as indicated by the hash mark (#) appearing in the first column. The remaining four lines have a simple structure consisting of three columns:

Regular expression
>Directories and files having a path matching the regular expression are labeled according to the specifications in columns two and three.

Flags
>The flags specify whether the regular expression matches directories, files, or either directories or files. The paired dashes specify that the regular expression can match only ordinary files.

Security context
>The security context specifies the SELinux user, role, and type with which the directory or file is to be labeled.

For instance, the Snort executable resides in the file */usr/sbin/snort*, a path matching the regular expression appearing in the second line of the FC file. When the *make relabel* command is executed in the policy source directory, the file */usr/sbin/snort* will be labeled with the security context system_u:object_r:snort_exec_t.

The regular expression appearing in the fourth line of the file includes several metacharacters:

```
/etc/snort(/.*)?           system_u:object_r:snort_etc_t
```

The metacharacters have the same meaning they take on in the *vi* editor and other Linux programs that use regular expressions. In particular, the parentheses indicate grouping, and the question mark (?) indicates that the preceding item or group is optional. The dot (.) can be replaced by any single character, and the asterisk (*) indicates that the preceding item or group can be repeated indefinitely. The slash (/) is not a metacharacter; it matches the slashes that separate the parts of a directory pathname. Therefore, the regular expression matches the path */etc/snort* and the path of any file or directory contained in */etc/snort*. Matching files and directories will be labeled with the security context system_u:object_r:snort_etc_t.

The snort.te File

Now, let's examine the TE file:

```
#DESC Snort - Network sniffer
#
# Author: Shaun Savage <savages@pcez.com>
# Modified by Russell Coker <russell@coker.com.au>
# X-Debian-Packages: snort-common
#

daemon_domain(snort)

log_domain(snort)
can_network(snort_t)
type snort_etc_t, file_type, sysadmfile;

# Create temporary files.
tmp_domain(snort)

# use iptable netlink
allow snort_t self:netlink_socket create_socket_perms;
allow snort_t self:packet_socket create_socket_perms;
allow snort_t self:capability { setgid setuid net_admin net_raw };

r_dir_file(snort_t, snort_etc_t)
allow snort_t etc_t:file { getattr read };
allow snort_t etc_t:lnk_file read;

allow snort_t self:unix_dgram_socket create_socket_perms;
allow snort_t self:unix_stream_socket create_socket_perms;

# for start script
allow initrc_t snort_etc_t:file read;
```

As you can see, the TE file is somewhat more complex than the FC file. In particular, whereas the FC file contains only one sort of noncomment line, this TE file contains several:

Type line
> Defines a type.

Allow lines
> Define an access vector rule.

Other lines
> Lines beginning with other identifiers, such as daemon_domain and can_network, are macro invocations.

The type line

The line:

```
type snort_etc_t, file_type, sysadmfile;
```

defines snort_etc_t as a type. The attributes file_type and sysadmfile mark this type as pertaining to file objects that can be accessed and modified by users associated with the sysadm_r (system administrator) role. Many such attributes are defined in the *attrib.te* file. If you look back to the FC file, you'll see that the */etc/snort* directory and its contents are labeled with the type snort_etc_t.

The allow lines

Lines beginning with the keyword allow specify access vector rules authorizing operations on various object types. For instance, the line:

```
allow snort_t etc_t:file { getattr read };
```

specifies that processes running in the snort_t domain can read and get the attributes of files labeled with the etc_t type. Notice the use of curly braces, { and }, to enclose the list.

Similarly, the line:

```
allow initrc_t snort_etc_t:file read;
```

specifies that processes running in the initrc_t domain can read files labeled with the snort_etc_t type. As it happens, the init process, which controls SysV daemons, runs in the initirc_t domain. Thus, the init process can read the contents of the */etc/snort* directory tree, which contains the Snort configuration files init must consult to start Snort with the user-specified options.

Notice that allow lines are the most common sort of line in the TE file. Recall that SELinux prohibits all operations not explicitly authorized. So, a typical domain contains several—perhaps many—allow lines that specify operations for which the domain is authorized.

 Not all access vector rules specify authorized access. For instance, as explained in Chapter 7, auditdeny and dontaudit rules specify prohibited operations. However, the *snort.te* file includes only allow rules.

Macro invocations

In addition to type and allow lines, the TE file contains a variety of other noncomment lines. These are macro invocations—statements that are expanded by the M4 macro processor into zero or more SELinux policy statements. If you administer a system running Sendmail, you're likely already familiar with M4, because Sendmail uses it to establish its configuration in much the same way as SELinux does. If you aren't familiar with macro definitions and invocations, you can think of a macro definition as a script and a macro invocation as a command invoking the script. Let's consider a simple example.

The file *macros/global_macros.te* defines many SELinux macros. Among them is the definition of the `can_network` macro, which is invoked on line 11 of the *snort.te* file (comment lines omitted for simplicity):

```
define(`can_network',`
allow $1 self:udp_socket create_socket_perms;
allow $1 self:tcp_socket create_stream_socket_perms;
allow $1 netif_type:netif { tcp_send udp_send rawip_send };
allow $1 netif_type:netif { tcp_recv udp_recv rawip_recv };
allow $1 node_type:node { tcp_send udp_send rawip_send };
allow $1 node_type:node { tcp_recv udp_recv rawip_recv };
allow $1 port_type:{ tcp_socket udp_socket } { send_msg recv_msg };
allow $1 mount_t:udp_socket rw_socket_perms;
allow $1 node_type: { tcp_socket udp_socket } node_bind;
allow $1 net_conf_t:file r_file_perms;
')dnl end can_network definition
```

When a macro is invoked, the invocation can supply the macro with arguments. Consider line 11 of *snort.te*:

```
can_network(snort_t)
```

This invocation of the `can_network` macro supplies the argument `snort_t`. When the macro is interpreted, its invocation is replaced with the lines from its definition. However, the symbol $1 appearing within the definition is replaced by the first supplied argument, the symbol $2 is replaced by the second supplied argument, and so on. In the macro invocation, notice that the left parenthesis immediately follows `can_network`, the name of the macro. M4 requires that no space appear between the name of a macro and the parenthesis that begins the macro's argument list.

In the case of the *snort.te* file, the invocation of `can_network` provides one argument, `snort_t`. This argument replaces the symbol $1 appearing in the macro definition. The result is that the following lines replace the macro invocation within the *snort.te* file:

```
allow snort_t self:udp_socket create_socket_perms;
allow snort_t self:tcp_socket create_stream_socket_perms;
allow snort_t netif_type:netif { tcp_send udp_send rawip_send };
allow snort_t netif_type:netif { tcp_recv udp_recv rawip_recv };
allow snort_t node_type:node { tcp_send udp_send rawip_send };
allow snort_t node_type:node { tcp_recv udp_recv rawip_recv };
allow snort_t port_type:{ tcp_socket udp_socket } { send_msg recv_msg };
allow snort_t mount_t:udp_socket rw_socket_perms;
allow snort_t node_type: { tcp_socket udp_socket } node_bind;
allow snort_t net_conf_t:file r_file_perms;
```

These `allow` lines authorize a variety of network-related operations.

The point of using macros is that they make policies more concise and therefore easier to read and understand. They also help prevent inconsistencies that may lead to policy errors. The section of this chapter titled "The macros Subdirectory" summarizes many of the standard macros defined for use in SELinux policies.

As shown in Figure 5-3, the M4 macro processor is invoked prior to the creation of the *policy.conf* file, so that file contains no macro invocations. Thus, the SELinux policy compiler does not actually process any macro invocations.

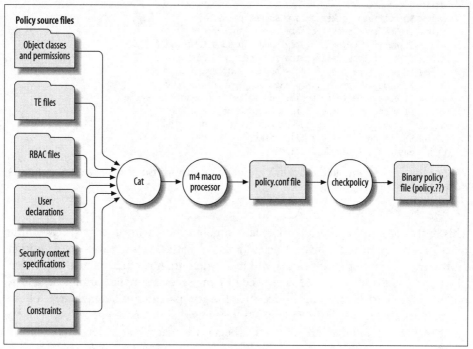

Figure 5-3. Transforming an SELinux policy, including M4 macro expansion

SELinux Policy Structure

Now that we've completed our close-up view of an SELinux policy component, let's return to a wide-angle view. This section explains the conventions observed by SELinux policy developers in choosing where to place policy statements of various types. The explanation is organized around the structure of the SELinux source directory tree, which is typically */etc/security/selinux/src/policy*. In good computer science fashion, we'll first visit the leaf nodes (that is, the subdirectories of the tree) and ultimately visit the root node (that is, the policy directory itself). However, we'll depart from computer science conventions in one key respect: rather than visit the nodes in lexicographic (alphabetical) order, we'll visit them in an order in which several nodes having fundamental content are visited first, to facilitate the exposition.

The flask Subdirectory

The *flask* directory, as implied by being the first subdirectory visited in our traversal of the policy source directory tree, is the most fundamental of the subdirectories. It contains three important files:

- *initial_sids*
- *security_classes*
- *access_vectors*

Like other policy source files, these files are read and processed during policy compilation. In addition, these files are used to generate C header files that are used during compilation of an SELinux-capable Linux kernel. In that context, the files specify symbol definitions for access vectors (that is, permissions), initial SIDs, and security classes. Because of their relationship to the kernel, changes to the contents of these files may require recompilation of the kernel. Therefore, in comparison to other policy source files, these files are relatively static.

> Although several policy source files are used in the compilation of the kernel, you don't need to have SELinux policy sources available during kernel compilation. The kernel sources include copies of the necessary SELinux policy source files.

The following subsections explain the purpose and contents of these files. The most interesting of the files is the *access_vectors* file, which is explained in the last of the three subsections.

The flask/initial_sids file

The *flask/initial_sids* file specifies about two dozen initial SID values. The values are used to label transient objects and objects used during system bootup. The file is also used to generate a C header file, *flask.h*, used during kernel compilation. System administrators do not generally need to modify the *initial_sids* file, nor should they do so.

The flask/security_classes file

The *flask/security_classes* file defines thirty security object classes, which are shown in Appendix A. The classes `file` and `dir` are among the most commonly used security classes. Like the *initial_sids* file, the file is used to create the C header file *flask.h*, which is used during kernel compilation. System administrators do not generally need to modify the *security_classes* file, nor should they do so.

The flask/access_vectors file

As explained in Chapter 2, access vectors specify the operations that can be performed by subjects upon objects. In other words, they specify permissions. The *flask/access_vectors* file defines the range of operations associated with each object class. In all, about 150 different operations are specified on the thirty defined classes of SELinux security objects. Among the most commonly used operations are read, which denotes reading a file or file-like object, and write, which denotes writing a file or file-like object. Appendix B summarizes the operations defined in the file. The *access_vectors* file generates a C header file, *av_permissions.h*, used during kernel compilation. System administrators do not generally need to modify the *access_vectors* file, nor should they do so.

You may find the large amount of detail appearing in Appendix B somewhat overwhelming. You certainly don't need to memorize the table in order to effectively use SELinux. But you will likely have to refer to it from time to time. You may do so, for example:

- To understand the log message generated when SELinux denies a requested operation. In this case, Appendix B will help you understand what the requesting program was attempting to do.

- To find the SELinux name of an operation so that you can create a policy rule that allows or denies it under particular circumstances.

The policy configuration provides the ability to specify some operations that are nonsensical, such as associating swap space with a socket file. Valid, real-world policies don't actually authorize such operations, even though it's possible to do so.

The descriptions of SELinux operations provided in Appendix B are approximate. The actual meaning of an operation is determined by the system calls that are enabled or disabled by the permissions corresponding to the operation. Precisely understanding or defining an operation therefore requires a detailed understanding of the related system calls and is beyond the scope of this book.

The macros Subdirectory

The *macros* directory contains several files that define M4 macros used primarily in the TE files that define domains. The files are:

admin_macros.te
> Defines the admin_domain macro.

base_user_macros.te
> Defines the base_user_domain macro.

core_macros.te
> Defines about five dozen fundamental macros, primarily defining sets of permissions and simple access vector rules.

global_macros.te

Defines about three dozen fundamental macros, primarily defining domain properties.

mini_user_macros.te

Defines the `mini_user_domain` macro.

user_macros.te

Defines the `user_domain`, `full_user_role`, and `in_user_role` macros.

Appendix C summarizes the macros defined in the *macros* subdirectory. A typical example of a macro is `r_file_perms`, which expands to the permissions needed to read files and file attributes, namely:

```
{ read getattr lock ioctl }
```

I suggest that you browse Table C-1 at this point. However, unless you have photographic recall, don't attempt to commit it to memory. You'll primarily use the table just as you use the tables presented earlier in this chapter: to understand log messages and to find SELinux names when coding your own policy rules. Please note that the descriptions given in Table C-1 are approximate. In drafting them, I emphasized conciseness over completeness. Once you more fully understand the SELinux policy language, you'll be able to develop your own, more sophisticated understanding of these macros.

In addition to the files defining macros, the *macros* directory also contains a subdirectory named *program*. This subdirectory contains about three dozen files that define M4 macros used in defining user domains. Their function is closely related to that of the TE files that define user domains, so they are not explained separately in this chapter.

The file_contexts Subdirectory

The *file_contexts* directory tree contains files, known as *file context files*, that specify the security context of persistent files. The *setfiles* program consults the file context files when labeling a filesystem.

The *file_contexts* directory contains two subdirectories:

program

Contains specifications of the security contexts of files that are part of installed packages or programs.

misc

Contains miscellaneous specifications.

Some implementations of SELinux are distributed with an empty *misc* directory. The absence of files is not a cause for concern.

In addition, the *file_contexts* directory contains two files:

file_contexts
> This file is automatically created when a policy is compiled. It aggregates the contents of all the file context files residing in the *misc* and *program* subdirectories.

types.fc
> This file contains security contexts for general system files and user home directories.

Security contexts are specified in *.fc* (file context) files, which have a simple syntax:

```
regex [ -type ] ( context | <<none>> )
```

That is, each line begins with a regular expression (*regex*), which is optionally followed by a token representing a type (*type*). Each line ends with a token representing a context (*context*) or the special token <<none>>.

> A file-context file may also contain comments. Any line beginning with a hash mark (#) is considered a comment and ignored by the *setfiles* program.

When files are being labeled, the path of each file is compared with the regular expressions of each successive file-context line. If a regular expression matches the path, the file is relabeled according to the specified security context; otherwise no action is performed. If multiple regular expressions match the path, the last matching regular expression determines the security context with which the file is labeled. The special token <<none>> specifies that files matching the associated regular expression should not be relabeled.

> The file context specifications generally have the form */path/.** (or its equivalent), which matches any path beginning with */path*. The associated security context, which is generally system_u:object_r:default_t, is used to label files not matching other regular expressions. Thus in practice, all files are labeled (unless the <<none>> token is used to direct otherwise).

For example, here's a typical file context specification:

```
/home/[^/]+/.+            system_u:object_r:user_home_t
```

This specification matches files in users' home directories and indicates they should be labeled with the security context system_u:object_r:user_home_t.

The optional token representing a type takes one of the following values:

--
> Matches only regular files.

-b
> Matches only block device files.

-c

Matches only character device files.

-d

Matches only directories.

-s

Matches only socket files.

If the type token does not appear in a line, the line matches directories and files of all types, including device files and other nonregular files.

The regular expressions appearing in file context specifications are implicitly anchored. That is, they behave as though ^ (the regular expression metacharacter matching the beginning of a string) appears as their first character and $ (the regular expression metacharacter matching the end of a string) appears as their last character. Thus, the regular expression given earlier for users' home directories does not match the path */root/home/homedir/roots-file.txt*, because the path does not begin with */home*. Because of the implicit anchoring, it's important to use absolute, rather than relative, paths in file context specifications.

 If you're unfamiliar with regular expressions—or rusty in working with them—I suggest that you consult *Mastering Regular Expressions* (O'Reilly).

The types Subdirectory

The *types* directory contains files that define *general types* and a few rules that govern their use. General types are types that are not associated with a particular domain. In all, over 150 general types are defined in 7 files:

device.te

Defines over two dozen types related to devices and device files. See Table D-1.

devpts.te

Defines two types related to the */dev/pts* filesystem: ptmx_t, the type of the pty master multiplexor, and devpts_t, the type of the *devpts* filesystem and its root directory.

file.te

Defines almost six dozen types related to files. See Table D-2.

network.te

Defines about three dozen types related to networks. See Table D-3.

nfs.te

Defines the type *nfs_t*, the type used for NFS filesystems and the files they contain.

procfs.te

Defines over one dozen types related to the */proc* filesystem, especially the sysctl parameters in */proc/sys*. See Table D-4.

security.te

Defines six types related to SELinux itself. See Table D-5.

The domains Subdirectory

The *domains* subdirectory contains two files and two subdirectories. The files are:

admin.te

Defines the sysadm_t general type, which is used by system administrators, and specifies several rules defining related permissions. Also defines several types related to the sysadm_t type.

user.te

Defines several general types used by ordinary users and specifies several rules defining related permissions.

The system administrator does not generally need to modify the *admin.te* or *user.te* file.

 Recall that a general type is one not related to a specific domain.

Like the *domains* directory, its subdirectories contain TE files defining domains. The subdirectories are:

misc

Defines several miscellaneous domains—that is, domains not related to specific programs. The particular domains vary across different SELinux policies and policy versions. However, the directory is likely to define the following domains:

auth-net

Policy for PAM LDAP authentication

fcron

Policy for the crond_t domain, associated with *cron*

kernel

Policy for the kernel_t domain, associated with the Linux kernel

startx

Policy for running X

The system administrator does not generally need to modify the files defining these domains.

program

Defines ordinary domains related to specific programs. A typical installation may contain over 100 TE files defining domains. The TE files are generally given names resembling those of the related package or program. For example, the TE file defining domains related to the Apache web server is commonly named *apache.te*.

Along with the *file_contexts/program* subdirectory and the policy sources directory itself, the *domains/program* subdirectory is one of the SELinux directories most important to the system administrator. Most SELinux directories contain static files that the system administrator need not—or must not—change. However, the system administrator often finds it necessary to modify or supplement the files contained in the *domains/program* subdirectory.

Most Linux distributions feature package managers that assist in the installation of software products. Generally, when SELinux is implemented for a particular distribution, the distribution's package manager is modified to interoperate with SELinux by automatically installing the TE and FC files related to a package when the package is installed.

However, system administrators often install programs for which their Linux distribution offers no officially supported package. In such a case—and in any case in which the package manager is unable to automatically install the FC and TE files related to a package—the system administrator must manually install the FC and TE files. In some cases, prebuilt FC and TE files may not exist; then the system administrator must create and install appropriate FC and TE files before the installed program will operate properly under SELinux. Chapter 9 explains how to do so.

A one-to-one relationship exists between files in the *file_contexts/program* and *domains/program* directories. The SELinux *Makefile* enforces this correspondence and refuses to build a binary policy if the correspondence is violated. So if you create a TE file in *domains/program*, you must create a corresponding FC file in *file_contexts/program*, and vice versa.

The appconfig Subdirectory

The *appconfig* subdirectory stores configuration information used by security-aware programs modified to work with SELinux. The configuration information consists of default contexts and types assigned to objects by security-aware programs. Typically, the subdirectory contains five files:

default_contexts

Used by *login*, *sshd*, and *crond* to determine the legal security contexts for a given user that are reachable from the security context of the current process

default_type

Used by *login* to determine the default type (domain) for each role

failsafe_context

Used in X failsafe operation

initrc_context

Used by the *run_init* program to determine the security context for running */etc/ rc.d* scripts

root_default_contexts

Used by *login* to determine the security contexts available to the root user

The system administrator does not generally need to modify these files, with one exception: the *root_default_contexts* file contains a commented line that can be uncommented to cause the root user to automatically log into the sysadm_r role. However, doing so may make you system somewhat less secure and is not a generally recommended practice.

The Policy Source Directory

In addition to its various subdirectories, the policy source directory contains several files, a few of which are important to the system administrator. Here are the most important files, i.e. those which often must be modified:

tunable.te

Contains various definitions that the system administrator can enable or disable to customize the SELinux security policy. This file is distribution-specific and may not exist on your SELinux system.

users

Defines the SELinux users. Described further in Chapter 6, this file generally must be modified to include the Linux user names of users who can act as system administrators. Optionally, the file can be modified to include the Linux user names of other users.

The other files within the policy source directory include:

assert.te

Defines assertions that safeguard the integrity of the SELinux security policy. Assertions are more fully explained in Chapter 7. Essentially, an assertion states a condition that must not be violated by the SELinux security policy. When a policy is compiled, assertions are checked; violation of an assertion terminates the compilation and suppresses binary policy generation. Assertions protect against unwise or incorrect policy revisions that might compromise the integrity of SELinux or the security policy.

attrib.te

Defines about six dozen type attributes. As more fully explained in Chapter 7, type attributes define sets of types and domains having common permissions.

constraints

Defines several constraints on M4 macro invocations. Like SELinux policy assertions, the constraints safeguard the integrity of the SELinux policy.

fs_use

Specifies how various filesystem types are labeled by SELinux.

genfs_contexts

Specifies how SELinux handles filesystem types that do not support extended attributes or an SELinux-supported fixed-labeling scheme.

initial_sid_contexts

Specifes the security context of several initial security context IDs (SIDs).

Makefile

Controls the labeling of filesystems and the compilation and installation of the SELinux security policy. Chapter 4 explains how to invoke the operations supported by the *Makefile*.

mls

Specifies configuration options related to multilevel security (MLS). MLS is not supported by the current release of SELinux.

net_contexts

Specifies the security contexts of ports, interfaces, and other network objects.

policy.??

The binary security policy file; for instance, *policy.17*.

policy.conf

A temporary file used during policy compilation, used to aggregate the source files involved in the compilation.

rbac

Defines legal role transitions. Currently, the only legal transition is from sysadm_r to system_r, a transition needed by the *run_init* program.

serviceusers

Specifies roles accessible by users that exist only if related optional packages are installed. For instance, the user cyrus is permitted to enter the role cyrus_r, but only if the cyrus.te domain is defined.

In addition, the policy sources directory includes several files that have no functional role but contain useful information for system administrators, including:

COPYING

Contains the license, currently the GNU General Public License, under which SELinux can be used.

ChangeLog

Summarizes changes made to SELinux versions.

policy.spec

The SPEC file associated with the source RPM containing the security policy. SPEC files specify how the RPM program builds source and binary RPM packages.

README

Provides a brief overview of the contents of the policy source directory tree.

VERSION

States the SELinux version.

## CHAPTER 6

Role-Based Access Control

Up to this point in the book, we've looked at the functions SELinux provides and the configuration files that direct its operation. However, we've merely glanced at the SELinux policy language that's used to specify the SELinux security policy. Our situation is akin to that of a 15th or 16th century explorer who has studied maps of the New World and dreamed of the exotic sights that may be found there but has not yet ventured to sea. In this chapter, we at last embark upon our sea voyage.

In this chapter and the following two chapters, you'll find a detailed explanation of the SELinux policy language and several related languages, such as those used to specify file and security contexts. This chapter explains the SELinux role-based access control policies, Chapter 7 explains the SELinux type-enforcement policies, and Chapter 8 explains other elements of the SELinux policy. Of course, most likely your goal is not merely to understand the SELinux policy language or SELinux security policies themselves, though such skills are useful to the SELinux system administrator. Instead, it's more likely that you want to be able to specify new and modified SELinux security policies. If that is your goal, Chapters 6–8 won't quite take you to the end of your voyage, though you'll make landfall near the end of Chapter 8. Then you'll be ready for Chapter 9, which explains how you can customize existing SELinux policies and implement your own policies.

The SELinux Role-Based Access Control Model

As explained in previous chapters, the SELinux security model is based primarily on a mechanism called *type enforcement* (TE). Type enforcement assigns processes to domains and restricts the operations each domain is permitted to perform. The SELinux policy, which can be customized by a system administrator, specifies the available domains and the operations that processes within them are authorized to perform. Chapter 7 explains the SELinux type-enforcement model in detail.

SELinux also includes a second security model, called *role-based access control* (RBAC). Role-based access control works alongside type enforcement: intended operations are prohibited unless they're explicitly authorized by both type enforcement and role-based access control. Of course, intended operations must also satisfy any requirements imposed by ordinary Linux discretionary access control mechanisms, such as file permissions.

Role-based access control works fairly simply and has three parts. First, each user is authorized for a set of roles. A user cannot enter a role other than one for which the user is authorized. Second, transitions between roles are authorized. A process can transition to a new role only if transitions between its current role and the new role are authorized. Finally, each role is authorized for a set of domains. Any attempt to enter a nonauthorized role or domain is prohibited by the SELinux security engine. Let's consider some concrete examples.

Users are assigned roles by the user statement. For instance, the following statement assigns the roles staff_r and sysadm_r to the user bill, permitting the user to enter either role:

```
user bill roles { staff_r sysadm_r };
```

Transitions between roles are governed by allow statements. For instance, the following allow statement authorizes processes running in the staff_r role to transition to the sysadm_r role:

```
allow staff_r sysadm_r;
```

Roles are authorized to enter domains by the role statement. For instance, the following statement authorizes the role sysadm_r to enter the ifconfig_t domain:

```
role sysadm_r types ifconfig_t;
```

A domain can include multiple role statements, each authorizing one or more roles to enter the domain. Unless a role statement authorizes a particular role to enter a domain, processes running in that role cannot enter the domain.

Both type enforcement and role-based access control work by inspecting security contexts. Recall that SELinux assigns a security context to each process, as well as to each instance of other objects, such as files. A security context includes three elements:

- A user
- A role
- A type (domain)

Thus, at any time, the security context of a process indicates its user identity and role identity, the characteristics considered by role-based access control. A process can change its user or role identity, but only if the current SELinux policy enables the specific transition. For instance, SELinux policies typically permit changing from the staff_r role to the sysadm_r role, but prohibit other roles (such as user_r) from changing to sysadm_r.

Similarly, SELinux policies restrict access to domains, allowing only processes running in specified roles to enter them. For instance, the `ifconfig_t` domain is authorized to perform various operations that concern network interfaces, which ordinary users should not generally be allowed to perform. Thus, entry to the domain is restricted to processes running in the `sysadm_r` role, which includes only users designated as system administrators.

Role-based access control governs processes rather than files or other objects. So the security contexts of files and other objects are simplified. Although these security contexts contain the three elements common to all security contexts, the role associated with objects other than processes is `object_r`, which is basically a mere placeholder.

The statements that express the SELinux role-based access control policy provide more elaborate options than shown in the preceding examples. To fully explain them, the following section introduces a visual representation of syntax: the railroad diagram.

Railroad Diagrams

In the film *Planes, Trains, and Automobiles*, characters played by Steve Martin and John Candy are faced with one improbable obstacle after another as they struggle to arrive home in time for the Thanksgiving holiday. Having compared this chapter with a sea voyage, it's reminiscent of that film to consider yet another mode of transportation, railways, as a means of understanding the SELinux policy language.

However, unlike many of the decisions of the film characters, my decision to introduce railroad diagrams is not capricious. Such diagrams were used in the 1970s by famous computer scientist Niklaus Wirth to develop and explain Pascal, one of the most successful programming languages. Since then, they've been used to explain many other programming languages. Although they can be cumbersome to create, they're quick to learn as well as easy to read and understand, so they're just about ideal as a means of explanation. Let's further mix our metaphors by diving into an exposition of railroad diagrams.

What Railroad Diagrams Do

Railroad diagrams are also known as *syntax diagrams* or *syntax charts*. They present the grammar of a formal language, such as one used for programming. However, formal languages also underlie the files used to configure systems and applications, such as the files that specify the SELinux security policy, so these diagrams are well suited to our immediate purpose.

Railroad diagrams specify two kinds of symbols:

Literal

A literal is a symbol that consists of one or more specific characters. Literals are generally punctuation marks, operators, or keywords of some sort.

Replaceable text

Replaceable text consists of text that has variable content.

These definitions will become clearer in the context of several small examples given in the following section.

How Railroad Diagrams Work

Figure 6-1 shows a railroad diagram that defines a literal representing the letter "a."

Figure 6-1. The letter "a"

The diagram contains two parts:

Line

The line guides you in reading the railroad diagram. If you're disappointed that the line doesn't more closely resemble a railroad track, I apologize. But, it's customary to draw the line in the simple fashion shown in the figure. You read the railroad diagram by following the line from left to right.

Oval

The oval represents a literal—that is, a specific character, namely the letter "a."

Literal symbols (text that appears in the file exactly as shown in the diagram) appear in lightly shaded boxes, while replaceable symbols (which should be replaced with appropriate values by the administrator) appear in darkly shaded boxes.

One way to use a railroad diagram is as a means of parsing sentences following the grammar represented by the diagram. To do so, follow the line from left to right and attempt to match each symbol you encounter with a corresponding token in the sentence. If you can do so, the sentence is grammatical; otherwise it's not.

The railroad diagram for the letter "a" is trivially simple, and therefore it is not much fun or valuable for practice. So, let's consider Figure 6-2, which presents a somewhat more sophisticated sentence, one that has the same form as an SELinux security policy attribute declaration. This sentence consists of three components that must appear in the indicated order:

- A literal representing the keyword `attribute`
- Replaceable text known as an *id*
- A literal representing a semicolon

Figure 6-2. Attribute declaration

The railroad diagram merely references—but doesn't define—the replaceable text *id*, which would be defined by another diagram. I'll present a diagram defining *id* shortly. For now, let's simply understand *id* as representing an identifier of the sort used in many programming languages, consisting of a letter followed by zero or more letters or digits.

Given our understanding of the replaceable text *id*, our railroad diagram tells us that sentences such as the following are grammatical attribute declarations:

```
attribute x;
attribute xyz;
attribute xyz123;
```

Similarly, our railroad diagram tells us that sentences such as the following are not grammatical attribute declarations:

```
attribute x        # lacks final semicolon
attrib x;          # abbreviates required literal "attribute"
attribute 123;     # contains integer rather than id
```

Let's now consider a somewhat more complex railroad diagram, shown in Figure 6-3, which represents a digit. Notice how multiple tracks branch off the main line, so that you can completely traverse the railroad diagram by matching any of the ten literals representing a digit.

If you're familiar with regular expressions, you may realize that the syntax represented by Figure 6-3 could easily be represented by the regular expression:

```
[0123456789]
```

or, more concisely:

```
[0-9]
```

Let's now consider a set of three railroad diagrams that, together with Figure 6-3, define the composition of a signed integer. Figure 6-4 tells us that a signed integer consists of a sign, consisting of the literal + or -, followed by replaceable text named Unsigned_Integer, which obviously represents an unsigned integer.

Figure 6-5 defines Unsigned_integer in terms of Digit, the replaceable text defined in Figure 6-3. In Figure 6-5, notice the track that leads from the right side of the second instance of Digit to the left side of the same instance. This track makes it possible to include multiple occurrences of the second instance of Digit. The railroad diagram tells us that an unsigned integer consists of a digit, followed by zero or more digits. Put more plainly, it tells us that an unsigned integer consists of one or more digits.

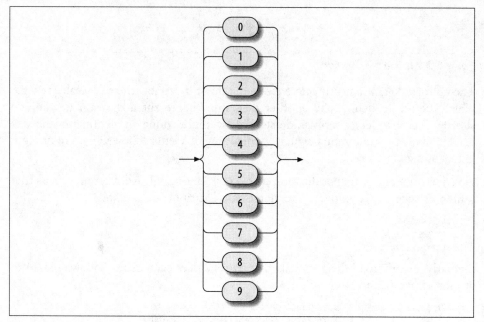

Figure 6-3. Digit

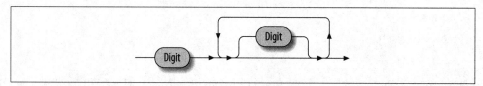

Figure 6-4. Signed_Integer

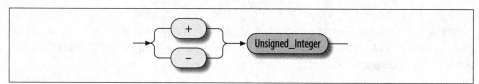

Figure 6-5. Unsigned_Integer

You might represent the syntax shown in Figures 6-4 and 6-5 by the regular expression:

    [+-]\d\d*

or the equivalent:

    [+-]\d+

Figure 6-6 puts together the definitions of Signed_Integer and Unsigned_Integer, telling us that an Integer consists of either a Signed_Integer or an Unsigned_Integer.

Figure 6-6. Integer

By now, you've seen everything necessary to understand the railroad diagrams we'll use to describe the SELinux security policy language. But, let's consider a couple additional railroad diagrams for good measure. Figure 6-7 shows another way of defining an Integer, one that consists of only a single railroad diagram. I suggest that you study the figure and convince yourself that the definition it offers is indeed equivalent to the previous definition that required three distinct railroad diagrams. Of course, like the three-diagram definition, the newer one references the diagram defining a Digit. So, it's not fully self-contained. But, including a definition of Digit rather than a reference to Digit in the newer definition would hopelessly clutter the definition.

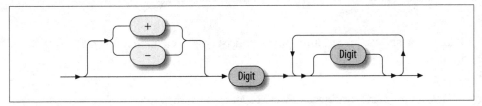

Figure 6-7. Another way of specifying an Integer

Finally, let's consider one more railroad diagram, given in Figure 6-8. This railroad diagram defines the composition of an Identifier, which consists of a letter, followed by zero or more digits, letters, or underscores, which can be freely intermingled. I trust that it's evident that the railroad is much faster and easier to read and understand than the equivalent English sentence.

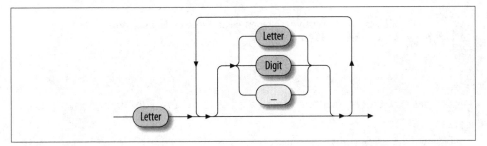

Figure 6-8. Identifier

I also presume you noticed that the replaceable text Letter, which is used in the railroad diagram, is defined neither by the diagram nor earlier in this chapter. I could give a railroad diagram defining this replaceable text, but it would be rather badly cluttered, since a letter can be any one of 52 literals: the lowercase and uppercase letters of the Roman alphabet.

SELinux Policy Syntax

The railroad diagram in Figure 6-9 represents an overview of the syntax of an SELinux policy.

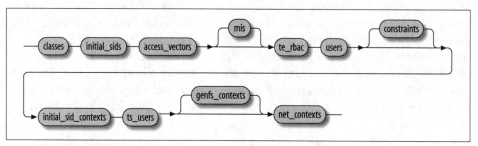

Figure 6-9. The SELinux Policy

As the figure shows, an SELinux policy consists of 11 elements, several of which are optional:

classes
> Defines the security object classes recognized by SELinux.

initial_sids
> Defines initial SIDs for important security objects.

access_vectors
> Defines access vectors associated with each security object class.

mls
> Defines MLS configuration (optional).

 MLS is not currently implemented in sample SELinux policies and is not covered in this book.

te_rbac
> Defines type enforcement and role-based access control configuration.

users
> Defines the user configuration.

constraints
> Defines constraints that the security policy must observe (optional).

`initial_sid_contexts`
> Defines the security contexts of important security objects.

`fs_use`
> Defines the method of labeling of filesystem inodes.

`genfs_contexts`
> Defines security contexts for filesystems lacking persistent labels (optional).

`net_contexts`
> Defines security contexts for network objects.

The policy elements must appear in the order indicated by the railroad diagram. However, you generally don't have to concern yourself with the order of policy statements, because each type of statement resides in a designated file or directory. As explained in Chapter 4, the SELinux policy *Makefile* assembles these files into a single file before compiling the policy source statements. The *Makefile* ensures that policy statements are presented to the policy compiler in the proper order. Table 6-1 shows the correspondence between the policy elements and files in the *src/policy* SELinux source tree.

Table 6-1. Policy elements and associated files

Element	File or directory (relative to *src/policy*)
`classes`	*flask/security_classes*
`initial_sids`	*initial_sid_contexts*
`access_vectors`	*flask/acess_vectors*
`opt_mls`	*mls*
`te_rbac`	*rbac*
	*.te
	domains/*.te
	domains/misc/*.te
	domains/programs/*.te
	macros/*.te
	macros/program/*.te
	types/*.te
`users`	*users*
	serviceusers (Fedora Core)
`opt_constraints`	*constraints*
`initial_sid_contexts`	*flask/initial_sids*
`fs_uses`	*fs_use*
`opt_genfs_contexts`	*genfs_contexts*
`net_contexts`	*net_contexts*

Table 6-1 shows files and directories used in the Fedora Core 2 SELinux implementation. The files may have different contents or locations under other implementations of SELinux.

One of the most important policy elements, te_rbac, contains type enforcement and role-based access control declarations. Along with the file context configuration, the TE and RBAC configuration is the part of an SELinux policy that is most often modified. Syntactically, the te_rbac element consists of a series that freely intermingles two subelements—te_decl and rbac_decl—as shown in Figure 6-10.

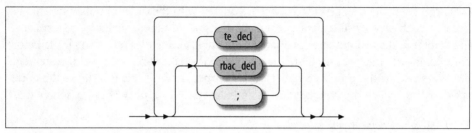

Figure 6-10. TE and RBAC declarations (te_rbac)

Basic Policy Elements

Before presenting the syntax of the SELinux user and role-based access control declarations, let's look at a few subelements that appear in a variety of SELinux policy elements and at a few principles that govern their use. Figure 6-11 shows the syntax of a subelement known as identifier_list. As its name suggests, the subelement represents a list of identifiers. An example of such a list appears in the following declaration from the *ping.te* file:

```
allow ping_t self:rawip_socket { create ioctl read write bind
   getopt setopt };
```

The curly braces enclose an identifier list specifying the permissions related to a raw IP socket: create, ioctl, read, write, bind, getopt, and setopt.

Figure 6-11. The identifier_list subelement

Notice that the identifiers are separated from one another by white space. Another subelement, id_comma_list, specifies a comma-separated list of identifiers. A railroad diagram for this subelement appears as Figure 6-12.

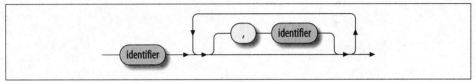

Figure 6-12. The id_comma_list subelement

Another statement of the *ping.te* file provides an example of this subelement:

```
type ping_exec_t, file_type, sysadmfile, exec_type;
```

In this statement, the identifiers `ping_exec_t`, `file_type`, `sysadmfile`, and `exec_type` appear as an `id_comma_list`.

Let's now consider some fine points of railroad diagrams. Literals do not need railroad diagrams to explain them, because they are labeled with the values they match. Though literals sometimes appear in railroad diagrams in uppercase form, the strings they represent can appear in the SELinux policy in either uppercase or lowercase. So, with reference to Figure 6-11, you can anticipate that most identifiers will appear in lowercase rather than uppercase. That is, you should expect the following:

```
create, ioctl, read, write, bind, getopt, setopt
```

rather than:

```
CREATE, IOCTL, READ, WRITE, BIND, GETOPT, SETOPT
```

However, it's entirely permissible to specify uppercase identifiers. It's just that SELinux policy developers generally prefer not to do so. What matters is consistency. The identifiers `create` and `CREATE` are both legal but also entirely distinct, because one uses lowercase letters whereas the other uses uppercase letters.

Let's consider one more common policy subelement, known as `names`, which appears in Figure 6-13. This element can represent such strings as:

- A single identifier
- A list of identifiers separated from one another by white space, enclosed within curly braces
- An asterisk (*)
- An identifier preceded by a tilde (~)
- A list of identifiers separated from one another by white space and enclosed within curly braces, and preceded by a tilde (~)
- Two identifiers separated by a hyphen (-)

Some rather bizarre extensions are also permissible. For instance, the following is a valid `nested_id_set` subelement:

```
{ x -y { a b c } }
```

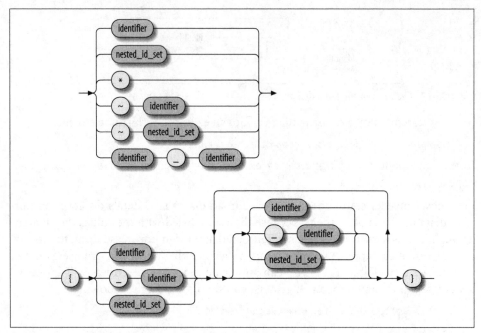

Figure 6-13. The names subelement and related subelements

You may be curious about the meaning or use of this subelement. But, for the moment, please focus merely on the syntax, not the meaning. The meaning of the subelement emerges from the context in which it is used. So rather than continue to examine subelements—a process that could be continued indefinitely—let's start looking at concrete examples by considering the users element, which is used to describe user declarations.

User Declarations

User declarations associate roles with SELinux users. A user cannot enter a role unless the role has been associated with the user's current identity.

Figure 6-14 shows the syntax of user declarations.

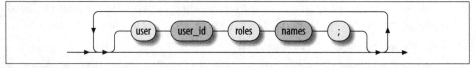

Figure 6-14. User declaration syntax

Here are typical user declarations found in the *src/policy/users* file:

```
user system_u roles system_r;
user user_u   roles { user_r };
user root     roles { staff_r };
```

In the Fedora Core 2 implementation of SELinux, the *src/policy/users* file includes M4 macros that can differently define the roles associated with the user_u and root users. If the user_canbe_sysadm symbol is defined, the user_u user is instead defined as:

```
user user_u    roles { user_r sysadm_r system_r };
```

And, if the direct_sysadm_daemon symbol is defined, the root user is instead defined as:

```
user root      roles { staff_r system_r };
```

Both the user_canbe_sysadm and direct_sysadm_daemon symbols are defined in the *tunable.te* file. They can be undefined by prefixing the appropriate lines with dnl, the M4 comment token.

If your system includes one or more user accounts other than root, you should update the *users* file so that it associates each user account with either the role user_r (for ordinary users) or staff_r (for user who administer the system). For instance, you might add declarations such as these:

```
user ordinary roles user_r;
user admin    roles staff_r;
```

Role-Based Access Control Declarations

As Figure 6-15 shows, there are four types of RBAC declarations:

role_type_def
>   Role type declarations

role_dominance
>   Role dominance declarations

roletrans_def
>   Role transition declarations

role_allow_def
>   Role allow declarations

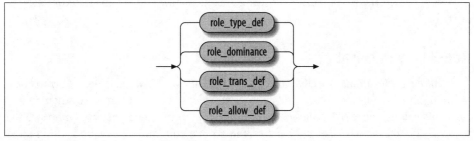

Figure 6-15. RBAC declarations (rbac_decl)

Role Type Declarations

A *role type declaration* specifies the set of domains for which a role is authorized. They have the form shown in Figure 6-16. The symbol identifier specifies the role and the symbol names specifies the authorized domain or domains.

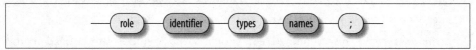

Figure 6-16. Role type declaration (role_type_def)

Role type declarations typically appear in type enforcement files, where they specify the roles that are authorized to enter the domains defined by the TE files. For instance, the *ping.te* file contains the following role-type declarations:

```
role sysadm_r types ping_t;
role system_r types ping_t;
```

The first declaration authorizes the sysadm_r role to enter the ping_t domain. The second declaration authorizes the system_r role to do likewise.

Role Dominance Declarations

Role dominance declarations can be used to specify a hierarchy among roles. However, existing implementations of SELinux policies do not specify role hierarchies.

Role Transition Declarations

At one time, role transition rules were used to specify the new role of a process based on its current role and the type of executable being executed. *Role transition declarations* were deprecated and dropped from SELinux, which used domain transitions instead. However, the Fedora Core 2 implementation of SELinux resumed use of role transitions. Fedora Core 2 provides a transition from sysadm_r to system_r designed to avoid the need for the administrator to execute *run_init* when invoking a SysV init script.

Role Allow Declarations

Role allow declarations specify authorized transitions between roles. A transition refers to someone in a source role (an existing role) choosing to enter a target role (a different role). Figure 6-17 shows their syntax. Two instances of names appear; the first, designated source_names, specifies the source role and the second, designated target_names, specifies the target role.

Role allow declarations appear in the *rbac* file and in TE files. However, if you inspect the TE files in *domains/program*, you likely won't find many role allow decla-

Figure 6-17. Role-allow declaration (role_allow_def)

rations. They're generally created indirectly, by invoking M4 macros such as the base_user_domain in *macros/base_user_macros.te*.

As an example, the *rbac* file contains the following role allow declaration:

```
allow sysadm_r system_r;
```

This declaration allows transition from the sysadm_r role to the system_r role.

If you inspect the *policy.conf* file, you can view policies after M4 macro expansion. There, you're likely to see role allow declarations such as these:

```
allow staff_r sysadm_r;

allow sysadm_r staff_r;
allow sysadm_r user_r;

allow system_r staff_r;
allow system_r sysadm_r;
allow system_r user_r;

allow user_r sysadm_r;
```

CHAPTER 7
Type Enforcement

The preceding chapter explained role-based access control in SELinux. Role-based access control is a secondary access control model that supplements the primary SELinux access control model, type enforcement. This chapter explains the syntax and meaning of SELinux policy declarations related to type enforcement. The chapter concludes with an analysis of a small but typical domain policy: the Fedora Core 2 policy for the ping domain, which resides in the file *ping.te*.

The SELinux Type-Enforcement Model

As explained in Chapter 2, the SELinux type-enforcement model associates each process with a domain and each nonprocess object with a type.* Permissions define the operations that can be performed upon objects. Thus, you can think of a domain as a set of related processes that share the same permissions. For instance, the Apache web server process runs within the httpd_t domain and therefore possesses the permissions associated with that domain. The SELinux policy grants permissions to domains and specifies rules for transitioning between domains.

Permissions are encoded as access vectors, which specify the operations that a domain is authorized to perform on objects of a given type, such as files. Thus, you can think of an object's type as implicitly referring to the set of rules—that is, the access vector—that specify the permissible operations on the object. For instance, access vector rules enable processes within the httpd_t domain to write to the web server log files.

Under Linux, processes fork new processes when they execute programs. The new process is called a *child process* and the process that forked the child process is called a *parent process*. The child process may run within the same domain as the parent.

---

* Recall that, in the context of SELinux, the words *domain* and *type* are synonymous; however, it's customary to use domain in reference to processes and type in reference to nonprocess objects.

Alternatively, the SELinux policy may specify a new domain to enter when the process is forked. Programs that can enter new domains upon execution are called *domain entry points*. For instance, the init run-control processes are associated with the initrc_t domain. However, when the init process starts the web server process, the web server process does not run in this domain. Instead, the web server process automatically transitions to the httpd_t domain, as specified by the SELinux policy.

Review of SELinux Policy Syntax

As explained in Chapter 6, an SELinux policy consists of 11 elements, several of which are optional:

classes
> Defines the security object classes recognized by SELinux.

initial_sids
> Defines initial SIDs for important security objects.

access_vectors
> Defines access vectors associated with each security object class.

mls
> Defines MLS configuration (optional).

te_rbac
> Defines type-enforcement and role-based access control configuration.

users
> Defines the user configuration.

constraints
> Defines constraints that the security policy must observe (optional).

initial_sid_contexts
> Defines the security contexts of important security objects.

fs_use
> Defines the method of labeling of filesystem inodes.

genfs_contexts
> Defines security contexts for filesystems lacking persistent labels (optional).

net_contexts
> Defines security contexts for network objects.

The te_rbac element specifies both the role-based access control policies and the type-enforcement policies. Within the element, role-based access control and type-enforcement declarations can be freely intermingled. The following section explains the SELinux type-enforcement declarations.

Type-Enforcement Declarations

Type-enforcement (TE) declarations are of seven types:

attribute_def
> Attribute declarations

type_def
> Type declarations

typealias_def
> Type alias declarations

bool_def
> Boolean declarations

transition_def
> Transition declarations

te_avtab_def
> TE access vector table declarations

cond_stmt_def
> Conditional statement declarations

Type Declarations

The SELinux policy language requires that all type names be explicitly defined. In the simplest possible form, a type declaration merely defines a name as a type. For instance, the type declaration:

```
type ping_t;
```

would mark ping_t as the name of a type. Type declarations need not precede all statements that refer to the types they define; you can place type declarations any place within a TE file.

Optionally, a type declaration may define one or more aliases for the type name. Any alias associated with a type can be freely used in place of the primary name of the type. A type declaration can also optionally associate one or more attributes with the type name.

Figure 7-1 shows the syntax of a type declaration. As an example, the *ping.te* file contains two type declarations:

```
type ping_t, domain, privlog;
type ping_exec_t, file_type, sysadmfile, exec_type;
```

The first declaration identifies ping_t as a type name, and associates the attributes domain and privlog with the type name, marking the type as a domain that communicates with the system log process. The second declaration identifies ping_exec_t as a type name, and associates the attributes file_type, sysadmfile, and exec_type with the type name, marking the type as one used to identify executable files accessible by system administrators.

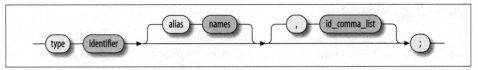

Figure 7-1. Type declaration (type_def)

To better understand how type attributes work with types, consider the definition of the syslogd domain, which contains the following declarations:

```
allow privlog devlog_t:sock_file { ioctl read getattr lock write append };
allow privlog syslogd_t:unix_dgram_socket sendto;
allow privlog syslogd_t:unix_stream_socket connectto;
allow privlog devlog_t:lnk_file read;
```

Notice how the type attribute privlog is used in these declarations in the same way that an actual type name might be used. Type attributes differ from types in that type attributes generally appear in multiple domains, whereas each type generally appears only in a single domain. You can think of a type attribute as simply an abbreviation standing for a set of access vector rules. You can associate these access vector rules with a type simply by binding the type attribute with the type, just as the domain and privlog type attributes are bound to the ping_t type.

The four allow declarations given earlier specify the range of permissible operations associated with the privlog type attribute, specifically:

- Perform various read and write operations on socket files having type devlog_t.
- Send data to datagram and stream sockets having type syslogd_t.
- Read files and symbolic links having type devlog_t.

As you'd likely guess, the types devlog_t and syslogd_t are used to label system log files, system log FIFOs, and the sockets used to communicate with the syslog process.

> The meanings of type attributes such as domain and privlog are not hardcoded in SELinux. Instead, the meaning of a type attribute is determined by policy statements. Consequently, the administrator of an SELinux system can create new type attributes or modify the meaning of type attributes that appear in sample policies. If the administrator of an SELinux system has added or modified many type attributes, it may be difficult to determine their meanings, as doing so would involve reading all the policy declarations related to each customized type attribute.
>
> Fortunately, the set of type attributes defined in sample policies is rich, and system administrators generally do not need, or choose, to extend or modify it substantially. And most domain attributes have names that suggest their meaning. Appendix E, explained in the upcoming section titled "Attribute Declarations," summarizes the meanings of principal SELinux type attributes.

Type-Alias Declarations

As explained in the preceding section, a type declaration can optionally bind one or more aliases to a type name. However, it's more common to use a special type-alias declaration to establish such a binding. Figure 7-2 shows the syntax of type-alias declarations.

Figure 7-2. Type-alias declaration (typealias_def)

Many M4 macros generate type alias declarations. However, a few TE files contain explicit type-alias declarations. For instance, the *cups.te* file contains the follow type-alias declaration:

```
typealias cupsd_etc_t alias etc_cupsd_t;
```

This declaration defines etc_cupsd_t as an alias for the type name cupsd_etc_t, allowing the two names to be used interchangeably.

Attribute Declarations

A type attribute is a name that is bound to one or more types and used to define a set of types sharing some property. For instance, a type attribute can be used to designate the types (domains) that are allowed to read the system log file.

Because type attributes can appear in allow declarations just as though they were types, permissions can be granted by referring either to types or type attributes. An allow declaration containing a type attribute refers to all types associated with the type attribute. Thus, type attributes make it convenient to specify policies that apply to multiple types. The relationship between types and attributes is a many-to-many relationship; an indefinite number of types can be associated with an attribute, and an indefinite number of attributes can be associated with a type.

Type attributes are defined in the file *attrib.te*. Appendix E summarizes the type attributes defined in the Fedora Core 2 implementation of SELinux.

Figure 7-3 shows the syntax of an attribute declaration, the SELinux policy statement that defines a type attribute. As you can see, the syntax is quite simple. A typical declaration is:

```
attrib admin;
```

This declaration identifies admin as an attribute. Appendix E explains that this attribute is used to identify administrator domain—domains that should be available only to system administrators.

Figure 7-3. Attribute declaration (attribute_def)

 Recall that the term *domain* refers to a type associated with a process.

TE Access-Vector Declarations

The permissions enforced by the SELinux security engine are held in kernel data space in an object known as the TE access matrix. As explained in Chapter 2, the TE access matrix includes four distinct access components, called vectors:

allow
> Operations that are allowed but are not logged

auditallow
> Operations that are allowed and are logged when they occur

auditdeny
> Operations that are denied and are logged when they are attempted

dontaudit
> Operations that are denied, but are not logged when they are attempted

Each TE access vector contains TE access-vector rules. A TE access-vector rule specifies permissible operations—based on a source type, a target type, and a security object class. Whenever an operation is attempted, the SELinux security engine searches the access vectors for a rule matching the source type, target type, and object class of the operation. If a matching rule is found, the access vector containing the rule determines the action taken by SELinux. For instance, if the matching rule resides in the allow access vector, the operation is allowed. However, if the matching rule resides in another access vector, or no matching rule exists, the operation is denied.

Figure 7-4 shows the syntax of access-vector rules. Notice that the diagram shows what seems to be a fifth type of access-vector rule, represented by the neverallow rule type. The neverallow rule defines constraints that the SELinux policy must observe. The policy compiler checks for violations of these constraints, and if it finds any violations, it terminates without producing a binary policy file. You can add or subtract neverallow rules from the SELinux policy. However, they're intended as a safety feature that prevents you from generating a grossly insecure policy, so it's generally best not to disturb them.

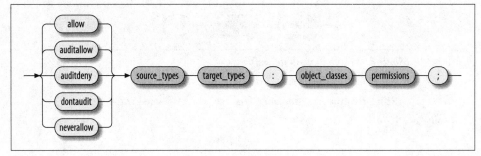

Figure 7-4. TE access vector rule declaration (te_avtab_def)

Each of the five forms of access vector rules contains four terms:

- The source type or types; this is generally the type associated with the process attempting to perform an operation.
- The target type or types; this is generally the type associated with the object that the process is attempting to manipulate.
- The object class or classes to which the rule applies.
- The permissions that the rule establishes.

The syntax of each of these terms is represented by the replaceable text names, which was explained in Chapter 6 and represented in Figure 6-13.

Here's a sample allow declaration associated with the ping_t domain:

```
allow ping_t ping_exec_t:file { read getattr lock execute ioctl };
```

The rule created by this declaration allows processes running in the ping_t domain to perform any of five operations (read, getattr, lock, execute, and ioctl) on files labeled as belonging to the ping_exec_t domain.

> If you check the *ping.te* file, you won't find this declaration there. Many access-vector declarations, including this one, are created by expansion of M4 macros, such as the domain_auto_trans macro explained later in this section.

The standard SELinux security policy includes fewer than six auditallow declarations. Here's a sample declaration:

```
auditallow kernel_t security_t:security load_policy;
```

Recall that auditallow rules don't actually enable any operations. Therefore, this rule is supplemented by an allow rule such as:

```
allow kernel_t security_t:security load_policy;
```

The allow rule authorizes processes running in the kernel_t domain (that is, kernel processes) to perform the load_policy operation on security objects labeled with the security_t domain. More plainly, the allow rule allows the kernel to load an

SELinux policy. The `auditallow` rule causes every such operation to be logged when it is performed. Thus, the system log contains a record of these important events.

The standard SELinux security policy does not include even one instance of an `auditdeny` rule. Since the default action of SELinux is to forbid unauthorized operations and make a log entry documenting the action, `auditdeny` rules are not generally needed. However, so that you can see how `auditdeny` rules work, here's a hypothetical `auditdeny` rule declaration:

```
auditdeny user_t security_t:security load_policy;
```

The rule created by this declaration forbids processes running in the `user_t` domain from performing the `load_policy` operation on `security` objects labeled with the `security_t` domain.

Here's a sample declaration of a `dontaudit` rule:

```
dontaudit ping_t var_t:dir search;
```

The rule created by this declaration suppresses log entries when processes in the `ping_t` domain attempt to search a directory labeled with the `var_t` domain, and are prohibited by the SELinux security engine from doing so.

> It's somewhat common for programs to attempt operations on security-sensitive objects, even though they don't need to do so. The `dontaudit` rule enables you to suppress such operations and avoid cluttering the log with a flood of routine entries associated with them.

As explained, the `neverallow` rule type enforces constraints on the SELinux security policy itself. It helps ensure the integrity of the policy, which might be inadvertently weakened by well-intentioned but erroneous changes. Operations forbidden by a `neverallow` constraint are prohibited *even if a conflicting* `allow` *rule exists within the SELinux security policy.*

Here's a hypothetical `neverallow` constraint declaration:

```
neverallow domain file_type:process transition;
```

The constraint created by this declaration would prevent a process having the `domain` attribute from transitioning to a type having the `file_type` attribute. The constraint would prevent an errant policy modification that allowed a process to be treated as a file, which might compromise system security.

Special notations for types, classes, and permissions

The hypothetical `neverallow` constraint just given is effective but incomplete. Ideally, we'd prohibit transitions from a `domain` type to any non-domain type, not just every type marked as a `file_type`. A special notation associated with the replaceable text names enables us to do so:

```
neverallow domain ~domain:process transition;
```

The constraint associated with this declaration forbids a process having the domain type attribute from transitioning to a type not having that attribute. For instance, the constraint prevents a malicious user from causing a process to transition to a file or another nondomain object.

Notice that the target type is specified as ~domain. This notation, known as *complementation*, provides a convenient means of referring to types that *do not* possess a specified attribute. In this case, the declaration refers to types that do not have the domain attribute. If complementation were not available, we'd find it cumbersome to write a constraint such as this, since the constraint would have to refer explicitly to every type that is not a domain. Many such types might exist. Moreover, having added a new nondomain type to the policy, we might neglect to modify the constraint appropriately. So complementation provides an important convenience.

Another convenient notation is known as *subtraction*. Here's an example of a constraint declaration that employs subtraction:

```
neverallow { domain -admin -anaconda_t -firstboot_t -unconfined_t -kernel_t
  -load_policy_t } security_t:security load_policy;
```

The constraint created by this declaration prevents any domain other than those listed with minus signs (admin, anaconda, firstboot_t, unconfined_t, kernel_t, and load_policy_t) from performing the load_policy operation on a security object having type security_t.

Occasionally, it's necessary to refer to *all* types, classes, or permissions. The asterisk (*) can be used to do so, as in the following constraint declaration:

```
neverallow domain file_type:process *;
```

The constraint created by this declaration prohibits any type having the domain attribute from performing *any* operation on processes having the file_type attribute.

Here's a somewhat more interesting example that includes two instances of the asterisk operator:

```
neverallow ~{ domain unlabeled_t } *:process *;
```

The constraint created by this declaration prevents types other than those having attributes domain or unlabeled_t from performing *any* operation on processes having *any* type.

Another special notation enables us to create rules where the target type is the same as the source type. Here's an example:

```
neverallow {domain -admin -insmod_t -kernel_t -anaconda_t -firstboot_t -unconfined_t }
  self:capability sys_module;
```

The rule created by this declaration applies to domains other than six specific domains (admin, anaconda, firstboot_t, unconfined_t, kernel_t, and load_policy_t). It prohibits these domains from performing the sys_module operation on capability objects labeled with domains other than the source domain.

These special notations can be used with `allow` rules as well as `neverallow` rules. For instance, consider the following rule:

```
allow sysadm_t self:process ~{ ptrace setexec setfscreate setrlimit };
```

This rule lets processes within the sysadm_t domain perform any operation on processes running within that domain, with the exception of the operations listed: ptrace, setexec, setfscreate, and setrlimit.

Table 7-1 summarizes the special notations used to specify types, classes, and permissions.

Table 7-1. Special notations for specification of types, classes, and permissions

Notation	Description
*	All members
~	Complementation
-	Subtraction
self	Target type same as source type

In addition to special notations, macros can be used to specify types, classes, or permissions. Appendix C summarizes a set of such macros, defined in the file *macros/core_macros.te*.

It's not necessary to specify all authorized permissions in a single access-vector rule. SELinux combines permissions pertaining to the same source type, target type, and object class into a single access-vector rule that authorizes all specified operations.

Macros that specify and authorize transitions

Two main types of rules govern transitions:

Type-transition rules
    Specify transitions that occur when a new object, such as a process or file, is created.

Access-vector rules
    Authorize transitions.

Type-transition rules do not authorize the transitions they specify. That is, they specify the transition that *would* occur, but don't actually give permission for the transition to occur. An access-vector rule must authorize the transition, or it will not be allowed to occur. Therefore, type transition and access vector rules both must be specified for most transitions. To avoid the associated tedium, several M4 macros conveniently generate type transition and access vector rule declarations from a single line of policy source code. Generally, the most useful of these macros are:

domain_auto_trans

> Specifies and authorizes a transition related to the execution of a program defined as a domain entry point.

file_type_auto_trans

> Specifies and authorizes a transition related to file creation.

For instance, the *ping.te* file of the Fedora Core 2 SELinux implementation invokes the domain_auto_trans macro three times:

```
domain_auto_trans(unpriv_userdomain, ping_exec_t, ping_t)
domain_auto_trans(sysadm_t, ping_exec_t, ping_t)
domain_auto_trans(initrc_t, ping_exec_t, ping_t)
```

The first invocation is executed conditionally, as explained in the next section. The second and third invocations are executed unconditionally. Each invocation defines a transition from a domain (unpriv_userdomain, sysadm_t, or initrc_t) to the ping_t domain when a ping_exec_t executable is loaded. The transition is also authorized by an access vector rule. For instance, the third invocation expands to the following policy declarations:

```
type_transition initrc_t ping_exec_t:process ping_t;
allow initrc_t ping_t:process transition;
```

Here's an example of a typical use of the file_type_auto_trans macro, occurring in the *ftpd.te* file of the Fedora Core 2 SELinux implementation:

```
file_type_auto_trans(ftpd_t, var_log_t, xferlog_t, file)
```

This macro invocation expands to the following policy declarations:

```
type_transition ftpd_t var_log_t:file xferlog_t;
allow ftpd_t var_log_t:dir rw_dir_perms;
allow ftpd_t var_log_t:file create_file_perms;
```

The file_type_auto_trans macro simplifies definition of the ftpd_t domain, by using a one-line macro invocation to specify that:

- When an ftpd_t process creates a file in a directory having type var_log_t (such as */var/log*), the file should be given the type xferlog_t. Thus, the FTP logs */var/log/xferlog* and */var/log/xferreport* will be properly labeled when created.

- Any ftpd_t process can read and write var_log_t directories (that is, perform any of the following operations associated with rw_dir_perms: read, getattr, lock, search, ioctl, add_name, remove_name, and write).

- Any ftpd_t process can create files within var_log_t directories (that is, perform any of the following operations associated with create_file_perms: create, ioctl, read, getattr, lock, write, setattr, append, link, unlink, and rename).

Occasionally, it's convenient to specify, but not authorize, a transition because the transition is already authorized elsewhere in the policy file or in another policy file. The following macros do so:

domain_trans
> Specifies, but does not authorize, a transition related to execution of a program defined as a domain entry point.

file_type_trans
> Specifies, but does not authorize, a transition related to file creation.

Transition Declarations

A transition rule specifies the new domains for a process or the security contexts for a newly created object, such as a file. Each transition rule has two types: a source type and a target type. For a process, the source type is the current domain of the process, and the target type is the type of the executable file. For an object, the source type is the domain of the process creating the object, and the target type is the type of a related object. For instance, if the object is a file, the target type is the type of the file's parent directory.

Figure 7-5 shows the syntax of type transitions. The railroad diagram contains three instances of replaceable text, each having the syntax of the now-familiar replaceable text names, originally described in Chapter 6 and represented in Figure 6-13:

- The source type or types
- The target type or types
- The object class or classes to which the transition rule applies

The diagram also includes the replaceable text new_type, which has the syntax of the familiar replaceable text identifier. The replaceable text new_type specifies the new type of the process or object.

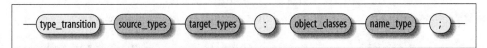

Figure 7-5. Transition declarations (transition_def)

Here's a typical type transition rule pertaining to a process:

```
type_transition sysadm_t ping_exec_t:process ping_t;
```

This rule affects the behavior of processes in the sysadm_t domain that execute a program having type ping_exec_t. Executing such a program causes the process to *attempt to* transition to the ping_t domain. I write *attempt to* because SELinux does not authorize operations, including transitions, by default. So if the transition is to succeed, an access-vector rule must authorize it; otherwise, unless SELinux is operating in permissive mode, the SELinux security engine will prohibit the transition.

Here's a typical type-transition rule pertaining to a file:

```
type_transition httpd_t var_log_t:file httpd_log_t;
```

This rule affects the behavior of processes in the `httpd_t` domain that create a file having a parent directory of the `var_log_t` type. Such files are created with the `httpd_log_t` type, unless the appropriate access vector rule does not exist.

The replaceable text `identifier` is always associated with a single identifier, whereas the replaceable text `names` can be associated with multiple identifiers, as shown in Figure 6-13. Because the railroad diagram refers to three instances of `names` and one instance of `identifier`—rather than four instances of `identifier`—a transition declaration can refer to multiple source types, target types, or classes. Here's a typical rule that does so:

```
type_transition httpd_t tmp_t:{ file lnk_file sock_file fifo_file } httpd_tmp_t;
```

Like the preceding rule, this rule also affects the behavior or processes in the `httpd_t` domain. When such a process creates a file, `lnk_file`, `sock_file`, or `fifo_file` object having a parent object of type `tmp_t`, the new object receives the type `http_tmp_t`, unless the appropriate access vector rule does not exist.

Because several sets of class names are commonly used, the file *macros/core_macros.te* defines eight convenient M4 macros, described in Table 7-2. Using the appropriate macro, the preceding type transition rule could be written more compactly as:

```
type_transition httpd_t tmp_t:notdevfile_class_set httpd_tmp_t;
```

Table 7-2. Class name M4 macros

Macro	Definition	Description
devfile_class_set	{ chr_file blk_file }	Device file classes
dgram_socket_class_set	{ udp_socket unix_dgram_socket }	Datagram socket classes
dir_file_class_set	{ dir file lnk_file sock_file fifo_file chr_file blk_file }	Directory and file classes
file_class_set	{ file lnk_file sock_file fifo_file chr_file blk_file }	File classes except `dir`
notdevfile_class_set	{ file lnk_file sock_file fifo_file }	File classes except `dir` and device files (`chr_file`, `blk_file`)
socket_class_set	{ tcp_socket udp_socket rawip_socket netlink_socket packet_socket unix_stream_socket unix_dgram_socket }	Socket classes
stream_socket_class_set	{ tcp_socket unix_stream_socket }	Stream socket classes
unpriv_socket_class_set	{ tcp_socket udp_socket unix_stream_socket unix_dgram_socket }	Unprivileged socket classes except raw IP socket class

Boolean Declarations

The Fedora Core 2 implementation of SELinux introduced a new feature: Boolean declarations. A Boolean is a true-false value that can be tested by policy statements. As explained in Chapter 4, the *setbool* command can set the value of a Boolean. Booleans make it possible to tailor dynamically the behavior of an SELinux policy.

Figure 7-6 shows the syntax of a Boolean declaration. The Fedora Core 2 SELinux policy defines one Boolean, user_ping:

```
bool user_ping false;
```

This Boolean controls nonprivileged user access to the *ping* and *traceroute* commands. This control is implemented by conditional declarations included in the *ping.te* and *traceroute.te* files, as explained in the next section.

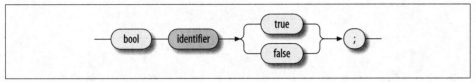

Figure 7-6. Boolean declaration (bool_def)

Conditional Declarations

The declarations explained so far in this chapter have been unconditional declarations. Recent implementations of SELinux, such as that included in Fedora Core 2, also support conditional declarations. A simple conditional declaration has two parts:

- A Boolean expression that is evaluated when the security engine makes policy decisions.
- A declaration that takes effect only if the Boolean expression evaluates true. The declaration is referred to as a subdeclaration, because it occurs inside the conditional declaration.

A more sophisticated conditional declaration includes a Boolean expression and two alternative subdeclarations. Depending on the result of dynamically evaluating the Boolean expression, the declaration has the force of either of the two subdeclarations.

Figure 7-7 shows the syntax of a conditional declaration. As the figure shows, the syntax of the associated conditional expression (cond_expr) is rich. The subdeclaration or subdeclarations have a familiar form, that of either a type transition or access-vector declaration of the following kinds:

- allow
- auditallow
- auditdeny
- dontaudit

 Although the railroad diagram in Figure 7-7 indicates that a subdeclaration can be an auditdeny declaration, SELinux does not support such subdeclarations at the time of writing. However, you can express equivalent policies by using one or more other declaration types rather than an auditdeny.

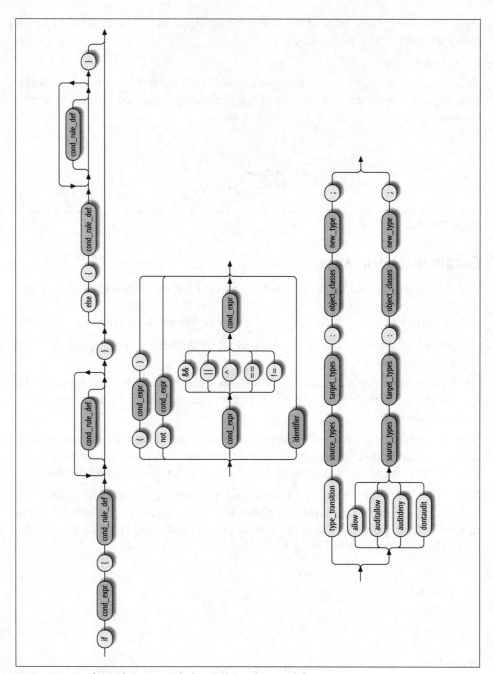

Figure 7-7. Conditional statement declaration (cond_stmt_def)

The conditional expression within a conditional statement declaration can use any of six relational operators, summarized in Table 7-3.

Table 7-3. Relational operators

Symbol	Description
&&	Logical AND
==	Logical equality
!	Logical negation
!=	Logical inequality
||	Logical OR
^	Logical exclusive OR

Here's a sample conditional statement declaration, taken from the *ping.te* file associated with the Fedora Core 2 implementation of SELinux:

```
if (user_ping) {
    domain_auto_trans(unpriv_userdomain, ping_exec_t, ping_t)
    # allow access to the terminal
    allow ping_t { ttyfile ptyfile }:chr_file rw_file_perms;
    ifdef(`gnome-pty-helper.te', `allow ping_t gphdomain:fd use;')
}
```

The `user_ping` conditional expression refers to a policy Boolean that indicates whether nonprivileged users are authorized to use the *ping* and *traceroute* commands, as explained earlier in this chapter. Only if the Boolean has the value `true` do the subdeclarations have effect. The subdeclarations:

- Authorize an automatic transition from a domain marked as an `unpriv_userdomain` to the `ping_t` domain upon execution of a `ping_exec_t` program.
- Authorize the `ping_t` domain to access the user's TTY or PTY.
- Invoke an M4 macro, `ifdef`, that conditionally allows the `ping_t` domain to use file descriptions passed by the Gnome PTY helper (`gphdomain`) domain.

Examining a Sample Policy

Seeing the syntax of individual policy declarations is not the same as seeing how they work together to establish a useful policy. In this section, we'll look at the policy that governs the `ping_t` domain, and the related domain `ping_exec_t`, as implemented in Fedora Core 2. Like most policies, this policy resides in two files:

file_contexts/program/ping.fc
> Specifies security contexts for files related to the domains.

domains/program/ping.te
> Specifies the RBAC declarations related to the domains.

The *ping.fc* file has these contents:

```
# ping
/bin/ping.*      -- system_u:object_r:ping_exec_t
/usr/sbin/hping2  --    system_u:object_r:ping_exec_t
```

When the filesystems are labeled, these specifications cause ordinary files matching the first regular expression */bin/ping.** to be labeled with the security context system_u:object_r:ping_exec_t. Ordinary files matching the second regular expression */usr/sbin/hping2* are also labeled with that security context. The *ping.te* file is considerably longer than the *ping.fc* file, so we'll analyze it a few lines at a time. The first several lines are merely comments:

```
#DESC Ping - Send ICMP messages to network hosts
#
# Author:  David A. Wheeler <dwheeler@ida.org>
# X-Debian-Packages: iputils-ping netkit-ping iputils-arping arping hping2
#

#################################
#
# Rules for the ping_t domain.
#
# ping_t is the domain for the ping program.
# ping_exec_t is the type of the corresponding program.
#
```

The comments point out that the domain has two associated types, ping_t and ping_exec_t. Most domains have at least two types such as these: a type synonymous with the domain (ping_t) and another type used for programs that serve as entry points to the domain (ping_exec_t).

The next line identifies ping_t as a type and gives it the domain and privlog attributes, marking the type as a domain that is authorized to communicate with the system log process.

```
type ping_t, domain, privlog;
```

The next two lines identify two roles, sysadm_r and system_r, authorized to access the ping_t domain:

```
role sysadm_r types ping_t;
role system_r types ping_t;
```

The next line invokes an M4 macro:

```
in_user_role(ping_t)
```

The macro definition resides in *macros/user_macros.te*. Its expansion generates the declarations:

```
role user_r  types ping_t;
role staff_r types ping_t;
```

These declarations extend the list of roles privileged to access the ping_t domain. However, as we will see, the role statement is not enough to ensure that ordinary users can execute a *ping*. A transition must also be authorized.

The next line defines the ping_exec_t type, marking it as a file type rather than a domain:

```
type ping_exec_t, file_type, sysadmfile, exec_type;
```

The declaration also marks the type as related to an executable file that is accessible to the system administrator.

The next line initializes a policy Boolean with the value false:

```
bool user_ping false;
```

This Boolean controls whether ordinary users are permitted to use the *ping* command and related commands.

The next several lines compose a conditional declaration that affects policy only if the policy Boolean user_ping has the value true:

```
if (user_ping) {
domain_auto_trans(unpriv_userdomain, ping_exec_t, ping_t)
# allow access to the terminal
allow ping_t { ttyfile ptyfile }:chr_file rw_file_perms;
ifdef(`gnome-pty-helper.te', `allow ping_t gphdomain:fd use;')
}
```

The conditional declaration uses an M4 macro to generate declarations authorizing processes in unprivileged domains to automatically enter the ping_t domain via execution of a ping_exec_t executable file. It also authorizes access to the TTY or PTY and authorizes use of a file descriptor marked with the gphdomain (Gnome PTY helper) attribute.

Access to the TTY or PTY file is granted through the ttyfile and ptyfile type attributes. These attributes, defined in the file *attrib.te*, are associated with the three types used to label all TTYs and PTYs: sysadm_tty_device_t, staff_tty_device_t, and user_tty_device_t. For instance, the *macros/admin_macros.te* file contains macros that expand upon invocation to the following declaration:

```
type sysadm_tty_device_t, file_type, sysadmfile, ttyfile;
```

The declaration binds the type attribute ttyfile to the type sysadm_tty_device_t. Thus, the allow declaration within the ping_t domain permits processes within that domain to permit read and write operations on device files labeled sysadm_tty_device_t.

The next several lines cause an automatic transition to the ping_t domain when a sysadm_t or initrc_t process loads a ping_exec_t executable:

```
# Transition into this domain when you run this program.
domain_auto_trans(sysadm_t, ping_exec_t, ping_t)
domain_auto_trans(initrc_t, ping_exec_t, ping_t)
```

Because these declarations are specified unconditionally, system administrators and processes running under *init* can always *ping*.

The next several lines invoke M4 macros that generate declarations enabling access to shared libraries, network resources, and use Network Information Service (NIS) (also known as yp):

```
uses_shlib(ping_t)
can_network(ping_t)
can_ypbind(ping_t)
```

Most of the remaining lines extend specific permissions to processes in the ping_t domain. First, such processes are allowed to get the attributes of and read etc_t files:

```
allow ping_t etc_t:file { getattr read };
```

Such processes are also allowed to create Unix stream sockets:

```
allow ping_t self:unix_stream_socket create_socket_perms;
```

Likewise, such processes can create and perform several other operations on raw IP sockets:

```
# Let ping create raw ICMP packets.
allow ping_t self:rawip_socket { create ioctl read write bind getopt setopt };
```

Processes in ping_t can send and receive raw IP packets using any interface and node:

```
allow ping_t netif_type:netif { rawip_send rawip_recv };
allow ping_t node_type:node { rawip_send rawip_recv };
```

Likewise, they can use the net_raw and setuid capabilities.

```
# Use capabilities.
allow ping_t self:capability { net_raw setuid };
```

Finally, they can access the terminal:

```
# Access the terminal.
allow ping_t admin_tty_type:chr_file rw_file_perms;
ifdef(`gnome-pty-helper.te', `allow ping_t sysadm_gph_t:fd use;')
allow ping_t { userdomain privfd kernel_t }:fd use;
```

Two additional declarations avoid cluttering the system log with useless chatter resulting from failed attempts to get filesystem attributes and search var_t directories:

```
dontaudit ping_t fs_t:filesystem getattr;
dontaudit ping_t var_t:dir search;
```

Exactly why *ping* wants to perform these operations isn't clear; presumably study of its source code would disclose the reason. But *ping* seems to work fine even when it is prohibited from performing these operations, so, consistent with the principle of least privilege, we choose not to enable them.

ping isn't alone in attempting unnecessary operations; quite a few programs do so. It's best to determine experimentally whether failed operations are really needed, rather than give a program free rein by enabling every operation it attempts.

The *ping.te* file, which contains 57 lines, is actually a bit longer than the median TE file size of 54 lines. So if you understand it, you're likely to experience no significant difficulty in understanding all but the most complex TE files. In Chapter 9, we move on to consider how to modify existing policies and create policies of your own.

CHAPTER 8

Ancillary Policy Statements

The most important SELinux policy statement types—role-based access control and type enforcement statements—were explained in the two preceding chapters. However, a typical SELinux policy contains several other statement types that the administrator of an SELinux system may want to understand. This chapter explains these statement types, including constraint declarations, context-related declarations, and Flask-related declarations. Most administrators will seldom need to refer to the material in this chapter, since these statement types are primarily important to SELinux developers rather than SELinux system administrators. However, occasionally a policy modification will fail because it violates a policy constraint. At these times, an understanding of policy constraint declarations is helpful.

Constraint Declarations

SELinux policy constraint declarations superficially resemble the constraints implemented via `neverallow` rules. However, they support a richer language for specifying constraints and, at the same time, have a narrower purpose: constraint declarations restrict the permissions that can be granted by an access-vector rule.

Figures 8-1 through 8-5 show the statement syntax, which is relatively complex. Fortunately, it's unusual for a system administrator to need to modify the constraint declarations supplied by a sample SELinux policy.

Figure 8-1. Constraint declaration

Constraint declarations impose restrictions on access-vector rules. Therefore, constraint declarations and access-vector rules share some syntactic elements. In particular, recall that access-vector rules involve two security contexts: a source context and a target context. In constraint declarations, you can refer to these contexts by using the special tokens summarized in Table 8-1.

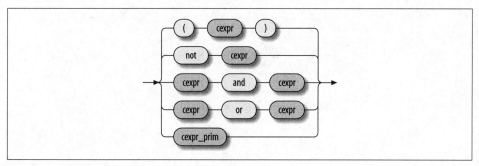

Figure 8-2. Syntax of cexpr

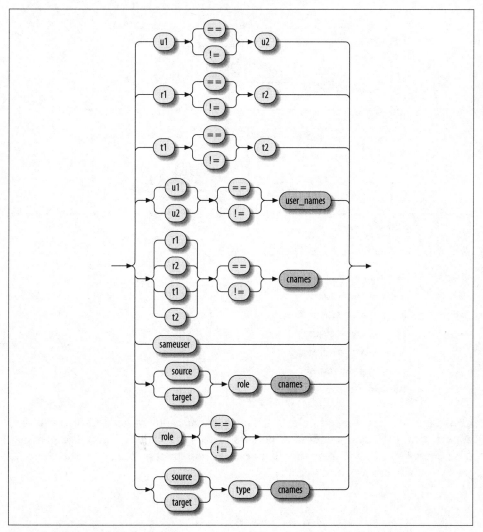

Figure 8-3. Syntax of cexpr_prim

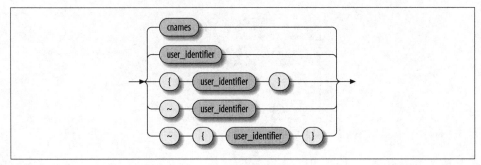

Figure 8-4. Syntax of user_names

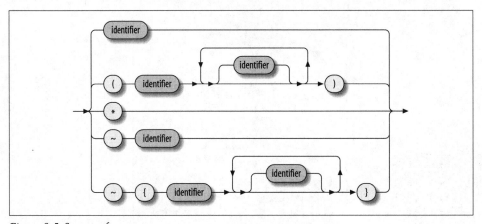

Figure 8-5. Syntax of cnames

Table 8-1. Special tokens used in constraint declarations

Token	Description
u1	User given in source context
u2	User given in target context
r1	Role given in source context
r2	Role given in target context
t1	Type given in source context
t2	Type given in target context

Constraints declarations reside in the file *constraints*. Only a handful of constraints appear within the sample SELinux policies distributed with SELinux. For instance, the Fedora Core 2 implementation defines two constraints that restrict the ability to transition between user and role identities:

```
constrain process transition
    ( u1 == u2
    or (t1 == privuser and t2 == userdomain )
    or (t1 == crond_t and t2 == user_crond_domain)
```

```
    or (t1 == userhelper_t)
    or (t1 == priv_system_role and u2 == system_u )
    );

constrain process transition
    ( r1 == r2
    or ( t1 == privrole and t2 == userdomain )
    or (t1 == crond_t and t2 == user_crond_domain)
    or (t1 == userhelper_t)
    or (t1 == priv_system_role and r2 == system_r )
    );
```

The first constraint allows these identity changes to occur only if one of the following circumstances exists:

- The user identity is unchanged.
- The source type has the privuser attribute and the target type has the userdomain attribute.
- The source type is crond_t and the target type has the attribute user_crond_domain (only the domains user_crond_t and sysadm_crond_t have this attribute).
- The source type is userhelper_t.
- The source type has the priv_system_role attribute and the target user is system_u.

  The priv_system_role attribute indicates domains that change role from a user role to system_r or change identity from a user identity to system_u.

The second constraint operates analogously but constrains changes of role rather user identity. These constraints are intended to allow only safe transitions between user identities and roles. Hence, with only the few identified exceptions, only privileged users can transition to new identities or roles.

The policy of Fedora Core 2 also defines two constraints that restrict the ability to label objects with a user identity other than the current identity:

```
constrain { dir file lnk_file sock_file fifo_file chr_file blk_file }
{ create relabelto relabelfrom }
    ( u1 == u2 or t1 == privowner );

constrain { tcp_socket udp_socket rawip_socket netlink_socket packet_socket unix_
stream_socket unix_dgram_socket }
{ create relabelto relabelfrom }
    ( u1 == u2 or t1 == privowner );
```

The first constraint restricts create, relabelto, and relabelfrom permissions over seven classes of file-like objects (dir, file, lnk_file, sock_file, fifo_file, chr_file, and blk_file). The operations are permitted only if they do not alter the user identity or the source type has the attribute privowner. The second constraint operates similarly but restricts operations over seven classes of network-related objects, rather than file-like objects.

Because constraints currently play a small role in typical SELinux policies, you likely don't need to understand them in complete detail. It's enough that you understand their function, which is to prevent certain changes to security contexts.

Other Context-Related Declarations

The SELinux policy language includes several declaration types that establish contexts for various objects:

- Objects having initial SIDs
- Filesystems supporting persistent labels
- Filesystems not supporting persistent labels
- Network-related objects

Some filesystems, such as ext2 and ext3, provide space in which SELinux can store persistent file labels. However, some filesystems do not have this capability. So that even uncooperative filesystems can be used with SELinux, SELinux lets you specify static labels that are applied to files within such filesystems.

The following subsections describe these declarations.

Syntax of Initial SID Context Declarations

Figure 8-6 shows the syntax of initial SID context declarations, which are used to specify the security context of objects having initial SIDs.

Figure 8-6. Initial SID context declaration

The example SELinux policy typically includes a bit more than two dozen initial SID declarations. A typical declaration is:

```
sid kernel      system_u:system_r:kernel_t
```

This declaration assigns the security context `system_u:system_r:kernel_t` to the kernel object. In general, it's not possible to change or add an initial SID declaration without making corresponding changes to SELinux itself, so changes and additions are generally made only by SELinux developers rather than system administrators.

Syntax of Filesystem Labeling Declarations

When an SELinux system mounts a filesystem, SELinux must determine whether the filesystem supports persistent labels. If so, SELinux processes the persistent labels according to the options specified in three types of declaration:

fs_use_xattr
: Specifies options for conventional filesystems.

fs_use_task
: Specifies options for pseudofilesystems associated with pipe and socket objects.

fs_use_trans
: Specifies options for pseudofilesystems associated with RAM disk devices, pseudoterminals, and shared memory objects.

Figure 8-7 shows the syntax for all three types of declarations.

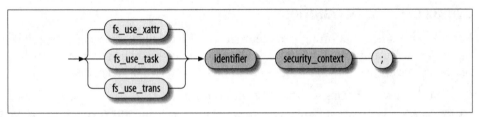

Figure 8-7. Filesystem labeling declaration

The `identifier` appearing in the syntax diagram denotes the filesystem type. Typical values include the following:

devpts
: Pseudoterminal filesystem

ext2
: Linux Ext2 filesystem

ext3
: Linux Ext3 filesystem

pipefs
: Pseudofilesystem associated with a pipe

shm
: Pseudofilesystem associated with a shared memory object

sockfs
: Pseudofilesystem associated with a socket

tmpfs
: Pseudofilesystem associated with a memory-resident filesystem

xfs
: Linux Xfs filesystem

Some typical filesystem labeling declarations appearing in sample policies include:

```
fs_use_xattr ext2    system_u:object_r:fs_t;
fs_use_xattr ext3    system_u:object_r:fs_t;
fs_use_xattr xfs     system_u:object_r:fs_t;
fs_use_task  pipefs system_u:object_r:fs_t;
fs_use_task  sockfs system_u:object_r:fs_t;
fs_use_trans devpts system_u:object_r:devpts_t;
fs_use_trans tmpfs   system_u:object_r:tmpfs_t;
fs_use_trans shm     system_u:object_r:tmpfs_t;
```

Thus, ext2, ext3, and xfs filesystems store file labels in their extended attribute space (fs_use_xattr); pipefs and sockfs filesystems use the special facility for pipe and socket pseudofilesystems (fs_use_task); and devpts, tmpfs, and shm filesystems use the special facility for pseudoterminal, memory-resident, and shared-memory filesystems (fs_use_trans).

Syntax of Genfs Declarations

For filesystems not supporting persistent labels, SELinux behavior can be specified using Genfs declarations. Figure 8-8 shows the syntax of such declarations, which resembles the syntax used in FC (file context) files, with two differences:

- The declaration begins with the keyword genfscon.
- The genfscon keyword is followed by an identifier giving the filesystem type.

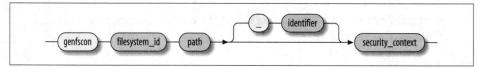

Figure 8-8. Genfs declaration

The replaceable text *path* gives the mount point of the filesystem. More precisely, it gives a prefix for the mount point, since any directory below the specified directory is considered to match the declaration. Specifying */nfs* matches any filesystem mounted at */nfs* or any subdirectory of */nfs*, and specifying / matches any mounted filesystem. When multiple declarations match an actual mount point, the longest matching declaration is used, and the others are ignored.

The optional identifier, which is preceded by a hyphen (-), also can be used to restrict the type of files to which the declaration applies. File types are specified using the codes displayed by the *ls* command; for instance, use *-c* to specify that the declaration applies only to character device files, or use *-b* to specify that the declaration applies only to block device files .

Genfs declarations reside in the genfs_contexts file, which contains about three dozen declarations in the example SELinux policy. These declarations assign security contexts to filesystems having types such as the following:

```
autofs
bdev
cifs
cramfs
eventpollfs
fat
futexfs
iso9660
msdos
nfs
nfsd
ntfs
proc
ramfs
romfs
rootfs
rpc_pipefs
selinuxfs
smbfs
sysfs
usbdevfs
usbfs
vfat
```

For example, a typical declaration assigning a security context to files residing on an nfs filesystem mounted somewhere below the root (/) directory is:

```
genfscon nfs / system_u:object_r:nfs_t
```

The related type nfs_t is defined in the file *types/nfs.te*. The proc filesystem receives special attention in the genfs_contexts file. Over one dozen of the entries in the file pertain to that filesystem.

Syntax of Network Declarations

Recent releases of SELinux support labeling of network objects, including ports, network interfaces, hosts (nodes), and received packets. This is useful in implementing the principle of least privilege, by restricting users and processes from unnecessarily accessing network objects. The labeling is specified by network declarations residing in the file *net_contexts*. Figure 8-9 shows the related syntax, which includes three declaration types:

portcon
    Specifies the security context of a port.

netifcon

> Specifies the security context of a network interface and the security context of packets it received.

nodecon

> Specifies the security context of a host (node).

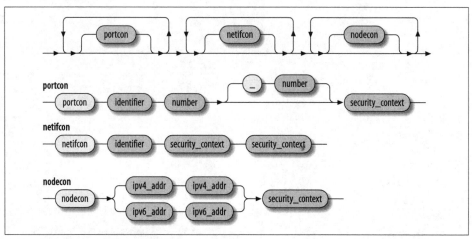

Figure 8-9. Network declaration

Portcon declarations

Portcon declarations specify security contexts of local ports. Here is a typical `portcon` declaration:

```
portcon tcp 80  system_u:object_r:http_port_t
```

The declaration assigns the security context `system_u:object_r:http_port_t` to port TCP/80. The related type `http_port_t` is defined in the file *domains/program/apache.te* by the declaration

```
type http_port_t, port_type;
```

An access-vector rule such as the following can restrict access to the port:

```
allow httpd_t { http_port_t http_cache_port_t }:tcp_socket name_bind;
```

This rule allows only the `httpd_t` domain to perform the `name_bind` operation on port TCP/80; thus, other domains are prohibited from binding to the port.

Netifcon declarations

Netifcon declarations specify security contexts of network interfaces. Here is a typical `netifcon` declaration:

```
netifcon eth0 system_u:object_r:netif_eth0_t system_u:object_r:netmsg_eth0_t
```

Notice that the declaration specifies two security contexts. The first security context pertains to the network interface itself, eth0. The second security context pertains to packets received on the network interface.

An access vector rule such as the following can restrict access to the network interface or packets received on it:

```
allow vmware_t netif_eth0_t:netif rawip_send;
```

This rule allows the vmware_t domain to send raw IP traffic with the eth0 interface.

Nodecon declarations

Nodecon declarations specify security contexts of hosts. Here is a typical nodecon declaration:

```
nodecon 127.0.0.1 255.0.0.0 system_u:object_r:node_lo_t
```

This declaration binds the security context system_u:object_r:node_lo_t to hosts having IP addresses 127.0.0.1 and netmask 255.0.0.0—that is, the local or loopback host.

 The sample policy related to nodecon declarations is relatively immature. For instance, the policy distributed with Fedora Core 2 includes no access vector rules related to types bound to hosts by nodecon declarations.

Flask-Related Declarations

The *flask* directory contains several files that are part of the SELinux policy:

security_classes
Specifies the SELinux security classes.

initial_sids
Specifies the initial SIDs.

access_vectors
Specifies the permissions includes in access vectors.

The following subsections explain the syntax of declarations residing in these files. Generally, only SELinux developers should change these declarations. However, administrators may find it helpful to understand these files and the declarations they contain.

Syntax of security_classes

The *flask/security_classes* file specifies the security classes handled by SELinux. Entries in the file have the syntax shown in Figure 8-10. A class declaration contains only the keyword class and an identifier giving the class name.

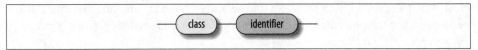

Figure 8-10. Flask class declaration

The example policy defines between two and three dozen classes. Here is a typical class declaration:

```
class security
```

Appendix A summarizes the standard security object classes.

Syntax of initial_sids

The *flask/initial_sids* file specifies the symbols corresponding to initial SIDs. Entries in the file have the syntax shown in Figure 8-11, consisting of the keyword sid and an identifier naming the SID.

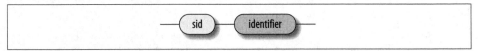

Figure 8-11. Flask initial SID declaration

The sample policy defines a few more than two dozen initial SIDs. A typical SID declaration follows:

```
sid kernel
```

 Don't confuse the *flask/initial_sids* file and its sid declarations with the sid declarations residing in the *initial_sid_contexts* file. The former declarations include no security context, whereas the latter declarations do.

Syntax of access_vectors

The *flask/access_vectors* file specifies the form of SELinux access vectors. Declarations in the *flask/access_vectors* file have the forms given in Figure 8-12 and 8-13. The common declaration, shown in Figure 8-12, is used to define access vector components common to multiple classes. The sample policy includes several such declarations. A typical common declaration is:

Figure 8-12. Common declaration

```
common file
{
    ioctl
    read
    write
    create
    getattr
    setattr
    lock
    relabelfrom
    relabelto
    append
    unlink
    link
    rename
    execute
    swapon
    quotaon
    mounton
}
```

This declaration specifies the permissions associated with file-like objects.

A second type of declaration, class, specifies the permissions associated with a class. Figure 8-13 shows the related syntax. The sample policy specifies between two and three dozen sets of permissions, one for each class.

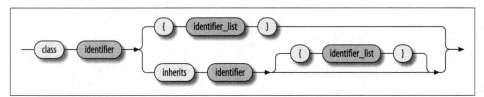

Figure 8-13. Access vector declaration

Within a class declaration, permissions can be enumerated directly, inherited from a common declaration, or both. For example, the class filesystem enumerates its permissions:

```
class filesystem
{
    mount
    remount
    unmount
    getattr
    relabelfrom
    relabelto
    transition
    associate
    quotamod
    quotaget
}
```

The lnk_file class, on the other hand, inherits all its permissions from the common declaration named file:

```
class lnk_file
inherits file
```

The dir class both enumerates and inherits permissions:

```
class dir
inherits file
{
    add_name
    remove_name
    reparent
    search
    rmdir
}
```

Appendix B summarizes the operations that appear in SELinux access vectors.

## CHAPTER 9

Customizing SELinux Policies

Chapter 8 explained the syntax and operation of the statements that make up the SELinux policy language. This chapter explains how to customize SELinux policies. It begins by reviewing the structure of the SELinux policy source tree and the *Makefile* that's used to compile, build, and load an SELinux policy. The chapter then explains several typical policy customizations of the sort you're most likely to perform. Most often, you'll use customizations recommended by the Audit2allow program. However, you'll need to carefully review such recommendations rather than blindly implement them. Otherwise, you may extend an unnecessarily broad set of permissions, thereby compromising system security. The chapter concludes with descriptions of some policy management tools, along with hints and procedures for using them.

The SELinux Policy Source Tree

Chapter 5 explained the structure of the SELinux policy source tree. The source tree typically resides in the directory */etc/security/selinux/src/policy*; however, your SELinux distribution may place it elsewhere. Table 9-1 recaps the structure of the policy source tree. You'll likely find it convenient to refer to this table as you read this chapter; it will help you locate the file that contains a particular type of declaration, the file to which you should add a particular type of declaration, or the directory in which you should create the file to hold a particular type of declaration. In other words, it's your roadmap to the policy source tree.

Table 9-1. The SELinux policy source tree

Directory/file	Description
appconfig/*	Defines contexts for special applications, such as `init`.
assert.te	Defines TE assertions.
attrib.te	Defines type attributes.
constraints	Defines Boolean constraints on permissions.

Table 9-1. The SELinux policy source tree (continued)

Directory/file	Description
domains/admin.te	Defines administrative domains.
domains/misc/*	Defines miscellaneous domains, such as the `kernel_t` domain.
. domains/program/*	Defines domains for specific programs.
domains/user.te	Defines user domains.
file_contexts/misc	Defines security contexts of miscellaneous domains.
file_contexts/program/*	Defines security contexts for files related to specific programs.
file_contexts/types.fc	Defines security contexts applied when the security policy is installed.
flask/*	Contains files—such as *security_classes*, *initial_sids*, and *access_vectors*—that define basic Flask elements and their characteristics. Generally, only SELinux developers modify the contents of this directory.
fs_use	Defines the labeling behavior for specific filesystem types.
genfs_contexts	Defines security contexts for filesystem types not supporting persistent labels or that use a fixed labeling scheme.
initial_sid_contexts	Defines the security context for each initial SID. Generally, only SELinux developers modify the contents of this file.
macros/admin_macros.te	Defines macros used in specifying administrative domains.
macros/base_user_ macros.te	Defines rules and types related to an ordinary user domain.
macros/core_macros.te	Defines core TE macros.
macros/global_macros.te	Defines macros used throughout the policy.
macros/mini_user_ macros.te	Defines macros used in specifying very simple user domains.
macros/program/*	Defines macros used to specify derived domains that support policy separation among multiple instances of a single program.
macros/user_macros.te	Defines macros used in specifying user domains.
Makefile	Supports common administrative operations, as explained in the section of this chapter titled "Using the SELinux Makefile."
mls	Defines the MLS configuration.
net_contexts	Defines the security contexts of network objects.
policy.??	The policy binary file; for example, *policy.17*.
policy.conf	The policy source file, assembled under control of the *Makefile*, from the component sources.
rbac	Defines the RBAC (Role-Based Access Control) configuration.
serviceusers	Defines users related to specific services (Fedora Core).
tmp/*	A working directory used during policy compilation. The *Makefile* assembles the component files of the TE configuration into the file *tmp/all.te*.
tunable.te	Provides tweakable macro definitions for tuning the policy (Fedora Core).
types/*	Contains files defining general types—types not associated with a particular domain—and related rules.
users	Defines the users.

On the Topics of Difficulty and Discretion

The SELinux source policy is a sophisticated software system. It includes dozens of object classes, scores of defined permissions, more than 1,000 type transitions, thousands of object instances, and tens of thousands of access-vector rules. You can think of the source policy as a computer program and the security engine as a CPU that executes the translated binary form of this program. So customizing the SELinux policy is akin to performing software maintenance on a program consisting of tens of thousands of noncomment source lines.

Using the SELinux Makefile

After you modify a policy source file, you must recompile the policy sources and load the translated binary policy into the kernel. These and other common administrative functions are performed by using the SELinux *Makefile*, which typically resides in */etc/security/selinux/src/policy*. Chapter 4 introduced the SELinux *Makefile*. Table 9-2 recaps the six operations the *Makefile* provides.

Table 9-2. SELinux Makefile operations

Operation	Description
policy	Compile the policy sources, but do not create a new policy binary.
install	Compile the policy sources and create—but do not load—a new policy binary (default).
load	Compile, create, and load a new binary policy.
reload	Compile and create a new binary policy if the policy sources have been recently modified; load the new binary policy.
clean	Delete temporary files created during policy compilation.
relabel	Relabel filesystems.

To perform an operation using the *Makefile*, move to the directory containing it. Then, issue the command:

    make operation

where *operation* is one of the six operations described in Table 9-2. For example, to compile, create, and load a new binary policy, issue the command:

    make load

To reload the current policy, issue the command:

    make reload

If the policy sources have been modified since the binary policy file was created, invoking *make* will also compile the policy sources and create a new binary policy file.

Creating an SELinux User

By default, only three SELinux users are defined:

`root`
Used by the system administrator

`system_u`
Used by system processes and objects

`user_u`
Used by generic users having no specific SELinux user identity

Unless your system has many users, you should generally create a specific SELinux user identity for each human user who will log in and use your SELinux system. To do so, modify the file *users* in the policy source directory.

Adding a System Administrator

It's important to add an SELinux user identity for each user who administers the system; otherwise, the user will be unable to transition to the `sysadm_r` role. To specify a user as a system administrator, add a declaration having the following form:

```
user wheel roles staff_r sysadm_r;
```

where `wheel` is the name of the user account. For example, to declare the user `bill` as an administrative user, add the following declaration:

```
user bill role staff_r sysadm_r;
```

The Fedora Core implementation of SELinux provides a feature that enables a system administrator to launch daemons without using the *run_init* program. As a result, user declarations under Fedora Core are slightly different, taking the form:

```
user wheel roles { staff_r sysadm_r ifdef(`direct_sysadm_daemon', `system_r') };
```

The `direct_sysadm_daemon` M4 macro, which implements the feature, can be enabled or disabled by tweaking the file *tunable.te*. The feature is enabled by default. If the feature is enabled, the expanded macro gives the declaration the following form:

```
user wheel roles {staff_r sysadm_r system_r};
```

which associates the user with the role `system_r`, as well as the two roles `staff_r` and `sysadm_r`.

The convenience provided by the `direct_sysadm_daemon` macro comes at the price of decreased system security. Unless you highly value the convenience provided by the macro, you should disable it in the same way `direct_sysadm_daemon` can be disabled.

Adding an Ordinary User

If the user to be added is not a system administrator, add a declaration having the following form:

```
user pleb roles user_r;
```

where *pleb* is the name of the user account. For example, to declare the user `patrick` as an ordinary user, add the following declaration:

```
user patrick role user_r;
```

The Fedora Core implementation of SELinux provides a feature that enables ordinary users to become system administrators. As a result, user declarations under Fedora Core are slightly different, taking the form:

```
user pleb roles { user_r ifdef(`user_canbe_sysadm', `sysadm_r system_r') };
```

The `user_canbe_sysadm` M4 macro, which implements the feature, can be enabled or disabled by tweaking the file *tunable.te*. By default, the feature is enabled. If the feature is enabled, the expanded macro gives the declaration the following form:

```
user pleb roles { user_r sysadm_r system_r };
```

which associates the user with the roles `sysadm_r` and `system_r` as well as the role `user_r`.

 Unless you highly value the convenience provided by the `user_canbe_sysadm` macro, you should disable it, by prefixing the appropriate line in *tunable.te* with the M4 comment token, `dnl`.

Customizing Roles

The SELinux RBAC associates roles with users and domains. A given user is authorized only for specific roles, and a given role is authorized only for specific domains. Thus, a user cannot enter a domain unless the user is associated with a role authorized for the domain.

By default, the SELinux policy defines four roles:

staff_r
: Used by users authorized to transition to the `sysadm_r` role

sysadm_r
: Used by the system administrator

system_r
: Used by system processes and objects

user_r
: Used by ordinary users, who are not authorized to transition to the `sysadm_r` role

The fact that many system processes and objects share the `system_r` role does not mean that SELinux violates the principle of least privilege. Processes and objects generally have discrete types that determine the operations that they can perform and that can be performed on them. As commonly used, roles don't authorize operations; instead they limit the types available to a process or object.

These roles are defined, and associated with users, by the `user` declarations appearing in the *users* file.

The Fedora Core SELinux policy defines two additional roles:

`cyrus_r`
Used by the Cyrus IMAP daemon

`mailman_r`
Used by the GNU mailing list manager application, Mailman

A role is defined by a `role` declaration that associates it with a domain. If multiple declarations associate a single role with multiple domains, the role is authorized to enter each of the domains specified. By convention, role declarations are not centralized in a single file; instead, the role declarations for a given domain generally appear in the TE file associated with the domain.

It's generally not necessary to create a new SELinux role. However, it's often necessary to authorize one of the predefined roles to enter a particular domain, particularly a customized domain. To do so, add a `role` declaration to the TE file associated with the domain. The declaration should have the form:

```
role role_name types domain_name;
```

where *role_name* is the name of the role, and *domain_name* is the name of the domain the role is to be authorized to enter. As explained, you can specify any number of role declarations for a given role.

Adding Permissions

At this point in the development of SELinux, it's common for policies to contain small bugs that cause operations to fail when applications or programs are used in unusual ways unanticipated by policy developers. As an SELinux administrator, one of the most frequent SELinux policy customizations you're likely to perform is adding permissions to coax the security engine into accepting an operation. Let's consider an actual situation based on Fedora Core 2's SELinux implementation and see how it's resolved. The procedure we'll follow isn't the only procedure or best procedure. Creating new policies typically entails a generous dollop of troubleshooting, which tends to be relatively unstructured. So rather than see our procedure as the universal norm, you should see it as merely an illustrative example.

Though unfamiliar to many, the Nmap program is a popular tool among those concerned with security that provides many useful functions. For instance, using Nmap, you can determine the ports on which a network host is listening and what service is running on each open port.

Suppose you install and run Nmap and obtain the following error message:

```
# nmap -sT 127.0.0.1

Starting nmap 3.50 ( http://www.insecure.org/nmap/ ) at 2004-06-01 17:23 UTC
Unable to find nmap-services!  Resorting to /etc/services
```

It seems that Nmap is unable to read the *nmap-services* file. Checking the system log, you find that SELinux recently logged eight denial messages:

```
avc:  denied  { read } for  pid=8682 exe=/usr/bin/nmap name=urandom dev=dm-0
ino=306563 scontext=root:sysadm_r:traceroute_t tcontext=system_u:object_r:urandom_
device_t tclass=chr_file
avc:  denied  { read } for  pid=8682 exe=/usr/bin/nmap name=random dev=dm-0
ino=301298 scontext=root:sysadm_r:traceroute_t tcontext=system_u:object_r:random_
device_t tclass=chr_file
avc:  denied  { read } for  pid=8682 exe=/usr/bin/nmap name=urandom dev=dm-0
ino=306563 scontext=root:sysadm_r:traceroute_t tcontext=system_u:object_r:urandom_
device_t tclass=chr_file
avc:  denied  { read } for  pid=8682 exe=/usr/bin/nmap name=random dev=dm-0
ino=301298 scontext=root:sysadm_r:traceroute_t tcontext=system_u:object_r:random_
device_t tclass=chr_file
avc:  denied  { read } for  pid=8682 exe=/usr/bin/nmap name=localtime dev=dm-0
ino=32810 scontext=root:sysadm_r:traceroute_t tcontext=system_u:object_r:locale_t
tclass=file
avc:  denied  { search } for  pid=8682 exe=/usr/bin/nmap name=root dev=dm-0
ino=262145 scontext=root:sysadm_r:traceroute_t tcontext=root:object_r:staff_home_dir_
t tclass=dir
avc:  denied  { read } for  pid=8682 exe=/usr/bin/nmap name=nmap-services dev=dm-4
ino=231156 scontext=root:sysadm_r:traceroute_t tcontext=system_u:object_r:usr_t
tclass=file
avc:  denied  { search } for  pid=8682 exe=/usr/bin/nmap name=policy dev=dm-0
ino=49161 scontext=root:sysadm_r:traceroute_t tcontext=system_u:object_r:policy_src_t
tclass=dir
```

Notice that Nmap runs in the domain traceroute_t; we'll use that information later. For now, focus on the seventh message, which is next to last. This message shows that the security engine denied read access to the *nmap-services* file. However, the message gives only the base filename, not the full path. You can find the location of the file by using the *locate* command:

```
# locate nmap-services
/usr/share/nmap/nmap-services
```

Next, double check the security context of the file:

```
# ls -Z /usr/share/nmap
-rw-r--r--  root    root    system_u:object_r:usr_t         nmap-os-fingerprints
-rw-r--r--  root    root    system_u:object_r:usr_t         nmap-protocols
-rw-r--r--+ root    root    system_u:object_r:usr_t         nmap-rpc
```

```
-rw-r--r--   root     root     system_u:object_r:usr_t              nmap-service-probes
-rw-r--r--   root     root     system_u:object_r:usr_t              nmap-services
```

The security context, system_u:object_r:usr_t, agrees with that shown in the log message. Apparently, the traceroute_t domain does not have permission to read files in the security context system_u:object_r:usr_t, including the *nmap-services* file.

Now that we understand the problem, let's fix it. We could give the traceroute_t domain read access to the system_u:object_r:usr_t security context by adding the following declaration to the SELinux policy:

```
allow traceroute_t usr_t:file { read };
```

However, adding this declaration would enable access to files other than *nmap-services* and might compromise system security. We need a more focused fix.

Let's examine the FC file for the traceroute_t domain, *file_contexts/program/traceroute.fc*:

```
# traceroute
/bin/traceroute.*         --       system_u:object_r:traceroute_exec_t
/usr/(s)?bin/traceroute.* --       system_u:object_r:traceroute_exec_t
/usr/bin/lft              --       system_u:object_r:traceroute_exec_t
/usr/bin/nmap             --       system_u:object_r:traceroute_exec_t
```

Notice that the only security context referenced in the FC file is system_u:object_r:traceroute_exec_t. This context is used to label the Nmap executable and other executable files. So, it doesn't seem to be an appropriate security context for the *nmap-services* file. However, it does seem appropriate to label the file with a security context based on the domain type traceroute_t. Let's add the following line to the FC file:

```
/usr/share/nmap.*                  system_u:object_r:traceroute_t
```

This line should cause the */usr/share/nmap* directory and the files it contains to be labeled with the security context system_u:object_r:traceroute_t. To relabel the directory, issue the commands:

```
# make load
# setfiles file_contexts/file_contexts /usr/share/nmap
```

Next, double check the result of the relabeling, which turned out okay:

```
# ls -Z /usr/share/nmap
-rw-r--r--  root     root     system_u:object_r:traceroute_t   nmap-os-fingerprints
-rw-r--r--  root     root     system_u:object_r:traceroute_t   nmap-protocols
-rw-r--r--+ root     root     system_u:object_r:traceroute_t   nmap-rpc
-rw-r--r--  root     root     system_u:object_r:traceroute_t   nmap-service-probes
-rw-r--r--  root     root     system_u:object_r:traceroute_t   nmap-services
```

Now, retry the command:

```
# nmap -sT 127.0.0.1

Starting nmap 3.50 ( http://www.insecure.org/nmap/ ) at 2004-06-01 17:46 UTC
Unable to find nmap-services!  Resorting to /etc/services
```

Again, the command fails. Checking the log, we find a relevant AVC message:

```
avc:  denied  { search } for  pid=8753 exe=/usr/bin/nmap name=nmap dev=dm-4
ino=100533 scontext=root:sysadm_r:traceroute_t tcontext=system_u:object_r:traceroute_
t tclass=dir
```

We've made progress, but we haven't yet resolved the problem. Now, we've run afoul of the traceroute_t domain, lacking permission to search the */usr/share/nmap* directory. Often it's convenient to avoid this sort of step-by-step discovery of successive problems by running the system in permissive mode. But since the system is attached to the Internet, we prefer to continue running in enforcing mode. We could temporarily take the system offline, but that could be inconvenient for some users. So we choose to continue as we've begun.

Let's authorize the traceroute_t domain to search traceroute_t directories. To do so, add the following line to the *domains/program/traceroute.te* file:

```
allow traceroute_t traceroute_t:dir { search };
```

After adding the line, load the revised policy and retry Nmap, which again fails:

```
# make load
# nmap -sT 127.0.0.1

Starting nmap 3.50 ( http://www.insecure.org/nmap/ ) at 2004-06-01 17:46 UTC
Unable to find nmap-services!  Resorting to /etc/services
```

This time, the log shows that Nmap was again prohibited from reading the *nmap-services* file but that the file is correctly labeled with the new security context:

```
avc:  denied  { read } for  pid=8822 exe=/usr/bin/nmap name=nmap-services dev=dm-4
ino=231156 scontext=root:sysadm_r:traceroute_t tcontext=system_u:object_r:traceroute_
t tclass=file
```

Apparently, the traceroute_t domain isn't authorized to read traceroute_t files. So we must add another line to *traceroute.te*, one authorizing the traceroute_t domain to read its own files:

```
allow traceroute_t traceroute_t:file { read };
```

Again, load the new policy and retry Nmap. This time, Nmap works as it should:

```
# nmap -sT 127.0.0.1

Starting nmap 3.50 ( http://www.insecure.org/nmap/ ) at 2004-06-01 18:02 UTC
Interesting ports on bill-a31 (127.0.0.1):
(The 1658 ports scanned but not shown below are in state: closed)
PORT    STATE SERVICE
22/tcp open  ssh

Nmap run completed -- 1 IP address (1 host up) scanned in 0.467 seconds
```

This case study is typical of what you may encounter when running programs with SELinux policies that are less than complete and error free.

Allowing a User Access to an Existing Domain

Let's continue the case study from the preceding section by observing that users other than the system administrator can't use Nmap:

```
# id -Z
root:staff_r:staff_t
# nmap -sT 127.0.0.1

Starting nmap 3.50 ( http://www.insecure.org/nmap/ ) at 2004-06-01 11:13 PDT
Unable to find nmap-services!  Resorting to /etc/services
socket troubles in massping : Permission denied
```

The relevant AVC log message is:

```
avc:  denied  { create } for  pid=8940 exe=/usr/bin/nmap scontext=root:staff_r:staff_
t tcontext=root:staff_r:staff_t tclass=rawip_socket
```

The message tells us that the staff_r role is not authorized to create a raw IP socket. We could authorize the domain to do so. But this naive approach would likely confer excessive permissions. Indeed, it's debatable whether we should allow staff_r access to Nmap at all. But let's presume that we do want to authorize access to Nmap without generally authorizing creation of raw IP sockets.

 Unless you have a good reason, I don't recommend that you authorize staff_r users to access Nmap. Limiting the permissions available to staff_r users is consistent with the principle of least privilege. If you do choose to authorize Nmap access, carefully consider whether to do so by using the approach explained here, which authorizes access to the entire traceroute_t domain, rather than only the Nmap program. The following section shows a more focused alternative approach.

Apparently, the problem is that staff_r is not authorized to enter the traceroute_t domain. Inspecting the *traceroute.te* file, we find the following two role declarations:

```
role sysadm_r types traceroute_t;
role system_r types traceroute_t;
```

Add a third declaration having the same form:

```
role staff_r  types traceroute_t;
```

To give effect to the change, load the revised policy. Then, retry Nmap:

```
# make load
# nmap -sT 127.0.0.1

Starting nmap 3.50 ( http://www.insecure.org/nmap/ ) at 2004-06-01 11:43 PDT
Interesting ports on bill-a31 (127.0.0.1):
(The 1658 ports scanned but not shown below are in state: closed)
PORT    STATE SERVICE
222/tcp open  rsh-spx

Nmap run completed -- 1 IP address (1 host up) scanned in 0.469 seconds
```

This time, Nmap works as expected.

In general, one additional step is often needed to add a user to an existing domain: a transition. In the case of the traceroute_t domain, a conditional transition exists:

```
ifdef(`ping.te', `
if (user_ping) {
    domain_auto_trans(unpriv_userdomain, traceroute_exec_t, traceroute_t)
    # allow access to the terminal
    allow traceroute_t { ttyfile ptyfile }:chr_file rw_file_perms;
}
')
```

This transition authorizes ordinary programs (programs labeled with the type unpriv_userdomain) to enter the traceroute_t domain by executing a program labeled with the traceroute_exec_t type. The Nmap program, which performs *ping* operations, benefits from this general-purpose transition. So we didn't find it necessary to add a new transition. Otherwise, we might have added a transition of the form:

```
domain_auto_trans(staff_t, traceroute_exec_t, traceroute_t)
```

The allow declaration in this conditional transition authorizes processes in the traceroute_t domain to access the pseudoterminal device. This allows messages to be written directly to the device, rather than writing them via the Unix standard output or standard error devices as *traceroute* requires.

Creating a New Domain

In general, it's unwise to create overly large domains, especially domains that include unrelated programs. The traceroute_t domain considered in the preceding sections is perhaps such an overweight domain, since it relates to both the *traceroute* and Nmap programs. These programs perform a few somewhat similar operations, but they're not closely related. Because they're part of a single domain, a vulnerability in either program could enable an intruder to gain control of the entire domain. Let's presume that we prefer to avoid that fate and see what's required to create a domain specific to the Nmap program.

To do so, we'll follow a procedure that also works in most similar cases:

1. Determine what files are related to the domain.
2. Determine the security contexts of these files.
3. Decide what security contexts are appropriate for the new domain.
4. Create a basic TE file.
5. Create a basic FC file that specifies proper labels for files related to the domain.
6. If necessary, delete conflicting specifications from other FC files.
7. Load the revised policy and label the domains.

8. Repeat the following steps as needed:

    a. Test the program.

    b. Tweak the TE or FC files as needed.

Determine What Files Are Related to the Domain

As the procedure directs, let's start by finding out what files are related to Nmap:

```
# rpm -ql nmap
/usr/bin/nmap
/usr/share/doc/nmap-3.50
/usr/share/doc/nmap-3.50/COPYING
/usr/share/doc/nmap-3.50/README
/usr/share/doc/nmap-3.50/copying.html
/usr/share/doc/nmap-3.50/nmap-fingerprinting-article.txt
/usr/share/doc/nmap-3.50/nmap.deprecated.txt
/usr/share/doc/nmap-3.50/nmap.usage.txt
/usr/share/doc/nmap-3.50/nmap_doc.html
/usr/share/doc/nmap-3.50/nmap_manpage.html
/usr/share/man/man1/nmap.1.gz
/usr/share/nmap
/usr/share/nmap/nmap-os-fingerprints
/usr/share/nmap/nmap-protocols
/usr/share/nmap/nmap-rpc
/usr/share/nmap/nmap-service-probes
/usr/share/nmap/nmap-services
```

We find four sorts of files:

- The Nmap executable, */usr/bin/nmap*
- Nmap documentation files, which live in */usr/share/doc/nmap*
- The Nmap man page, */usr/share/man/man1/nmap.1.gz*
- Nmap data files, which live in */usr/share/nmap*

Determine the Security Contexts of the Files

Next, let's see what security contexts are currently assigned:

```
# ls -Z /usr/bin/nmap
-rwxr-xr-x+ root     root       system_u:object_r:traceroute_exec_t /usr/bin/nmap
# ls -Z /usr/share/doc/nmap-3.50/
-rw-r--r--+ root     root       system_u:object_r:usr_t         COPYING
-rw-r--r-- root      root       system_u:object_r:usr_t         copying.html
-rw-r--r-- root      root       system_u:object_r:usr_t         nmap.deprecated.txt
-rw-r--r-- root      root       system_u:object_r:usr_t         nmap_doc.html
-rw-r--r-- root      root       system_u:object_r:usr_t         nmap-fingerprinting-
article.txt
-rw-r--r-- root      root       system_u:object_r:usr_t         nmap_manpage.html
-rw-r--r-- root      root       system_u:object_r:usr_t         nmap.usage.txt
-rw-r--r-- root      root       system_u:object_r:usr_t         README
# ls -Z /usr/share/man/man1/nmap.1.gz
```

```
-rw-r--r--+ root     root       system_u:object_r:man_t              /usr/share/man/man1/
nmap.1.gz
# ls -Z /usr/share/nmap/
-rw-r--r-- root      root       system_u:object_r:traceroute_t       nmap-os-fingerprints
-rw-r--r-- root      root       system_u:object_r:traceroute_t       nmap-protocols
-rw-r--r--+ root     root       system_u:object_r:traceroute_t       nmap-rpc
-rw-r--r-- root      root       system_u:object_r:traceroute_t       nmap-service-probes
-rw-r--r-- root      root       system_u:object_r:traceroute_t       nmap-services
```

Decide on Appropriate Security Contexts for the New Domain

Files having the usr_t and man_t types are readable by ordinary users, but writable only by privileged users. So it appears that the documentation files and the man page have reasonable security contexts.

Let's establish new contexts for the executable and data files. We'll use nmap_t as the type of the data files and nmap_exec_t as the type of the executable.

Create a Basic TE File

To assign the proper security contexts, let's first create a simple TE file, *domains/program/nmap.te*:

```
###################################
#
# Rules for the nmap_t domain.
#
# nmap_t is the domain for the nmap program.
# nmap_exec_t is the type of the corresponding program.
#
type nmap_t, domain;
type nmap_exec_t, file_type, sysadmfile, exec_type;
```

Our TE file currently does nothing more than define the types we'll use to properly label the files related to the domain. We'll add additional declarations later. In particular, we'll add a declaration that allows processes executing nmap_exec_t programs to transition to the nmap_t domain. We'll also add declarations that specify the operations processes in the nmap_t domain are authorized to perform and the operations that other domains can perform on nmap_t objects. Like the nmap_t domain, most domains have at least two associated types: one associated with the domain itself and one used as an entry point to the domain. Many domains have additional types used to restrict permissions further.

Create a Basic FC File

Next, let's create the FC file, *file_contexts/program/nmap.fc*:

```
# nmap
/usr/bin/nmap        --  system_u:object_r:nmap_exec_t
/usr/share/nmap.*        system_u:object_r:nmap_t
```

When the filesystem is labeled, the FC file will cause the Nmap program and its associated documentation files to be assigned the specified contexts.

Delete Conflicting Specifications from Other FC Files

Conflicting FC specifications could result in incorrectly labeled files. To avoid conflicts, let's remove the following extraneous lines from the *traceroute.fc* file:

```
/usr/bin/nmap        --  system_u:object_r:traceroute_exec_t
/usr/share/nmap.*        system_u:object_r:traceroute_t
```

Load the Revised Policy and Label the Domains

Now, let's install our new policy and relabel the related files:

```
# make load
# setfiles file_contexts/file_contexts /usr/bin/nmap
# setfiles file_contexts/file_contexts /usr/share/nmap
# ls -dZ /usr/bin/nmap /usr/share/nmap/
-rwxr-xr-x+ root    root     system_u:object_r:nmap_exec_t    /usr/bin/nmap
drwxr-xr-x  root    root     system_u:object_r:nmap_t         /usr/share/nmap/
```

The output of the *ls* command verifies that the security contexts were correctly revised.

Test and Revise the TE and FC Files as Needed

Now, let's try executing the Nmap command and see what sorts of errors arise:

```
# id -Z
root:sysadm_r:sysadm_t
# nmap -sT 127.0.0.1

Starting nmap 3.50 ( http://www.insecure.org/nmap/ ) at 2004-06-01 13:49 PDT
Interesting ports on bill-a31 (127.0.0.1):
(The 1658 ports scanned but not shown below are in state: closed)
PORT    STATE SERVICE
22/tcp open  ssh

Nmap run completed -- 1 IP address (1 host up) scanned in 0.510 seconds
```

When we run the program as system administrator, it appears to work fine. However, let's see what happens when we run the program as a user other than the administrator:

```
# id -Z
root:staff_r:staff_t
# nmap -sT 127.0.0.1

Starting nmap 3.50 ( http://www.insecure.org/nmap/ ) at 2004-06-01 13:50 PDT
Unable to find nmap-services!  Resorting to /etc/services
socket trobles in massping : Permission denied
```

As you might expect, the program fails. Indeed, we should hope that it does so, because otherwise SELinux would not be properly enforcing its policies. Let's discover what's necessary to coax our new nmap_t domain into working for a nonadministrative user.

First, let's examine the system log for relevant AVC messages. We find a message similar to the one we found in the situation described in the preceding section:

```
avc: denied { create } for pid=9533 exe=/usr/bin/nmap scontext=root:staff_r:staff_
t tcontext=root:staff_r:staff_t tclass=rawip_socket
```

Resolve the problem as we did earlier, by authorizing users in the staff_r role to access the domain.

```
role staff_r types nmap_t;
```

Also authorize an automatic type transition to nmap_t when the Nmap executable is loaded:

```
domain_auto_trans(staff_t, nmap_exec_t, nmap_t)
```

Again, load the revised policy and test the program. This time, it segfaults:

```
# nmap -sT 127.0.0.1
Segmentation fault
```

Inspecting the system log, we find the relevant AVC message:

```
avc: denied { use } for pid=9607 exe=/usr/bin/nmap path=/dev/pts/1 dev= ino=3
scontext=root:staff_r:nmap_t tcontext=root:system_r:sshd_t tclass=fd
```

This message indicates that the program was unable to access the pseudoterminal device, */dev/pts/1*. Recall that before moving Nmap to its own domain, it executed from the traceroute_t domain without problems. So the traceroute_t domain probably contains a declaration that authorizes access to the pseudoterminal. By studying the TE file for the traceroute_t domain, we discover the declaration needed in our new domain:

```
allow traceroute_t privfd:fd use;
```

Add the declaration, load the revised policy, and try again. The program appears to suffer from the same problem. But inspecting the system log turns up a new AVC message:

```
avc: denied { read write } for pid=9661 exe=/usr/bin/nmap path=/dev/pts/1 dev=
ino=3 scontext=root:staff_r:nmap_t tcontext=root:object_r:staff_devpts_t tclass=chr_
file
```

Now that Nmap can use the file descriptor, it needs read and write access to the related device file. Again consulting the TE file for traceroute_t, we discover and add a declaration authorizing read and write access to the terminal:

```
allow nmap_t { ttyfile ptyfile }:chr_file rw_file_perms;
```

This time, after loading the new policy, we obtain an unfamiliar error:

```
# nmap -sT 127.0.0.1
nmap: error while loading shared libraries: libssl.so.4: cannot open shared object
file: Permission denied
```

This message indicates that our domain is unable to access shared libraries. Let's add a macro invocation that authorizes such access:

```
uses_shlib(nmap_t)
```

After loading the new policy, we obtain a somewhat familiar error:

```
# nmap -sT 127.0.0.1

Starting nmap 3.50 ( http://www.insecure.org/nmap/ ) at 2004-06-01 21:21 UTC
Unable to find nmap-services!  Resorting to /etc/services
Unable to open /etc/services for reading service information
QUITTING!
```

This resembles the error we encountered in the preceding section, when Nmap was unable to read */usr/share/nmap/nmap-services*. However, now Nmap also seems unable to read */etc/services*. Inspecting the system log uncovers related log entries:

```
avc: denied  { create } for pid=9821 exe=/usr/bin/nmap scontext=root:staff_r:nmap_t
tcontext=root:staff_r:nmap_t tclass=unix_stream_socket
avc:  denied   { read } for  pid=9821 exe=/usr/bin/nmap name=localtime dev=dm-0
ino=32810 scontext=root:staff_r:nmap_t tcontext=system_u:object_r:locale_t
tclass=file
avc:  denied   { create } for  pid=9821 exe=/usr/bin/nmap scontext=root:staff_r:nmap_t
tcontext=root:staff_r:nmap_t tclass=unix_stream_socket
avc:  denied   { read } for  pid=9821 exe=/usr/bin/nmap name=nsswitch.conf dev=dm-0
ino=32811 scontext=root:staff_r:nmap_t tcontext=system_u:object_r:etc_t tclass=file
avc:  denied   { read } for  pid=9821 exe=/usr/bin/nmap name=passwd dev=dm-0 ino=34492
scontext=root:staff_r:nmap_t tcontext=system_u:object_r:etc_t tclass=file
avc:  denied   { search } for  pid=9821 exe=/usr/bin/nmap name=nmap dev=dm-4
ino=100533 scontext=root:staff_r:nmap_t tcontext=system_u:object_r:nmap_t tclass=dir
avc:  denied   { search } for  pid=9821 exe=/usr/bin/nmap name=root dev=dm-0
ino=262145 scontext=root:staff_r:nmap_t tcontext=root:object_r:staff_home_dir_t
tclass=dir
avc:  denied   { read } for  pid=9821 exe=/usr/bin/nmap name=services dev=dm-0
ino=32797 scontext=root:staff_r:nmap_t tcontext=system_u:object_r:etc_t tclass=file
```

Understanding how to resolve these errors might be overwhelming, were it not for our strategy of studying the domain traceroute_t. After some consideration, we settle on the following additional lines:

```
can_network(nmap_t)
allow nmap_t self:{ rawip_socket netlink_socket } create_socket_perms;
allow nmap_t self:unix_stream_socket create_socket_perms;
read_locale(nmap_t)
allow nmap_t etc_t:file  { getattr read };
allow nmap_t nmap_t:dir  { search };
allow nmap_t nmap_t:file { getattr read };
```

The first line invokes a macro that generates declarations authorizing network access. The second and third lines authorize specific network operations—namely, creating raw and stream sockets. The fourth line authorizes reading locale information, such as *localtime*. The fifth line authorizes access to etc_t files, such as *nsswitch.conf*. Finally, the sixth and seventh lines authorize access to nmap_t directories and files.

Unfortunately, after loading the new policy, we discover that our work is not yet done:

```
# nmap -sT 127.0.0.1

Starting nmap 3.50 ( http://www.insecure.org/nmap/ ) at 2004-06-01 14:36 PDT
socket trobles in massping : Operation not permitted
```

At least Nmap now prints a different error message. That's some indication of progress. Studying the system log turns up the following AVC messages:

```
avc:  denied  { search } for  pid=9972 exe=/usr/bin/nmap name=root dev=dm-0
ino=262145 scontext=root:staff_r:nmap_t tcontext=root:object_r:staff_home_dir_t
tclass=dir
avc:  denied  { search } for  pid=9972 exe=/usr/bin/nmap name=root dev=dm-0
ino=262145 scontext=root:staff_r:nmap_t tcontext=root:object_r:staff_home_dir_t
tclass=dir
avc:  denied  { search } for  pid=9972 exe=/usr/bin/nmap dev= ino=1 scontext=root:
staff_r:nmap_t tcontext=system_u:object_r:proc_t tclass=dir
avc:  denied  { net_raw } for  pid=9972 exe=/usr/bin/nmap capability=13
scontext=root:staff_r:nmap_t tcontext=root:staff_r:nmap_t tclass=capability
```

Our problems now seem to relate to accessing our home directory, which has type staff_home_dir_t; accessing */proc*; and using special capabilities. Address the home directory problem by adding

```
allow nmap_t staff_home_dir_t:dir {search };
```

To access the files within a directory, a process must be able to:

- Search the directory.
- Get the attributes of, and read, the files contained in the directory.

So, to fix the problem accessing */proc*, add:

```
allow nmap_t proc_t:dir search;
allow nmap_t proc_t:file { getattr read };
```

However, it's not necessary to be prescient. If we failed to authorize the getattr and read operations, Nmap would fail with an AVC message that would prompt us to authorize them.

Finally, to authorize use of special capabilities, add:

```
allow nmap_t nmap_t:capability { net_raw };
```

After compiling and loading the revised policy and testing Nmap, we find a new error message:

```
# nmap -sT 127.0.0.1

Starting nmap 3.50 ( http://www.insecure.org/nmap/ ) at 2004-06-01 14:47 PDT
pcap_open_live: socket: Permission denied
```

```
There are several possible reasons for this, depending on your operating system:
LINUX: If you are getting Socket type not supported, try modprobe af_packet or
recompile your kernel with SOCK_PACKET enabled.
*BSD: If you are getting device not configured, you need to recompile your kernel
with Berkeley Packet Filter support.  If you are getting No such file or directory,
try creating the device (eg cd /dev; MAKEDEV <device>; or use mknod).
SOLARIS: If you are trying to scan localhost and getting '/dev/lo0: No such file or
directory', complain to Sun.  I don't think Solaris can support advanced localhost
scans.  You can probably use "-P0 -sT localhost" though.

QUITTING!
```

It appears that our new domain lacks the ability to create sockets. A glance at the log confirms this hypothesis. Add a declaration authorizing the creation of sockets:

```
allow nmap_t self:packet_socket create_socket_perms;
```

After compiling and loading the policy, we find that Nmap now works correctly:

```
# nmap -sT 127.0.0.1

Starting nmap 3.50 ( http://www.insecure.org/nmap/ ) at 2004-06-01 14:49 PDT
Interesting ports on bill-a31 (127.0.0.1):
(The 1658 ports scanned but not shown below are in state: closed)
PORT    STATE SERVICE
22/tcp open  ssh

Nmap run completed -- 1 IP address (1 host up) scanned in 0.473 seconds
```

Because we implemented our domain iteratively, it may be hard to grasp the big picture. So that you can review the result of our effort, here's the complete TE file for the nmap_t domain:

```
################################
#
# Rules for the nmap_t domain.
#
# nmap_t is the domain for the nmap program.
# nmap_exec_t is the type of the corresponding program.
#
type nmap_t, domain;
type nmap_exec_t, file_type, sysadmfile, exec_type;
role staff_r types nmap_t;
domain_auto_trans(staff_t, nmap_exec_t, nmap_t)
allow nmap_t privfd:fd use;
allow nmap_t { ttyfile ptyfile }:chr_file rw_file_perms;
uses_shlib(nmap_t)
can_network(nmap_t)
allow nmap_t self:{ rawip_socket netlink_socket } create_socket_perms;
allow nmap_t self:unix_stream_socket create_socket_perms;
read_locale(nmap_t)
allow nmap_t etc_t:file  { getattr read };
allow nmap_t nmap_t:dir  { search };
allow nmap_t nmap_t:file { getattr read };
allow nmap_t staff_home_dir_t:dir {search };
```

```
allow nmap_t proc_t:dir search;
allow nmap_t proc_t:file { getattr read };
allow nmap_t nmap_t:capability { net_raw };
allow nmap_t self:packet_socket create_socket_perms;
```

However, unless we're very lucky, we're not yet done. It's likely that additional testing will disclose other permissions that must be added to the TE file. You can now see why many SELinux policies work less than perfectly. Like almost all computer software, they're generally developed using a write-test-revise process that doesn't differ much from cut-and-try. Unusual inputs or circumstances can reveal the need for permissions that haven't been anticipated or provided.

Using Audit2allow

Most implementations of SELinux include Audit2allow, a tool that can help you create or customize a domain. Some fledgling SELinux administrators use Audit2allow indiscriminately, rendering their system less secure. One technical reviewer of this book terms Audit2allow "evil," not so much because of problems with the tool itself as because of the way it's often misused. In this section, I'll explain how to use Audit2allow more carefully, so that you can avoid this pitfall.

Audit2allow is a Perl script that processes recent AVC messages. It analyzes the messages it finds and prints allow rules that—if added to the current policy—would authorize the denied operations. Hence, you can go badly wrong by blindly accepting its recommendations. For instance, perhaps someone has attempted a prohibited operation. Adding the rules generated by Audit2allow will authorize the prohibited operation, but may also compromise system security. Another more subtle source of problems is that Audit2allow takes the current type architecture and file labels as given. Often it's appropriate—or even necessary—to create a new domain that encapsulates a program or operation, as I did in the preceding section. But Audit2allow provides no help in doing so.

Audit2allow is less than perfect in other ways. For instance, it is sometimes blind to prohibited operations. This can occur if the operation is covered by a dontaudit rule. It can also occur if AVC message caching has caused one or more messages to be suppressed.

A related weakness of Audit2allow is that it's not aware of the M4 macros used in implementing policies. So rules recommended by Audit2allow tend to be quite wordy and can result in cluttered policy files that are hard to understand.

However, despite its weaknesses, Audit2allow is a very useful tool when properly used.

The Audit2allow command has the following form:

```
audit2allow [-d] [-v] [-l] [-i inputfile ] [-o outputfile]
```

The command takes the following options:

-d

Read input from the *dmesg* command, rather than a log file.

-v

Print verbose output.

-l

Ignore input preceding the most recent loading of the SELinux policy.

-i inputfile

Read input from *inputfile*.

-o outputfile

Append output to *outputfile*.

Typically use of Audit2allow takes the form:

```
make reload
# test program or operation here
audit2allow -l -i /var/log/kernel
```

By reloading the SELinux policy, you define a starting point before which Audit2allow, when run with the –l option, will ignore log entries. You then test the subject program or operation, generating AVC messages. Finally, Audit2allow analyzes these messages and prints recommended rules. You can capture these rules by redirecting Audit2allow's output to a file:

```
audit2allow -l -i /var/log/kernel > /tmp/audit2allow
```

 You may be tempted to incorporate the rules generated by Audit2allow into your SELinux policy just to see what happens. Stifle this urge: it's likely that the generated rules include several that will weaken the security of your system.

It's often useful to set permissive mode before using Audit2allow. Doing so may avoid early termination of the test program. In general, it's best if the program runs to completion, since this generates more AVC messages than otherwise. However, setting permissive mode may compromise system security.

Let's consider the same case study in the preceding section, the Nmap program. But this time, let's use Audit2allow to help us create the nmap_t domain.

Let's begin, as before, with an FC file that refers to the nmap_t and nmap_exec_t domains:

```
# nmap
/usr/bin/nmap        --   system_u:object_r:nmap_exec_t
/usr/share/nmap.*         system_u:object_r:nmap_t
```

And let's create a basic TE file that defines these domains. This time, we'll also include a role declaration and a domain_auto_trans macro invocation. We'll need these because Audit2allow generates only AVC declarations. In particular, without the domain_auto_trans macro, Audit2allow will recommend authorizing the staff_t domain or another general-purpose domain to perform operations that we prefer to authorize only for the nmap_t domain. Here's our primitive TE file:

```
###############################
#
# Rules for the nmap_t domain.
#
# nmap_t is the domain for the nmap program.
# nmap_exec_t is the type of the corresponding program.
#
type nmap_t, domain;
type nmap_exec_t, file_type, sysadmfile, exec_type;

role staff_r types nmap_t;
domain_auto_trans(staff_t, nmap_exec_t, nmap_t)
```

Let's now load the revised policy, set permissive mode, test Nmap, and examine the recommendations provided by Audit2allow:

```
# make load
# setenforce 0
# nmap -sT 127.0.0.1

Starting nmap 3.50 ( http://www.insecure.org/nmap/ ) at 2004-06-01 14:52 PDT
Interesting ports on bill-a31 (127.0.0.1):
(The 1658 ports scanned but not shown below are in state: closed)
PORT    STATE SERVICE
22/tcp open  ssh

Nmap run completed -- 1 IP address (1 host up) scanned in 0.475 seconds
# setenforce 1
# audit2allow -l -i /var/log/kernel
allow nmap_t amandaidx_port_t:tcp_socket { recv_msg send_msg };
allow nmap_t amidxtape_port_t:tcp_socket { recv_msg send_msg };
allow nmap_t biff_port_t:tcp_socket { recv_msg send_msg };
allow nmap_t device_t:dir { search };
allow nmap_t dict_port_t:tcp_socket { recv_msg send_msg };
allow nmap_t dns_port_t:tcp_socket { recv_msg send_msg };
allow nmap_t etc_t:dir { search };
allow nmap_t etc_t:file { getattr read };
allow nmap_t fingerd_port_t:tcp_socket { recv_msg send_msg };
allow nmap_t ftp_data_port_t:tcp_socket { recv_msg send_msg };
allow nmap_t ftp_port_t:tcp_socket { recv_msg send_msg };
allow nmap_t http_cache_port_t:tcp_socket { recv_msg send_msg };
allow nmap_t http_port_t:tcp_socket { recv_msg send_msg };
allow nmap_t inetd_port_t:tcp_socket { recv_msg send_msg };
allow nmap_t innd_port_t:tcp_socket { recv_msg send_msg };
allow nmap_t ipp_port_t:tcp_socket { recv_msg send_msg };
allow nmap_t ircd_port_t:tcp_socket { recv_msg send_msg };
allow nmap_t ld_so_cache_t:file { getattr read };
allow nmap_t ld_so_t:file { read };
allow nmap_t ldap_port_t:tcp_socket { recv_msg send_msg };
```

```
allow nmap_t lib_t:dir { search };
allow nmap_t lib_t:lnk_file { read };
allow nmap_t locale_t:file { getattr read };
allow nmap_t monopd_port_t:tcp_socket { recv_msg send_msg };
allow nmap_t net_conf_t:file { getattr read };
allow nmap_t netif_lo_t:netif { rawip_send tcp_recv tcp_send };
allow nmap_t nmap_t:capability { net_raw };
allow nmap_t nmap_t:dir { search };
allow nmap_t nmap_t:file { getattr read };
allow nmap_t nmap_t:packet_socket { bind create getopt ioctl read setopt };
allow nmap_t nmap_t:rawip_socket { create setopt write };
allow nmap_t nmap_t:tcp_socket { connect create getopt setopt };
allow nmap_t nmap_t:udp_socket { create ioctl };
allow nmap_t nmap_t:unix_stream_socket { connect create };
allow nmap_t node_lo_t:node { rawip_send tcp_recv tcp_send };
allow nmap_t pop_port_t:tcp_socket { recv_msg send_msg };
allow nmap_t port_t:tcp_socket { recv_msg send_msg };
allow nmap_t portmap_port_t:tcp_socket { recv_msg send_msg };
allow nmap_t postgresql_port_t:tcp_socket { recv_msg send_msg };
allow nmap_t printer_port_t:tcp_socket { recv_msg send_msg };
allow nmap_t proc_t:dir { search };
allow nmap_t proc_t:file { getattr read };
allow nmap_t rlogin_port_t:tcp_socket { recv_msg send_msg };
allow nmap_t rndc_port_t:tcp_socket { recv_msg send_msg };
allow nmap_t root_t:dir { search };
allow nmap_t rsh_port_t:tcp_socket { recv_msg send_msg };
allow nmap_t shlib_t:file { execute getattr read };
allow nmap_t smbd_port_t:tcp_socket { recv_msg send_msg };
allow nmap_t smtp_port_t:tcp_socket { recv_msg send_msg };
allow nmap_t snmp_port_t:tcp_socket { recv_msg send_msg };
allow nmap_t soundd_port_t:tcp_socket { recv_msg send_msg };
allow nmap_t spamd_port_t:tcp_socket { recv_msg send_msg };
allow nmap_t ssh_port_t:tcp_socket { recv_msg send_msg };
allow nmap_t sshd_t:fd { use };
allow nmap_t staff_devpts_t:chr_file { getattr read write };
allow nmap_t staff_home_dir_t:dir { search };
allow nmap_t telnet_port_t:tcp_socket { recv_msg send_msg };
allow nmap_t transproxy_port_t:tcp_socket { recv_msg send_msg };
allow nmap_t urandom_device_t:chr_file { getattr ioctl read };
allow nmap_t usr_t:dir { search };
allow nmap_t vnc_port_t:tcp_socket { recv_msg send_msg };
allow nmap_t xserver_port_t:tcp_socket { recv_msg send_msg };
```

Audit2allow produces many recommended rules. But notice that most of them have the same form:

```
allow nmap_t port:tcp_socket { recv_msg send_msg };
```

where *port* refers to some TCP port. As it happens, these rules would work fine if added to the domain. But they're wordy and complicated because they don't take advantage of available M4 macros.

Using our knowledge of the macros available, which we can deepen by studying TE files distributed with SELinux, let's start over with a revised primitive TE file. Our revised TE file features a macro invocation, `can_network`, that authorizes network access:

```
################################
#
# Rules for the nmap_t domain.
#
# nmap_t is the domain for the nmap program.
# nmap_exec_t is the type of the corresponding program.
#
type nmap_t, domain;
type nmap_exec_t, file_type, sysadmfile, exec_type;

role staff_r types nmap_t;
domain_auto_trans(staff_t, nmap_exec_t, nmap_t)
can_network(nmap_t)
```

After loading the new policy, testing Nmap, and running Audit2allow, we obtain the following set of recommended rules:

```
allow nmap_t device_t:dir { search };
allow nmap_t etc_t:dir { search };
allow nmap_t etc_t:file { getattr read };
allow nmap_t ld_so_cache_t:file { getattr read };
allow nmap_t ld_so_t:file { read };
allow nmap_t lib_t:dir { search };
allow nmap_t lib_t:lnk_file { read };
allow nmap_t locale_t:file { getattr read };
allow nmap_t nmap_t:capability { net_raw };
allow nmap_t nmap_t:dir { search };
allow nmap_t nmap_t:file { getattr read };
allow nmap_t nmap_t:packet_socket { bind create getopt ioctl read setopt };
allow nmap_t nmap_t:rawip_socket { create setopt write };
allow nmap_t nmap_t:unix_stream_socket { connect create };
allow nmap_t proc_t:dir { search };
allow nmap_t proc_t:file { getattr read };
allow nmap_t root_t:dir { search };
allow nmap_t shlib_t:file { execute getattr read };
allow nmap_t sshd_t:fd { use };
allow nmap_t staff_devpts_t:chr_file { getattr read write };
allow nmap_t staff_home_dir_t:dir { search };
allow nmap_t urandom_device_t:chr_file { getattr ioctl read };
allow nmap_t usr_t:dir { search };
```

This set of recommended rules is substantially smaller than the original set, consisting of between one-third and one-half the number of lines.

Our next step is to review the recommendations to ensure that none is overly broad. We notice that all the rules pertain to the `nmap_t` domain. This is encouraging, since we were trying to ensure that we authorize only that domain for the special operations performed by Nmap. Ultimately, after careful study, we convince ourselves that the recommendations are appropriate and safe and add them to the *nmap.te* file, completing our task.

As you see, Audit2allow is no substitute for a solid understanding of the SELinux policy language, since intelligent use of Audit2allow requires such an understanding. But used judiciously, Audit2allow expedites and facilitates creation and customization of policies.

 When customizing an existing policy, it's often helpful to avoid modifying the associated TE file. Otherwise, installing an updated policy may overwrite changes you've painstakingly devised. To avoid this problem, consider placing your changes in a file named *domains/program/local.te*. Be sure to create the corresponding FC file, *file_contexts/program/local.fc*; otherwise, policy compilation may fail. Either file can be empty or contain only comments if no related specifications or declarations are needed.

Policy Management Tools

Tresys Technology, a network services company, has published a set of open source GUI tools for SELinux policy management. Most releases of SELinux include at least one of the Tresys tools, which are:

Apol
Supports analysis of the SELinux *policy.conf* file.

Seaudit
Supports searching, sorting, and viewing AVC log messages.

Sepcut
Supports browsing and editing of SELinux policy components.

Seuserx
Supports adding, changing, and removing Linux and SELinux users.

The following subsections briefly describe these tools. My intention is not to show you *how* to use the tools but to help you understand what they do, so that you can decide *when* to use them and *which* tool to use. Because the tools are regularly improved, I advise you to refer to the tools' help files for information on operating them. If your SELinux release does not include the Tresys tools, you can obtain them at *http://www.tresys.com/*.

Apol

The Apol tool enables you to analyze an SELinux policy. It does not work with the component files that compose the policy, but only with *policy.conf*. So you should compile the SELinux policy before using Apol. You can do so by issuing the command:

```
make load
```

from within the SELinux *src/policy* directory. Figure 9-1 shows Apol's main window after using its File menu to open the *policy.conf* file.

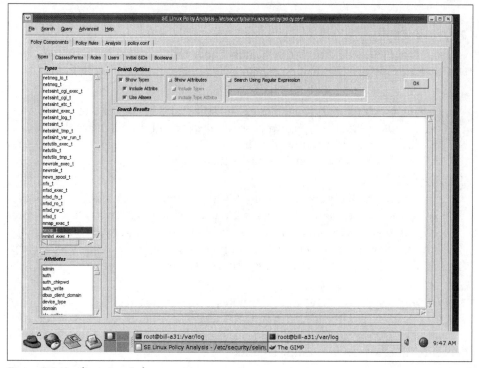

Figure 9-1. Apol's main window

Apol's main window contains four primary tabs:

Policy Components

Supports searching and viewing policy components: types, type attributes, type aliases, object classes, object permissions, roles, users, initial SIDs, and SElinux Booleans.

Policy Rules

Supports working with policy rules: allow, neverallow, auditallow, dontaudit, type_transition, and type_change declarations.

Analysis

Supports several analysis operations, including forward and reverse domain transition analyses, direct information flow analysis, and indirect (transitive) information flow analysis.

policy.conf

Enables you to view the *policy.conf* file.

The following subsections describe the operations associated with Apol's first three tabs. You can learn more about Apol by studying its help file, available via the Help menu.

Policy components

As shown in Figure 9-1, the Policy Components tab contains six secondary tabs related to the policy component types:

Types
> Lets you search types, type attributes, and aliases by specifying a regular expression. Double-clicking a type, attribute, or alias provides a summary description. The Search Results window displays *policy.conf* lines related to types and attributes having names matching the regular expression.

Classes/Perms
> Lets you search object classes, common permissions, and permissions by specifying a regular expression. The Search Results window displays *policy.conf* lines related to object classes having names matching the regular expression. Double-clicking a class, common permission, or permission provides a summary description. Figure 9-2 shows a sample query and its result.

Roles
> Lets you search roles and their attributes by specifying regular expressions for role or type. The tab makes it simple to identify all roles that include a specified type. Double-clicking a role provides a summary description. Figure 9-3 shows the result of a query requesting all roles.

Users
> Lets you search SELinux user identities and their associated roles. Figure 9-4 shows the result of a query requesting all users.

Initial SIDs
> Lets you search initial SIDs and their associated security contexts. Figure 9-5 shows the result of a query requesting all initial SIDs.

Booleans
> Lets you search SELinux Booleans. Figure 9-6 shows the result of a query requesting all Booleans.

Policy rules

Figure 9-7 shows Apol's Policy Rules tab, which contains three secondary tabs:

TE Rules
> This tab lets you search type-enforcement rules. The tab supports several search criteria:
>
> *Rule Selection*
> > Lets you narrow the scope of a search to include only specified rules.

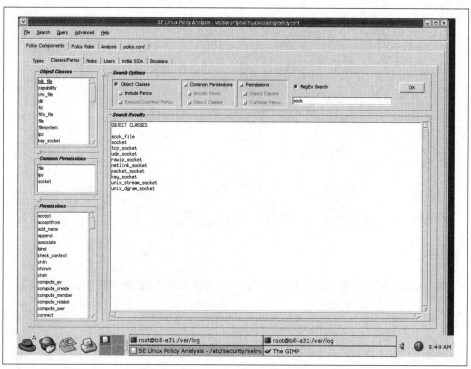

Figure 9-2. Apol's Classes/Perms tab

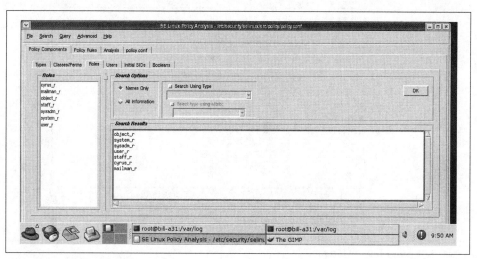

Figure 9-3. Apol's Roles tab

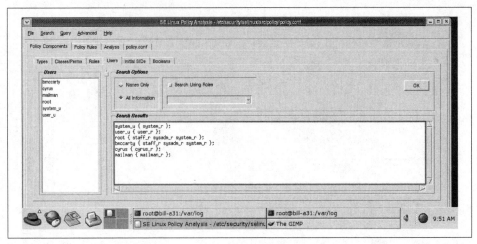

Figure 9-4. Apol's Users tab

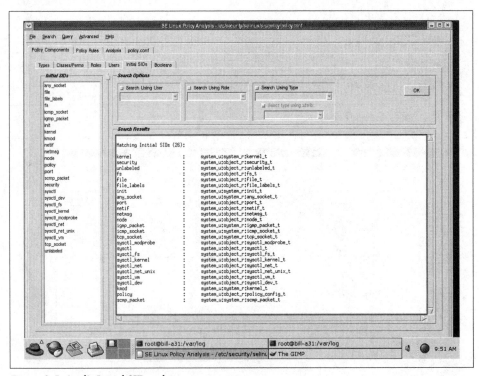

Figure 9-5. Apol's Initial SIDs tab

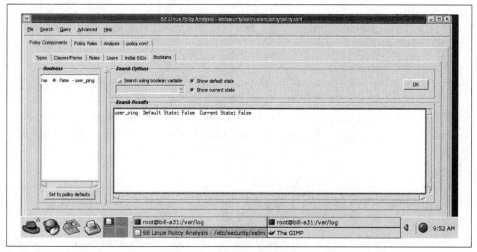

Figure 9-6. Apol's Booleans tab

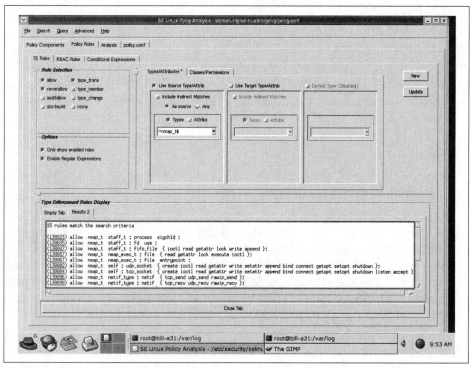

Figure 9-7. Apol's Policy Rules tab

Type/Attributes
> Lets you search by types and type attributes used as source, target, or default types in rules.

Classes/Permissions
> Lets you search by object classes and permissions, returning only rules that reference the specified classes and permissions.

The results window displays all rules matching the specified search criteria. Each displayed rule includes a hyperlink that points to the rule's place in the *policy.conf* file.

RBAC Rules
> Figure 9-8 shows the RBAC tab, which lets you search role-based access control rules in much the same way as the TE tab lets you search type enforcement rules.

Conditional Expressions
> Figure 9-9 shows the Conditional Expressions tab, which lets you search conditional expressions for the following rule types:
>
> * `audit` rules
> * `allow` rules
> * `transition` rules

You can search by specifying a regular expression that matches the name of a Boolean appearing within a conditional expression. Each rule displayed in the results window include a hyperlink that points to the rule's location within the *policy.conf* file.

Analysis

The Analysis tab is perhaps the most interesting and useful of Apol's tabs. It enables you to perform three types of analysis:

Domain transition analysis
> We generally think of a domain transition as a single step involving two domains: the source (beginning) domain and the target (ending) domain. But suppose your SELinux policy permits domain A to transition to domain B and also permits domain B to transition to domain C. There's no single-step path between domains A and C. Nevertheless, by executing two transitions a process can move from domain A to domain C.
>
> A forward domain analysis shows the domains that can be reached in one or more transition steps from a given domain. To perform a forward domain transition analysis, you first specify a source domain. Apol then presents a tree identifying the target domains that can be reached directly from the specified source domain. Using a mouse or other pointing device, you can walk the tree, inspecting the rules that authorize each transition. Figure 9-10 shows the result of a simple forward domain analysis.

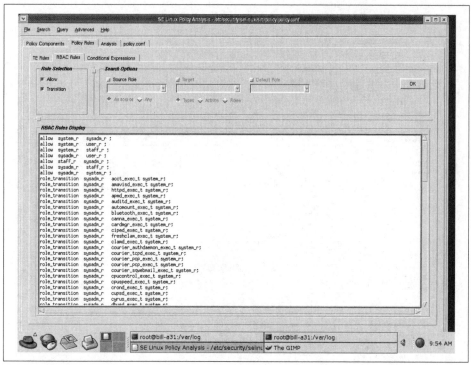

Figure 9-8. Apol's RBAC Rules tab

A reverse domain analysis simply goes in the opposite direction. You specify a target domain, and Apol identifies the source domains that can reach the specified source domain in one or more transition steps.

Direct information flow analysis

Direct information flow analysis generalizes the domain analysis operation in two respects. First, it lets you specify the direction of the relationship between domains as IN, OUT, EITHER, or BOTH. Second, the relationship extends beyond domain transitions to include information flows. Roughly speaking, an information flow exists between two domains if one member of the pair can read or write objects having the type of the other member of the pair. For a more precise explanation of information flows, see the white paper titled *An Overview of Information Flow Analysis*, available on the Tresys web site.

Indirect (transitive) information flow analysis

Indirect information flow analysis generalizes direct information flow analysis by showing relationships along indirect paths between pairs of domains. For instance, suppose that no information flow exists between domains A and C. If an information flow exists between domains A and B, and another exists between domains B and C, an indirect information flow may exist between

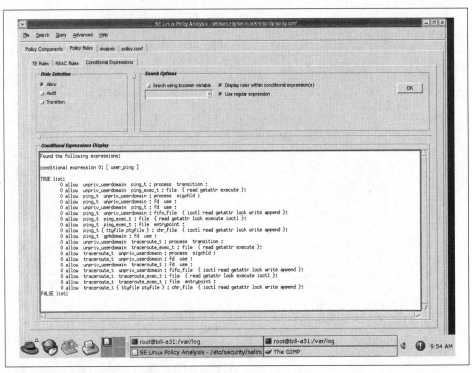

Figure 9-9. Apol's Conditional Expressions tab

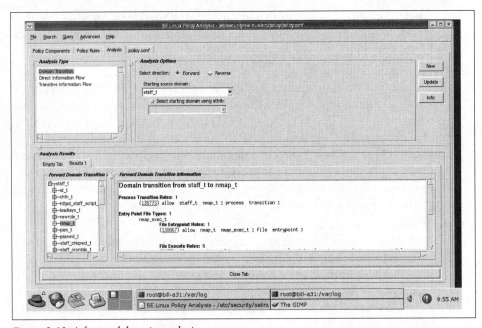

Figure 9-10. A forward domain analysis

domains A and C. Informally, indirect information flow analysis shows which domains interact with other domains. See the Apol help file for more information on indirect information flow analysis.

Seaudit

Figure 9-11 shows the main window of Seaudit, a GUI tool for viewing AVC messages within system logs. Seaudit can display results in real or nonreal time. Menu items let you specify the columns to be displayed, and search buttons let you construct, save, and run queries that select only a subset of log messages. You can also query the SELinux policy based on information contained within a log entry.

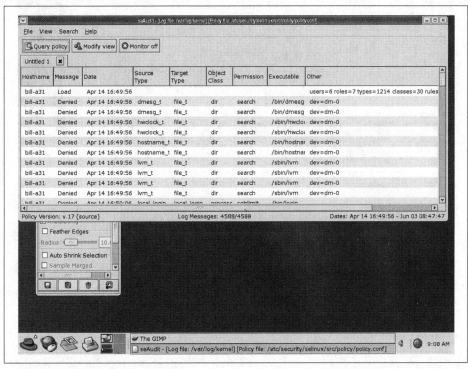

Figure 9-11. The Seaudit main window

Sepcut

Sepcut helps you browse and edit policy component files. Figure 9-12 shows Sepcut's main window. The window includes three main tabs:

Browse Policy
    Lets you view and modify policy component files.

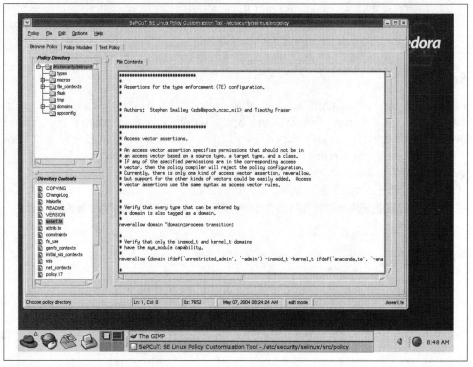

Figure 9-12. Sepcut's main window

Policy Modules

Lets you view or edit policy modules and individually enable or disable them. The term *policy module* refers to a pair of files consisting of an FC file and a TE file.

Test Policy

Lets you compile and load a policy.

Seuserx

Seuserx lets you add, change, and delete Linux and SELinux users. Its main window, shown in Figure 9-13, includes five buttons, as well as an Exit button:

Add

Lets you add a new user.

View/Change

Lets you view and change user characteristics.

Delete

Lets you delete a user.

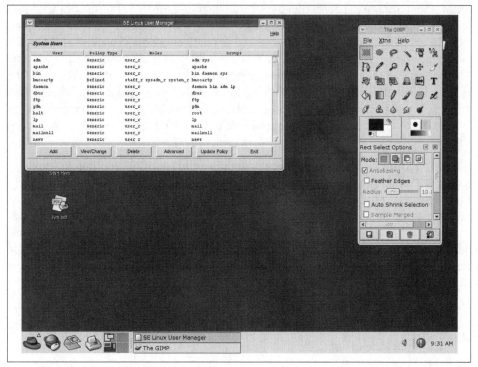

Figure 9-13. Seuserx's main window

Advanced

Lets you configure characteristics of generic users—users who don't have specific SELinux identities and are therefore associated with the user_u SELinux identity.

Update Policy

When you exit Suserx, it automatically loads a new security policy reflecting any changes you've made. However, you can use the Update Policy button to manually load a new policy whenever you like

The Road Ahead

Having completed this chapter, you know quite a bit about SELinux and typical SELinux policies. If you're content to run only relatively popular applications and prefer to rely on others for assistance in troubleshooting and fixing the occasional problems that you're likely to run into when using SELinux, you'll know pretty much all you need to know.

But typical Linux users are seldom so complacent. Those that desire even greater control over their computing affairs have merely begun to learn what they need to know about SELinux. This book has covered the fundamentals. But the SELinux policy is a sophisticated software unit whose mastery demands significant study and experimentation. Moreover, SELinux is still a relatively new software product and is constantly undergoing change. So in working with SELinux, you should anticipate that you will encounter many interesting puzzles and challenges. If you resemble the typical Linux user, you'll enjoy tackling and overcoming these. You should also anticipate that your growing SELinux expertise will enable you to better secure your systems and applications, which should help you—and your management—sleep more soundly.

SELinux and the SELinux sample policy are powerful tools for securing systems. But like other security tools, their proper installation and ongoing use demand significant expertise. From this book, you can learn how SELinux works and the syntax and semantics of the SELinux policy language. But mastery of SELinux demands thorough understanding of the policy domains associated with principal programs and applications installed on your systems. And since SELinux and its policies are regularly updated and improved, understanding arises only from an ongoing process of study and learning.

Here are some tips for developing a progressively greater understanding of SELinux:

- Maintain at least one system dedicated for testing new and revised SELinux policies and releases.

- Begin a study of the TE files associated with important programs and applications.

- Regularly review postings to relevant e-mail lists such as *fedora-selinux-list@redhat.com* and *SELinux@tycho.nsa.gov*.

- Experiment by creating new policies and observing the results.

May all your policies build correctly the first time and authorize neither too few nor too many permissions!

Security Object Classes

Table 2-1 has been reproduced here as Table A-1 for convenient reference. Table A-1 summarizes the object classes defined by the current release of SELinux. The table is organized by object class within object class type. SELinux developers may change the roster of object classes in future releases of SELinux.

Table A-1. Security object classes

Class	Description
File classes	
blk_file	Block device file
chr_file	Character device file
dir	Directory
fd	File descriptor
fifo_file	FIFO file
file	File
filesystem	Formatted filesystem residing on disk partition
lnk_file	Hard or symbolic link
sock_file	Network socket file
Interprocess communication classes	
ipc	(Obsolete)
msg	Interprocess communication message within queue
msgq	Interprocess communication queue
sem	Interprocess communication semaphore
shm	Interprocess communication shared memory
Network classes	
key_socket	IPSec socket
netif	Network interface
netlink_socket	Socket used to communicate with kernel via the netlink syscall

Table A-1. Security object classes (continued)

Class	Description
node	TCP/IP network host, as represented by IP address
packet_socket	Obsolete object type used by Linux 2.0 programs invoking the socket syscall
rawip_socket	Raw IP socket
socket	Generic socket
tcp_socket	TCP socket
udp_socket	UDP socket
unix_dgram_socket	Unix-domain datagram socket
unix_stream_socket	Unix-domain stream socket
Object class	
passwd	Linux password file
System classes	
capability	SELinux capability
process	Process
security	Security-related objects, such as the SELinux policy
system	Kernel and system objects

SELinux Operations

Table B-1 summarizes SELinux operations, identifying their related object classes and giving an approximate description of them. In future SELinux releases, SELinux developers may change the roster of operations, associate operations with object classes differently, or modify the function performed by an operation. The table is sorted alphabetically by the name of the operation. The SELinux file *src/policy/flask/access_vectors* shows the relationship between object classes and operations and is sorted by object class.

Table B-1. SELinux operations

Operation	Object classes	Description
accept	key_socket, netlink_socket, packet_socket, raw_ipsocket, socket, tcp_socket, udp_socket, unix_dgram_socket, unix_stream_socket	Accept a connection.
acceptfrom	tcp_socket, unix_stream_socket	Accept connection from client socket.
add_name	dir	Add a name.
append	blk_file, chr_file, dir, fifo_file, file, key_socket, lnk_file, netlink_socket, packet_socket, rawip_socket, sock_file, socket, tcp_socket, udp_socket, unix_dgram_socket, unix_stream_socket	Write or append file or socket contents.
associate	filesystem, ipc, msgq, sem, shm	Associate a file or key with a filesystem, queue, semaphore set, or memory segment.
avc_toggle	system	Toggle between permissive and enforcing modes.
bdflush	system	Control the buffer-dirty-flush daemon.

Table B-1. SELinux operations (continued)

Operation	Object classes	Description
bind	key_socket, netlink_socket, packet_socket, rawip_socket, socket, tcp_socket, udp_socket, unix_dgram_socket, unix_stream_socket	Bind name to socket.
change_sid	security	Determine the SID of an object during relabeling.
check_context	security	Write context in selinuxfs filesystem.
chfn	passwd	Change user account information (real name, work room and phone, and home phone).
chown	capability	Change file ownership and group ownership.
chsh	passwd	Change login shell.
compute_av	security	Compute an access vector given a source, target, and class.
compute_create	security	Set create information in selinuxfs filesystem.
compute_member	security	Set member information in selinuxfs filesystem.
compute_relabel	security	Set relabel information in selinuxfs filesystem.
compute_user	security	Set user information in selinuxfs filesystem.
connect	key_socket, netlink_socket, packet_socket, rawip_socket, socket, tcp_socket, udp_socket, unix_dgram_socket, unix_stream_socket	Initiate connection.
connectto	tcp_socket, unix_stream_socket	Connect to server socket.
context_to_sid	security	Convert a context to an SID.
create	blk_file, chr_file, dir, fifo_file, file, ipc, key_socket, lnk_file, msgq, netlink_socket, packet_socket, rawip_socket, sem, shm, sock_file, socket, tcp_socket, udp_socket, unix_dgram_socket, unix_stream_socket	Create new file, IPC object, queue, semaphore set, or shared memory segment.
dac_override	capability	Override discretionary access control except LINUX_IMMUTABLE.
dac_read_search	capability	Overrides all discretionary access control.

Operation	Object classes	Description
destroy	ipc, msgq, sem, shm	Destroy IPC object, message queue, semaphore set, or shared memory segment.
enforce_dest	node	Destination node can enforce restrictions on the destination socket.
enqueue	msgq	Message may reside on queue.
entrypoint	file	Enter a new domain via this program.
execute	blk_file, chr_file, dir, fifo_file, file, lnk_file, sock_file	Execute.
execute_no_trans	file	Execute file without a domain transition.
fork	process	Fork into two processes.
fowner	capability	Grant file operations otherwise restricted due to ownership.
fsetid	capability	overrides effective user ID checks for set user ID and set group ID files
get_sids, get_user_sids	security	Get the list of active SIDs.
getattr	blk_file, chr_file, dir, fifo_file, file, filesystem, ipc, key_socket, lnk_file, msgq, netlink_socket, packet_socket, process, rawip_socket, sem, shm, sock_file, socket, tcp_socket, udp_socket, unix_dgram_socket, unix_stream_socket	Get file, process, message queue, or shared memory segment attributes.
getcap	process	Get process capabilities.
getopt	key_socket, netlink_socket, packet_socket, rawip_socket, socket, tcp_socket, udp_socket, unix_dgram_socket, unix_stream_socket	Get socket options.
getpgid	process	Get process group ID.
getsched	process	Get process priority.
getsession	process	Get session ID.
ioctl	blk_file, chr_file, dir, fifo_file, file, key_socket, lnk_file, netlink_socket, packet_socket, rawip_socket, sock_file, socket, tcp_socket, udp_socket, unix_dgram_socket, unix_stream_socket	I/O control system call requests not addressed by other permissions.
ipc_info	system	Get information for an IPC socket.

Table B-1. SELinux operations (continued)

Operation	Object classes	Description
ipc_lock	capability	Lock nonshared and shared memory segments.
ipc_owner	capability	Ignore IPC ownership checks.
kill	capability	Raise signal any process.
lease	capability	Take fcntl( ) leases on a file.
link	blk_file, chr_file, dir, fifo_ file, file, lnk_file, sock_file	Create hard link to file.
linux_immutable	capability	Modify S_IMMUTABLE and S_APPEND file attributes on supporting filesystems.
listen	key_socket, netlink_socket, packet_socket, rawip_socket, socket, tcp_socket, udp_socket, unix_dgram_socket, unix_ stream_socket	Listen for connections.
load_policy	security	Load the security policy.
lock	blk_file, chr_file, dir, fifo_ file, file, key_socket, lnk_ file, netlink_socket, packet_ socket, rawip_socket, sh, sock_ file, socket, tcp_socket, udp_ socket, unix_dgram_socket, unix_stream_socket	Set and unset file or memory page locks.
member_sid	security	Determine SID to use when selecting a member of a polyinstantiated object .
mknod	capability	Create character or block device nodes.
mount	filesystem	Mount a filesystem.
mounton	blk_file, chr_file, dir, fifo_ file, file, lnk_file, sock_file	Use as filesystem mount point.
name_bind	key_socket, netlink_socket, packet_socket, rawip_socket, socket, tcp_socket, udp_socket, unix_dgram_socket, unix_ stream_socket	Bind port to IP or file to Unix socket.
net_admin	capability	Network configuration changes.
net_bind_service	capability	Bind to privileged port.
net_raw	capability	Open raw socket or packet socket.
netbroadcast	capability	Send network broadcast or listen to incoming multicasts.
newconn	tcp_socket, unix_stream_socket	Create new socket for connection.
nfsd_control	system	Control the NFS server.
noatsecure	process	Allow GLibc secure mode.

Table B-1. SELinux operations (continued)

Operation	Object classes	Description
node_bind	rawip_socket, tcp_socket, udp_socket	Bind socket.
passwd	passwd	Change user password.
ptrace	process	Trace program execution of parent or child.
quotaget	filesystem	Get quota information.
quotamod	filesystem	Modify quota information.
quotaon	blk_file, chr_file, dir, fifo_file, file, lnk_file, sock_file	Enable quotas.
rawip_recv	netif, node	Receive raw IP packet.
rawip_send	netif, node	Send raw IP packet.
read	blk_file, chr_file, dir, fifo_file, file, ipc, key_socket, lnk_file, msgq, netlink_socket, packet_socket, rawip_socket, sem, shm, sock_file, socket, tcp_socket, udp_socket, unix_dgram_socket, unix_stream_socket	Read file, IPC, message queue, or shared memory segment contents.
receive	msg	Remove message from a queue.
recv_msg	key_socket, netlink_socket, packet_socket, rawip_socket, socket, tcp_socket, udp_socket, unix_dgram_socket, unix_stream_socket	Receive datagram message having SID unequal to socket.
recvfrom	key_socket, netlink_socket, packet_socket, rawip-socket, socket, tcp_socket, udp-socket, unix_dgram_socket, unix_stream_socket	Receive datagrams from socket.
relabelfrom	blk_file, chr_file, dir, fifo_file, file, filesystem, key_socket, lnk_file, netlink_socket, packet_socket, rawip_socket, sock_file, socket, tcp_socket, udp_socket, unix_dgram_socket, unix_stream_socket	Change the security context based on existing type.
relabelto	blk_file, chr_file, dir, fifo_file, file, filesystem, key_socket, lnk_file, netlink_socket, packet_socket, rawip_socket, sock_file, socket, tcp_socket, udp_socket, unix_dgram_socket, unix_stream_socket	Change the security context based on the new type.

Table B-1. SELinux operations (continued)

Operation	Object classes	Description
remount	filesystem	Change mounted filesystem options.
remove_name	dir	Remove a name.
rename	blk_file, chr_file, dir, fifo_file, lnk_file, sock_file	Rename a hard link.
reparent	dir	Change parent directory.
rlimitinh	process	Inherit resource limits from old SID.
rmdir	dir	Remove directory.
rootok	passwd	Update password if the user is root and the process has the rootok permission.
search	dir	Search directory.
send	msg	Add message to a queue.
send_msg	key_socket, netlink_socket, packet_socket, rawip_socket, socket, tcp_socket, udp_socket, unix_dgram_socket, unix_stream_socket	Send datagram message having SID unequal to that of sending socket.
sendto	key_socket, netlink_socket, packet_socket, rawip_socket, socket, tcp_socket, udp_socket, unix_dgram_socket, unix_stream_socket	Send datagrams to socket.
setattr	blk_file, chr_file, dir, fifo_file, file, ipc, key_socket, lnk_file, msgq, netlink_socket, packet_socket, rawip_socket, sem, shm, sock_file, socket, tcp_socket, udp_socket, unix_dgram_socket, unix_stream_socket	Change attributes of file, shared memory segment, or message queue.
setbool	security	Set a boolean value.
setcap	process	Set process capabilities.
setenforce	security	Change the SELinux enforcement mode.
setfscreate	process	Set fscreate context.
setgid	capability	Allow setgid( ) calls, and fake group IDs on credentials passed over a socket.
setopt	key_socket, netlink_socket, packet_socket, rawip_socket, socket, tcp_socket, udp_socket, unix_dgram_socket, unix_stream_socket	Set IPSec or socket options socket.
setpcap	capability	Transfer process capability map.
setpgid	process	Set process group ID.
setrlimit	process	Change process hard limits.

Table B-1. SELinux operations (continued)

Operation	Object classes	Description
setsched	process	Set process priority.
setuid	capability	Allow `setsuid( )` and fake UIDs on credentials passed over a socket.
share	process	Allow state sharing with cloned or forked process.
shutdown	key_socket, netlink_socket, packet_socket, rawip_socket, socket, tcp_socket, udp_socket, unix_dgram_socket, unix_stream_socket	Shutdown connection.
sid_to_context	security	Convert a SID to a context.
sigchld	process	Send `SIGCHLD` signal.
siginh	process	Inherit signal state from old SID.
sigkill	process	Send `SIGKILL` signal.
signal	process	Send a signal other than `SIGKILL`, `SIGSTOP`, or `SIGCHLD`.
signull	process	Test for existence of another process without sending a signal.
sigstop	process	Send `SIGSTOP` signal.
swapon	blk_file, chr_file, dir, fifo_file, lnk_file, sock_file	Allow file to be used for swap space.
sys_admin	capability	Various system capabilities (see */usr/include/linux/capability.h*).
sys_boot	capability	Reboot the system.
sys_chroot	capability	Use `chroot( )`.
sys_module	capability	Load and remove kernel modules and otherwise modify kernel.
sys_nice	capability	Change process priority and scheduling options.
sys_pacct	capability	Change process accounting state.
sys_ptrace	capability	Trace any process.
sys_rawio	capability	Perform raw I/O.
sys_resource	capability	Various capabilities (see */usr/include/linux/capability.h*).
sys_time	capability	Set system time and real-time clock.
sys_tty_config	capability	Configure tty devices.
syslog_console	system	Log to `syslog` console.
syslog_mod	system	Perform `syslog` operation other than reading `syslog` or logging to console.
syslog_read	system	Read `syslog`

Table B-1. SELinux operations (continued)

Operation	Object classes	Description
tcp_recv	netif, node	Receive TCP packet.
tcp_send	netif, node	Send TCP packet.
transition	filesystem, process	Transition to a new SID.
transition_sid	security	Determine SID for a new object.
udp_recv	netif, node	Receive UDP packet.
udp_send	netif, node	Send UDP packet.
unix_read	ipc, msgq, sem, shm	Perform IPC read.
unix_write	ipc, msgq, sem, shm	Perform IPC write or append.
unlink	blk_file, chr_file, dir, fifo_file, file, lnk_file, sock_file	Remove (delete) hard link.
unmount	filesystem	Unmount filesystem.
use	fd	Use an inherited file descriptor.
write	blk_file, chr_file, dir, fifo_file, file, ipc, key_socket, lnk_file, msgq, netlink_socket, packet_socket, rawip_socket, sem, shm, sock_file, socket, tcp_socket, udp_socket, unix_dgram_socket, unix_stream_socket	Write or append file or IPC object contents.

SELinux Macros Defined in src/policy/macros

Table C-1 describes principal macros defined in the *src/policy/macros* subdirectory. The macros included in the table are those present in the Fedora Core 2 implementation of SELinux. Other implementations may define different macros or alter the operation of macros appearing in the table.

Table C-1. SELinux macros defined in the macros subdirectory

Macro	Description
admin_domain	Defines a domain for an administrative user.
append_logdir_domain	Authorizes a specified domain to create, read, and append to logfiles within its own specially labeled logging directory.
append_log_domain	Authorizes a specified domain to read and append to its own specially labeled logfiles.
application_domain	Authorizes a specified domain to perform operations common to simple applications.
base_file_read_access	Authorizes a specified domain to read and search several system file types.
base_pty_perms	Authorizes a specified domain to access the pty master multiplexer domain and to search */dev/pts*.
base_user_domain	Defines a domain for a nonadministrative user.
can_create_other_pty	Authorizes a specified domain to create new ptys for another specified domain.
can_create_pty	Authorizes a specified domain to create new ptys.
can_exec	Authorizes a specified domain to execute files having a specified type (domain) without transitioning to a new domain.
can_exec_any	Authorizes a specified domain to execute a variety of executable types.
can_getcon	Authorizes a specified domain to obtain its execution context.
can_getsecurity	Authorizes a specified domain to query the security server.
can_loadpol	Authorizes a specified domain to load a policy.
can_network	Authorizes a specified domain to access the network.
can_ps	Authorizes a process in a specified domain to see */proc* entries for processes in another specified domain.

Table C-1. SELinux macros defined in the macros subdirectory (continued)

Macro	Description
can_ptrace	Authorizes a specified domain to trace processes executing in another specified domain.
can_setbool	Authorizes a specified domain to set a policy Boolean.
can_setenforce	Authorizes a specified domain to set the SELinux enforcement mode.
can_setexec	Authorizes a specified domain to set its exec context.
can_setfscreate	Authorizes a domain to set its fscreate context.
can_sysctl	Authorizes a specified domain to modify sysctl parameters.
can_tcp_connect	Authorizes a specified domain to establish a TCP connection with another specified domain.
can_udp_send	Authorizes a specified domain to send UDP datagrams to another specified domain.
can_unix_connect	Authorizes two specified domains to establish a Unix stream connection.
can_unix_send	Authorizes a specified domain to send Unix datagrams to another specified domain.
create_append_log_file	Authorizes a domain to read, write, and add names to directories and create and append to files.
create_dir_file	Authorizes a specified domain to create and use directories and files.
create_dir_notdevfile	Defines access-vector rules for creating and using directories and nondevice files.
create_dir_perms	Defines permissions needed to create and use directories.
create_file_perms	Defines permissions needed to create and use files.
create_msgq_perms	Defines permissions needed to create message queues and read and write message queues and their attributes.
create_sem_perms	Defines permissions needed to create semaphores and read and write semaphores and their attributes.
create_shm_perms	Defines permissions needed to create shared memory segments and read and write shared memory segments and their attributes.
create_socket_perms	Defines permissions needed to create, read, write, and otherwise use sockets.
create_stream_socket_perms	Defines permissions needed to create, read, write, and otherwise use stream sockets.
daemon_base_domain	Authorizes a specified domain to perform a variety of operations useful to daemons, including those authorized by daemon_core_rules.
daemon_core_rules	Authorizes a specified domain to access a variety of types useful to daemons.
daemon_domain	Authorizes a specified domain to use PID files.
daemon_sub_domain	Defines a child domain of a specified domain.
devfile_class_set	Defines a class that includes all device file classes.
dgram_socket_class_set	Defines a class that includes all datagram socket classes.
dir_file_class_set	Defines a class that includes all directory and file classes.
domain_auto_trans	Authorizes a specified domain to automatically transition to another specified domain.

Table C-1. SELinux macros defined in the macros subdirectory (continued)

Macro	Description
domain_trans	Authorizes a specified domain to transition to another specified domain.
etcdir_domain	Authorizes a specified domain to read files within its own specially labeled configuration subdirectory of directories labeled etc_t.
etc_domain	Authorizes a specified domain to read its own specially labeled configuration files residing in directories labeled etc_t.
file_class_set	Defines a class including all nondirectory file classes.
file_type_auto_trans	Authorizes a specified domain to automatically label with a specified type files created within directories having another specified type.
file_type_trans	Authorizes a specified domain to label with a specified type files created within directories having another specified type.
full_user_role	Defines a role for a user who logs in to the system and has full user status.
general_domain_access	Authorizes a specified domain to access processes, PID files, file descriptors, pipes, Unix sockets, and IPC objects belonging to the domain.
general_proc_read_access	Authorizes a specified domain to access most nodes in the */proc* filesystem.
init_service_domain	Authorizes a specified domain to perform operations useful to programs that are run from *init*.
in_user_role	Defines a type as accessible to the user_r and staff_r roles.
link_file_perms	Defines permissions needed to link, unlink, and rename files.
lock_domain	Authorizes a specified domain to use its own specially labeled lock files within directories labeled var_lock_t.
logdir_domain	Authorizes a specified domain to create private logfiles.
log_domain	Authorizes a specified domain to use files having type var_log_t.
mini_user_domain	Defines a simple domain for a nonadministrative user having minimal privileges.
mount_fs_perms	Defines permissions needed to mount and unmount filesystems.
notdevfile_class_set	Defines a class including all nondevice file classes.
packet_perms	Defines permissions needed to send and receive network packets.
pty_slave_label	Authorizes a specified domain to access a slave pty, but not to create new ptys.
r_dir_file	Authorizes a specified domain to read directories and files.
r_dir_perms	Defines permissions needed to read directories and directory attributes.
r_file_perms	Defines permissions needed to read files and file attributes.
r_msgq_perms	Defines permissions needed to read message queues and message queue attributes.
r_sem_perms	Defines permissions needed to read semaphores and semaphore attributes.
r_shm_perms	Defines permissions needed to read shared memory segments and shared memory segment attributes.
ra_dir_create_file	Defines access-vector rules for reading directories and files, creating and appending to files, and adding names to directories.
ra_dir_file	Defines access vector rules for reading directories and files, appending to files, and adding names to directories.

Table C-1. SELinux macros defined in the macros subdirectory (continued)

Macro	Description
ra_dir_perms	Defines permissions needed to read directories and add names to directories.
ra_file_perms	Defines permissions needed to read and append to files.
read_locale	Authorizes a specified domain to read the locale data, */etc/localtime*, and the file to which it links.
read_sysctl	Authorizes a specified domain to read *sysctl* variables.
rw_dir_create_file	Authorizes a specified domain to read and write directories and create and use files.
rw_dir_file	Defines access vector rules for reading and writing files and directories.
rw_dir_perms	Defines permissions needed to read and write directories and directory attributes.
rw_file_perms	Defines permissions needed to read and write files and file attributes.
rw_msgq_perms	Defines permissions needed to read and write message queues and their attributes.
rw_sem_perms	Defines permissions needed to read and write semaphores and their attributes.
rw_shm_perms	Defines permissions needed to read and write shared memory segments and their attributes.
rw_socket_perms	Defines permissions needed to read, write, and otherwise use (but not create) sockets.
rw_stream_socket_perms	Defines permissions needed to read, write, and otherwise use (but not create) stream sockets.
rx_file_perms	Defines permissions needed to read and execute files.
signal_perms	Defines permissions needed to send signals to processes.
socket_class_set	Defines a class including all socket classes.
stat_file_perms	Defines permissions needed to get file attributes.
stream_socket_class_set	Defines a class including all stream socket classes.
system_domain	Authorizes a specified domain to use shared libraries, the system log, access system administration files, and perform other operations common to system processes.
tmp_domain	Authorizes a specified domain to create and use files having type tmp_t.
tmpfs_domain	Authorizes a specified domain to create and use files having type tmpfs_t.
unconfined_domain	Authorize a domain to perform any operation permitted by Linux DAC, effectively bypassing all SELinux policy checks.
unpriv_socket_class_set	Defines a class including all nonprivileged socket classes (excludes rawip-, netlink-, and packet-related classes).
user_application_domain	Authorizes a specified domain to perform operations common to simple applications and defines the domain as a user domain.
user_domain	Defines a domain for a nonadministrative user.
uses_authbind	Authorizes a specified domain to use services provided by the authbind_t domain.
uses_shlib	Authorizes a specified domain to use shared libraries.

Table C-1. SELinux macros defined in the macros subdirectory (continued)

Macro	Description
`var_lib_domain`	Authorizes a specified domain to use files having type `var_lib_t`.
`var_run_domain`	Authorizes a specified domain to create files in */var/run* files and other directories created for the domain.
`x_file_perms`	Defines permissions needed to execute files.

APPENDIX D
SELinux General Types

This appendix includes several tables describing SELinux general types: types that tend to be referenced by multiple domains. The types shown in Tables D-1 through D-5 are those present in the Fedora Core 2 implementation of SELinux. SELinux developers may introduce new types or delete existing types in other SELinux releases.

Table D-1. Device-related types

Type	Description
agp_device_t	AGP video device: */dev/agpgart*
apm_bios_t	APM BIOS
clock_device_t	Hardware clock device: */dev/rtc*
console_device_t	Console device: */dev/console*
cpu_device_t	CPU device: */dev/cpu/**
devfs_control_t	Devfs filesystem.
device_t	Device
devtty_t	tty device
dri_device_t	DRI device: */dev/dri, /dev/dri/.**
event_device_t	Event device: */dev/input/event.**
fixed_disk_device_t	Fixed disk drive
framebuf_device_t	Framebuffer device: */dev/fb[0-9]**
memory_device_t	Memory device: */dev/kmem, /dev/mem, /dev/port, /dev/nvram*
misc_device_t	Miscellaneous device (for instance, */dev/sequencer*)
mouse_device_t	Mouse
mtrr_device_t	Memory type range register device: */dev/cpu/mtrr*
null_device_t	*/dev/null*
ppp_device_t	*/dev/ppp, /dev/pppox, /dev/ippp*
random_device_t	Entropy generator: */dev/random*

Table D-1. Device-related types (continued)

Type	Description
removable_device_t	Device having removable media (for instance, a CD-ROM device)
scanner_device_t	Scanner
scsi_generic_device_t	Generic SCSI device: */dev/sg[0-9]+*
sound_device_t	Sound device
tape_device_t	Magnetic tape device
tty_device_t	tty device
tun_tap_device_t	Network tunnel or tap device: */dev/net/tun/**, */dev/net/tap/**
urandom_device_t	Entropy generator: */dev/urandom*
v4l_device_t	Radio or tuner device
zero_device_t	*/dev/zero*

Table D-2. File-related types

Type	Description
at_spool_t	*At*-related files in */var/spool/at*
bdev_t	Bdev filesystem
bin_t	Binary executables in */bin*
boot_runtime_t	Boot configuration files, such as *grub.conf*
boot_t	Bootable kernel and RAM disk files such as */vmlinuz*
catman_t	Man page catalog files
cifs_t	Alias for sambafs_t
cron_spool_t	*cron* files
default_t	A default file context
dosfs_t	MSDOS, FAT, VFAT, or NTFS filesystem
etc_aliases_t	*/etc/aliases* and related files
etc_runtime_t	Volatile files in */etc* and subdirectories
etc_t	Nonvolatile files in */etc* and subdirectories
eventpollfs_t	Event-poll filesystem
faillog_t	*/var/log/faillog* and related login failure log files
file_t	Default type of unlabeled file
fonts_t	Font file
fs_t	Default type for filesystems
futexfs_t	Futex filesystem
home_root_t	Type for directory containing user home directories
iso9660_t	ISO9660 filesystem
krb5_conf_t	*/etc/krb5.conf* and related Kerberos files
lastlog_t	*/var/log/lastlog* and related login log files

Table D-2. File-related types (continued)

Type	Description
ld_so_cache_t	*/etc/ld.so.cache* and related shared library cache files
ld_so_t	*/etc/ld.so.conf* and related shared library configuration files
lib_t	Modules, libraries, and related files in */lib*
locale_t	*/usr/share/locale*, */usr/share/zoneinfo* and localization files
lost_found_t	Lost and found directories and the files they contain
ls_exec_t	*/bin/ls*
mail_spool_t	*/var/mail*, */var/spool/mail*, and related files
man_t	*/usr/man*, */usr/share/man*, and related files
mnt_t	*/mnt* and related files
mqueue_spool_t	*/var/spool/mqueue* and related files.
net_conf_t	Network configuration files, such as */etc/resolv.conf*
nfsd_fs_t	NFSD filesystem
poly_t	Polyinstantiated directory (defined, but not used, in sample policy)
print_spool_t	*/var/spool/lpd*, */var/spool/cups*, and related files
ramfs_t	RAMFS filesystem
readable_t	Files and directories readable by ordinary users
resolv_conf_t	Alias for net_conf_t
romfs_t	ROMFS or CRAMFS filesystem
root_t	Root filesystem
rpc_pipefs_t	RPC pipe filesystem
sambafs_t	Samba (CIFS) filesystem
sbin_t	*/sbin*, */usr/sbin*, and related files
shadow_t	*/etc/shadow* and related files
shell_exec_t	Executable shell, such as */bin/bash*
shlib_t	Shared libraries in */lib*, */usr/lib*, and elsewhere
src_t	*/usr/local/src* and related files
swapfile_t	Swap file
sysfs_t	SYS filesystem
system_map_t	*/boot/System.map* and related files
test_file_t	(Defined, but not used, in sample policy)
tetex_data_t	Texmf-related files in */var/spool/texmf*, */var/lib/texmf*, and elsewhere
tmpfs_t	TMPFS filesystem
tmp_t	User-created files in */tmp* and elsewhere
udev_runtime_t	UDEV table file
unlabeled_t	Unlabeled file
usbdevfs_t	USB DEV filesystem

Table D-2. File-related types (continued)

Type	Description
usbfs_t	USB filesystem
usr_t	*/usr, /opt* and related files
var_lib_nfs_t	*/var/lib/nfs* and related files
var_lib_t	*/var/lib* and related files
var_lock_t	*/var/lock* and related files
var_log_ksyms_t	*/var/log/ksyms* and related files
var_log_t	*/var/log/dmesg, /var/log/syslog*, and related files
var_run_t	*/var/run* and related files
var_spool_t	*/var/spool* and related files
var_t	*/var* and related files
var_yp_t	*/var/yp* and related files
wtmp_t	*/var/log/wtmp* and related files

The descriptions given in Table D-2 are abbreviated. The types listed in the table are often used to label a variety of files beyond those identified in the concise descriptions given in the table.

Table D-3. Types related to networking

Type	Description
any_socket_t	Obsolete type used to refer to UDP or raw IP socket
icmp_socket_t	Socket used to send ICMP messages
igmp_packet_t	IGMP packet
netif_eth0_t	Network interface *eth0*
netif_eth1_t	Network interface *eth1*
netif_eth2_t	Network interface *eth2*
netif_ippp0_t	Network interface *ippp0*
netif_ipsec0_t	Network interface *ipsec0*
netif_ipsec1_t	Network interface *ipsec1*
netif_ipsec2_t	Network interface *ipsec2*
netif_lo_t	Network interface *lo*
netif_t	A network interface
netmsg_eth0_t	Network message arriving on interface *eth0*
netmsg_eth1_t	Network message arriving on interface *eth1*
netmsg_eth2_t	Network message arriving on interface *eth2*
netmsg_ippp0_t	Network message arriving on interface *ippp0*
netmsg_ipsec0_t	Network message arriving on interface *ipsec0*

Table D-3. Types related to networking (continued)

Type	Description
netmsg_ipsec1_t	Network message arriving on interface *ipsec1*
netmsg_ipsec2_t	Network message arriving on interface *ipsec2*
netmsg_lo_t	Network message arriving on interface *lo*
netmsg_t	Network message arriving on any interface
node_compat_ipv4_t	IP address of IPv4-compatible host
node_inaddr_any_t	IP address of any host
node_internal_t	IP address of LAN host
node_link_local_t	IP address of LAN host
node_lo_t	IP address of loopback interface
node_mapped_ipv4_t	IP address of host having a mapped IPv4 address
node_multicast_t	IP address of host having a multicast address
node_site_local_t	IP address of host associated with local site
node_t	Default type of network node
node_unspec_t	Network node of unspecified type
pop_port_t	Post Office Protocol port
port_t	TCP/IP port
scmp_packet_t	SCMP (ST Control Message Protocol) packet
tcp_socket_t	Socket used to send TCP data
xserver_port_t	X server port

Table D-4. Types related to /proc

Type	Description
proc_kcore_t	*/proc/kcore* and related files
proc_kmsg_t	*/proc/kmsg* and related files
proc_t	*/proc* filesystem and related files
sysctl_dev_t	*/proc/sys/dev* and related files
sysctl_fs_t	*/proc/sys/fs* and related files
sysctl_hotplug_t	*/proc/sys/kernel/hotplug* and related files
sysctl_irq_t	*/proc/irq* and related procfs files
sysctl_kernel_t	*/proc/sys/kernel* and related files
sysctl_modprobe_t	*/proc/sys/kernel/modprobe* and related files
sysctl_net_t	*/proc/sys/net* and related files
sysctl_net_unix_t	*/proc/sys/net/unix* and related files
sysctl_rpc_t	*/proc/net/rpc* and related files
sysctl_t	*/proc/sys* and related files
sysctl_vm_t	*/proc/sys/vm* and related files

Table D-5. Types related to SELinux

Type	Description
default_context_t	Type of */etc/security/default_contexts* file
file_labels_t	Type of the persistent label mapping stored in a filesystem
no_access_t	Type of objects that should be accessed only administratively
policy_config_t	Type of */etc/security/selinux/**
policy_src_t	Type of the policy source files
security_t	Target type used when checking permissions in the security class; also the type of *selinuxfs* i-nodes

SELinux Type Attributes

Table E-1 summarizes the SELinux type attributes appearing in the Fedora Core 2 implementation of SELinux. Other implementations may define different type attributes or assign different meaning to attributes shown in the table.

Table E-1. SELinux type attributes

Type attribute	Description
admin	Administrator domain, such as `sysadm_t`
auth	Domain that can read */etc/shadow*
auth_chkpwd	Domain that can authenticate users by running *unix_chkpwd*
auth_write	Domain that can write or relabel */etc/shadow*
dbus_client_domain	Domain of dbus client
device_type	Type assigned to device nodes
domain	Type that can be assigned to a process
etc_writer	Domain that can write to *etc_t*
exec_type	Type assigned to executables that are domain entry points
file_type	Type assigned to files in persistent filesystems
fs_domain	Domain that can directly access a fixed disk
fs_type	Type assigned to filesystems, including nonpersistent filesystems
gphdomain	Domain derived from *gnome-pty-helper*
home_dir_type	Type assigned to the parent directory holding user home directories
home_type	Type assigned to home directories
homedirfile	Type of special file in home directory, used to associate mount points with home directories
lockfile	Type assigned to lock files or directories
logfile	Type assigned to log files or directories
login_contexts	Type assigned to files used to define default contexts for login type
mail_server_domain	Domain that can accept inbound TCP port 25 connection

Type attribute	Description
mail_server_sender	Domain that can make outbound TCP port 25 connection
mini_pty_type	pty used for a *user_mini_domain*
mlstrustedobject	Type that can be accessed irrespective of MLS restrictions (not used)
mlstrustedreader	Domain that can override MLS restrictions on reading (not used)
mlstrustedwriter	Domain that can override MLS restrictions on writing (not used)
mta_delivery_agent	Mail server domain that can deliver messages
mta_user_agent	Mail server domain that can read user files and FIFOs and inherit file handles for mail spool
netif_type	Type assigned to network interfaces
netmsg_type	Type assigned to packets received on network interfaces
node_type	Type assigned to network nodes (hosts)
noexattrfile	Type of filesystem not supporting extended attributes
pidfile	Type assigned to PID files
port_type	Type assigned to TCP/IP port numbers
priv_system_role	Domain that can change role from a user role to a system_r role, and user from a user identity to system_u
privfd	Domain whose file handles can be widely inherited
privhome	Domain that can act on behalf of a user by creating files under the user's home directory
privlog	Domain that can communicate with the system logger daemon via its Unix domain socket
privmail	Domain that can transition to system_mail_t
privmem	Domain that can access kernel memory
privmodule	Domain that can run *modprobe*
privowner	Domain that can assign a nondefault SELinux user identity to a file, or create a file having an SELinux user identity other than that of the current process
privrole	Domain that can change the SELinux role identity
privuser	Domain that can change the SELinux user identity
ptyfile	Type assigned to ptys
root_dir_type	Type assigned to filesystem root directories, including those of nonpersistent filesystems
server_pty	Type of pty created by a server, such as *sshd*
socket_type	Type assigned to kernel-created sockets (ordinary sockets are labeled with the type of the creating process)
sysadmfile	Type assigned to files fully controlled by administrators
sysctl_kernel_writer	Domain (other than admin Domain) that can write to sysctl_kernel_t
sysctl_net_writer	Domain that can write to sysctl_net_t
sysctl_type	Type assigned to a sysctl entry; that is, a configuration item appearing in */proc/sys*

Table E-1. SELinux type attributes (continued)

Type attribute	Description
tmpfile	Type assigned to temporary files
tmpfsfile	Type defined for `tmpfs` type translations
ttyfile	Type assigned to ttys
unpriv_userdomain	Type of nonadministrative users, such as `user_t`
user_crond_domain	Type of user *crond* domain, such as `user_crond_t` and `system_crond_t`
user_home_dir_type	Type of user home directory of `unpriv_userdomain` user
user_home_type	Type of nonadministrator home directory
user_mail_domain	Domain used by `sendmail -t`
user_mini_domain	Small Domain used for *newrole*
user_tmpfile	Type assigned to temporary files of `unpriv_userdomain` domain
usercanread	Type of files that user can read
userdomain	User domain, such as `user_t` and `sysadm_t`
userpty_type	Type of nonadministrative pty (devpts)
web_client_domain	Domain of web client, such as Netscape and Squid
xserver_tmpfile	Type assigned to temporary files of `user_xserver_t` domain

Index

Numbers

0-day vulnerabilities and patch cycles, 5–7

Symbols

* (asterisk), special notation for specifying
types/classes/permissions, 139
&& (logical AND), used in conditional
expressions, 145
= = (logical equality), used in conditional
expressions, 145
^ (logical exclusive OR), used in conditional
expressions, 145
!= (logical inequality), used in conditional
expressions, 145
! (logical negation), used in conditional
expressions, 145
| | (logical OR), used in conditional
expressions, 145
- (minus sign), special notation for specifying
types/classes/permissions, 139
~ (tilde), special notation for specifying
types/classes/permissions, 139

A

accept operation, 201
acceptfrom operation, 201
access controls, discretionary/mandatory, 11
access decisions, 26–28
access vector cache (AVC), 28
access vectors, 27
    TE access-vector declarations, 135–141

access-control lists (ACLs), protecting
memory with, 10
access-vector rules
    authorizing transitions with, 139
    restrictions imposed on, by constraint
declarations, 150
    syntax of, 135
access_vectors file in flask subdirectory, 106,
160
access_vectors policy element, 122, 131
ACLs (access-control lists), protecting
memory with, 10
actions performed by subjects, 22
active content, contributing to software
threats, 3
Add button (Seuserx window), 196
adding user accounts, 84–86, 167
add_name operation, 201
Address Space Layout Randomization
(ASLR), 17
adduser command, 52
admin type attribute, 220
admin_domain macro, 209
admin_macros.te file, 106, 164
admin.te file, 110, 164
Advanced button (Seuserx window), 197
agp_device_t type, 214
aliases for type names, defining with type
declarations, 132, 134
allow access vector, 27, 135
    conditional declarations and, 143, 173
    sample declaration, 136
allow lines in snort.te file, 102

We'd like to hear your suggestions for improving our indexes. Send email to *index@oreilly.com*.

About the Author

Bill McCarty is a Professor of Information Technology at Azusa Pacific University, Azusa, California. Bill is also the author of more than fifteen technical books and numerous papers and presentations. He serves as editor of the Honeynet Files department of the journal *IEEE Security and Privacy* and directs the Azusa Pacific University Honeynet Research Project, which is affiliated with the Honeynet Project's Honeynet Research Alliance. Bill has briefed members of U.S. organizations such as the CIA, DISA, FBI, NASA, and NSA, and non-U.S. organizations such as the United Kingdom's CESG and GCHQ, on his Honeynet research. He has worked with the FBI to prevent and detect computer crimes.

Colophon

Our look is the result of reader comments, our own experimentation, and feedback from distribution channels. Distinctive covers complement our distinctive approach to technical topics, breathing personality and life into potentially dry subjects.

The image on the cover of *SELinux: NSA's Open Source Security Enhanced Linux* depicts surveying soldiers. During the second half of the nineteenth century, following the Civil War, the U.S. military dispatched troops to the American West to subdue hostilities between Native Americans and settlers. These intrepid soldiers braved a chaotic environment; they were frequently confronted with shoot-outs, ambushes, and snipers in their struggle to bring order to the American frontier. Among these troops were the Buffalo soldiers, the first peacetime regiments of African-American cavalry in the military. Despite being stationed in extremely dangerous terrain with inferior supplies, the Buffalo soldiers became one of the most distinguished military units in the Old West. To future generations of soldiers, they were models of courage and dedication in the face of adversity.

Sanders Kleinfeld was the production editor and copyeditor for *SELinux: NSA's Open Source Security Enhanced Linux*. Jamie Peppard was the proofreader. Mary Anne Weeks Mayo and Claire Cloutier provided quality control. Caitrin McCullough provided production assistance. Judy Hoer wrote the index.

Emma Colby designed the cover of this book, based on a series design by Hanna Dyer and Edie Freedman. The cover image is a 19th-century engraving from the Dover Pictorial Archive. Clay Fernald produced the cover layout with QuarkXPress 4.1 using Adobe's ITC Garamond font.

Melanie Wang designed the interior layout, based on a series design by David Futato. The chapter opening images are from the Dover Pictorial Archive, *Marvels of the New West: A Vivid Portrayal of the Stupendous Marvels in the Vast Wonderland West of the Missouri River*, by William Thayer (The Henry Bill Publishing Co., 1888); and *The Pioneer History of America: A Popular Account of the Heroes and Adventures*, by Augustus Lynch Mason, A.M. (The Jones Brothers Publishing Company,

1884). This book was converted by Julie Hawks to FrameMaker 5.5.6 with a format conversion tool created by Erik Ray, Jason McIntosh, Neil Walls, and Mike Sierra that uses Perl and XML technologies. The text font is Linotype Birka; the heading font is Adobe Myriad Condensed; and the code font is LucasFont's TheSans Mono Condensed. The illustrations that appear in the book were produced by Robert Romano and Jessamyn Read using Macromedia FreeHand 9 and Adobe Photoshop 6. The tip and warning icons were drawn by Christopher Bing. This colophon was written by Sanders Kleinfeld.

Related Titles Available from O'Reilly

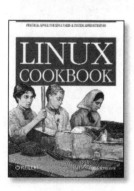

Linux

Building Embedded Linux Systems

Building Secure Servers with Linux

The Complete FreeBSD, *4th Edition*

Even Grues Get Full

Exploring the JDS Linux Desktop

Extreme Programming Pocket Guide

Knoppix Hacks

Learning Red Hat Enterprise Linux and Fedora, *4th Edition*

Linux Cookbook

Linux Device Drivers, *3rd Edition*

Linux in a Nutshell, *4th Edition*

Linux iptables Pocket Reference

Linux Network Administrator's Guide, *3rd Edition*

Linux Pocket Guide

Linux Security Cookbook

Linux Server Hacks

Linux Unwired

Linux Web Server CD Bookshelf, *Version 2.0*

LPI Linux Certification in a Nutshell, *2nd Edition*

Managing RAID on Linux

OpenOffice.org Writer

Programming with Qt, *2nd Edition*

Root of all Evil

Running Linux, *4th Edition*

Samba Pocket Reference, *2nd Edition*

Test Driving Linux

Understanding the Linux Kernel, *2nd Edition*

Understanding Open Source & Free Software Licensing

User Friendly

Using Samba, *3rd Edition*

Keep in touch with O'Reilly

1. Download examples from our books

To find example files for a book, go to:

www.oreilly.com/catalog

select the book, and follow the "Examples" link.

2. Register your O'Reilly books

Register your book

Why register your b

Once you've registered

- Win O'Reilly books, T-shirts or discount coupons in our monthly drawing.
- Get special offers available only to registered O'Reilly customers.
- Get catalogs announcing new books (US and UK only).
- Get email notification of new editions of the O'Reilly books you own.

3. Join our email lists

Sign up to get topic-specific email announcements of new books and conferences, special offers, and O'Reilly Network technology newsletters at:

elists.oreilly.com

It's easy to customize your free elists subscription so you'll get exactly the O'Reilly news you want.

4. Get the latest news, tips, and tools

www.oreilly.com

- "Top 100 Sites on the Web"—PC Magazine
- CIO Magazine's Web Business 50 Awards

Our web site contains a library of comprehensive product information (including book excerpts and tables of contents), downloadable software, background articles, interviews with technology leaders, links to relevant sites, book cover art, and more.

5. Work for O'Reilly

Check out our web site for current employment opportunities:

jobs.oreilly.com

6. Contact us

O'Reilly & Associates
1005 Gravenstein Hwy North
Sebastopol, CA 95472 USA

TEL: 707-827-7000 or 800-998-9938
(6am to 5pm PST)

ns regarding your order or our
ook order online, visit:

www.oreil_____new

catalog@oreilly.co.
To request a copy   ur latest catalog.

booktech@oreilly.com
For book content technical questions or corrections.

corporate@oreilly.com
For educational, library, government, and corporate sales.

proposals@oreilly.com
To submit new book proposals to our editors and product managers.

international@oreilly.com
For information about our international distributors or translation queries. For a list of our distributors outside of North America check out:

international.oreilly.com/distributors.html

adoption@oreilly.com
For information about academic use of O'Reilly books, visit:

academic.oreilly.com